The Action Française
and Revolutionary Syndicalism

by Paul Mazgaj

The University of North Carolina Press
Chapel Hill

Paul Mazgaj is assistant professor of history
at The University of North Carolina at Greensboro.

© 1979 *The University of North Carolina Press*
All rights reserved
Manufactured in the United States of America
ISBN 0-8078-1316-8
Library of Congress Catalog Card Number 79-4229

Library of Congress Cataloging in Publication Data

Mazgaj, Paul, 1942–
    The Action française and revolutionary syndicalism.

    Bibliography: p.
    Includes index.
    1. Syndicalism—France—History.   2. L'Action
française—History.   I. Title.
HD6684.M28   335'.82'0944   79-4229
ISBN 0-8078-1316-8

The Action Française and Revolutionary Syndicalism

*To my parents who, through thick and thin,
have believed in their children's education*

Contents

Acknowledgments

I wish to express my gratitude to the faculty of the University of Iowa for their kind help at every stage of this study. I am in debt, first, to Ralph Giesey and David Schoenbaum for, although they have had no direct hand in this project, their approach to historical problems has deeply influenced me. To Allan D. Megill, whose expenditure of time with the manuscript went far beyond the call of duty, I owe special thanks. Most directly involved in this project at every stage has been Alan B. Spitzer, who has always combined, with rare grace, the roles of tough-minded critic and generous friend.

I am also grateful to Stanford University for a Teaching and Research Fellowship, which facilitated or—more accurately—made possible the writing of the original manuscript.

My greatest debt, however, is to Nicole Marcon-Mazgaj. While alternating as debating partner, grammarian, critic, part-time therapist, and full-time companion, she has managed to complain only occasionally. I owe more than can be expressed to her unshakable conviction that a study such as this can be completed within the span of a single human lifetime.

The Action Française and Revolutionary Syndicalism

[1]

The Historiographical
Backdrop

> One of the most characteristic traits of our time . . . is
> certainly the attack directed from the Right and from
> the Left, with arguments divergent in their source
> but convergent in their effects, by adversaries equally
> resolute, against democracy.   Georges Guy-Grand

"Our time," one hazards a guess, is the era between the two world
wars. A reasonable conjecture. Everywhere in Europe, fascism and
communism were on the march; everywhere, parliamentary democracy was on the defensive, if not in full retreat.

In fact, "our time" was 1911. The author was a discouraged
French democrat.[1] The movements that he feared were, on the
Right, the royalists of the Action française and, on the Left, the
revolutionary syndicalists.

The Action française, founded during the Dreyfus affair, attracted national attention only gradually, after almost a decade of quiet
preparation. Recognition came with the publication of the daily
Action française in 1908 and the organization, shortly afterward, of
the Camelots du roi. The newspaper, which had something for
everyone from the gutter to the academy, combined—often in the
same column—the popular vituperation of an Edouard Drumont
with the kind of serious conservative political analysis not seen in
France since the days of de Bonald and de Maistre. Meanwhile, the
Camelots were busy capturing headlines. They not only proved
that they could prevent a professor from giving a class at the Sor-

bonne, which was relatively easy, but made themselves masters of the streets of the Latin Quarter, something a good deal more difficult. At the same time, the leader of the Action française, Charles Maurras, was openly discussing a coup d'état against a Republic whose best defenders, the aging Dreyfusards, were publicly expressing apathy over its very existence.

While the Action française was resuscitating the French Right, a new force had been at work on the Left. Men who called themselves revolutionary syndicalists came to dominate the French labor movement, and, under their auspices from about 1904 to the eve of the First World War, a wave of violent strikes upset the nervous calm that had characterized class relations in France since the Commune. Even more than their actions, the rhetoric of these men had an unsettling effect: they claimed that the current strike activity was simply a prelude to the vaunted general strike, which would bring in its train the overturning of existing society. With the publication of Georges Sorel's *Reflections on Violence*,[2] the ideas of the revolutionary syndicalists not only were given a certain intellectual respectability but—even more importantly, perhaps—benefited from seeming avant-garde. Revolutionary syndicalism—not unlike the royalism of the Action française—seemed, by 1906, a movement whose time was about to come.

With the advantage of hindsight, one can detect weaknesses in both movements and strengths in the Republic that were more difficult for contemporaries to perceive. The Third Republic, historians now would agree, was in no immediate danger from either royalists or syndicalists. Contemporary perceptions, however, were less sanguine about the future of the Republic. It had almost become a cliché that the Republic had lost its ability to inspire: nationalists saw it as spineless, workers as repressive, and intellectuals —more influential than ever after the Dreyfus affair—were taken up with antidemocratic critics like Maurras and Sorel.

It was under these circumstances, worrisome to all good republicans, that the Action française unveiled a new strategy. Royalists began to flatter syndicalists, to speak with great enthusiasm about syndicalist doctrines, and, in fact, to incorporate bits and pieces of these doctrines into what now had become the "social" monarchy. Influenced especially by the writings of Sorel, the new social program of the royalists was a blatant call for working-class support: the real danger, the royalists claimed, came not from exploitation by the capitalist but from exploitation by the democratic politician. Largely discarding corporative theories, long the staple of royalist programs, the Action française formulated what can only be described as a working-class fascism. Developed most fully by Georges Valois, later to organize France's first fascist party, this program became a major preoccupation—in terms of both time and money—of the prewar Action française.

This royalist initiative toward the Left was pursued at two levels: a highly theoretical polemic directed largely at leading syndicalist intellectuals and a more pedestrian search for syndicalist leaders willing to collaborate with the royalists. Both had their results. At the intellectual level, royalist efforts were rewarded by the conversion of Edouard Berth, Sorel's closest disciple, the cooperation of Sorel himself for a time, and the foundation of a joint nationalist-syndicalist study group, the Cercle Proudhon. At the level of working-class organizations, the royalists succeeded in finding certain syndicalists willing not only to sponsor a newspaper that would echo royalist themes but to mount a virulent anti-Semitic campaign among the workers. In the end the venture failed, but before it ran its course it affected—and certainly more than has been conceded by the historians of the Third Republic—not only revolutionary syndicalism and royalism but the political environment in which both operated.

The primary aim of this study is to describe the inspiration, the process, and the results of this royalist initiative. Needless to say, much of the royalist effort was not a matter of public record. Because it took on the quality of an intrigue—sometimes quite self-consciously—the attempt has been made to reconstruct it as such. Much of the context was that of the exotic web of Parisian politics during the Belle Epoque; it makes little sense outside that complex and rather self-contained universe. All this is by way of apology for both the whodunit quality of the narrative and the seemingly endless parade of political ne'er-do-wells.

It is hoped, however, that beyond this admittedly dense thicket there emerges a forest of larger historical concerns. Because they are sometimes only implicit in the narrative, it may be well, before beginning, to outline their general character and their relation to this study.

The historiography of revolutionary syndicalism in France has suffered more than it deserves from a good press. French historians of labor have generally ended—or, worse yet, started out—with a rather uncritical fondness for the subjects of their inquiry. The classic model here has been the second volume of Edouard Dolléans's *Histoire du mouvement ouvrier*, now in its sixth printing.[3] The rise, flowering, and decline of revolutionary syndicalism, as Dolléans described them, took on the proportions of an epic myth. Revolutionary syndicalism was born of the covetousness of the socialist parties, all scheming to subdue French labor; it grew to a robust manhood believing in the vision of the independent *syndicat* as the cell of a new society; and it was brought low, prematurely, mainly through the connivance of Machiavellian politicians. Dolléans's heroic syndicalism, albeit in modified form, has survived down to present-day French treatment of revolutionary syndicalism. Especially marked has been the tendency to take syndicalist leaders at their own words, to accept rather obvious rationalizations at face value, and, most importantly, to seriously distort the historical import of revolutionary syndicalism.

The result has been a misrepresentation of the significance of the syndicalist movement in the history of the Third Republic. Despite Dolléans's claim of a golden age—a *temps héroïque*—syndicalism was never very successful: it could neither rally workers in large numbers[4] nor settle ideological differences within its own leadership ranks.[5] The Amiens congress in 1906, which purportedly gave the movement its charter, was in reality a papering over of differences that could not be bridged.[6] Finally, as troubles began to multiply after 1909, even syndicalists themselves began to talk of a *crise du syndicalisme*. The crisis, in fact, was to spell the end of revolutionary syndicalism as a viable ideology for the French labor movement. Dolléans claimed that this premature end—coming as it did scarcely ten years after revolutionary syndicalism had been launched—was largely external: it was not so much the responsibility of the syndicalist leadership as a successful job of sabotage engineered by enemies of the movement.

French historical accounts of revolutionary syndicalism, with some notable exceptions, still bear the imprint of Dolléans's pioneering work.[7] The most influential contemporary French historian of revolutionary syndicalism, Jacques Julliard, stands firmly in the heroic tradition, although he has contributed rather important modifications.[8] The modifications are the result of Julliard's careful scholarship. He has made, for example, rich use of police archives, an operation suspect to certain defenders of heroic syndicalism. With a more balanced array of sources than Dolléans had at his disposal, Julliard has been able to illuminate the importance of certain trends that had escaped the scrutiny of earlier historians. His work has led to a keener appreciation of the Confédération générale du travail, France's leading pre-1914 labor organization and bulwark of the revolutionary syndicalist position.

Most importantly from the perspective of this study, Julliard has contributed a much more sophisticated understanding of the factional disputes that split the confederation and worked to deepen the crisis of syndicalism. Traditionally, the division in the Confédération générale du travail has been seen as one between revolutionaries, who controlled the apparatus and gave the movement its revolutionary syndicalist ideology, and reformists, who fought, unsuccessfully, to capture the movement and bring it to an accommodation with the Republic. But beyond this division, as Julliard has demonstrated, there was a struggle taking place within the revolutionary faction itself. As it became increasingly apparent that the confederation could not live up to the revolutionary expectations of certain segments of the working class, two strategies were devised by adherents of the revolutionary faction to meet the situation: one group, those whom Julliard calls *les politiques* and who had most responsibility for decisions, took a prudent line and urged caution, although they still insisted that they were revolutionary; a second group, *les ultras*, feeling the revolution betrayed, argued that the impasse could be overcome only by increased revolutionary élan.[9] This second group found in Gustave Hervé a valuable ally outside the syndicalist movement proper. His lively *Guerre sociale* was the most popular publication of the revolutionary Left. Much of the disarray among syndicalist leaders themselves, which contributed no small amount to the crisis, can be attributed directly to this conflict in the revolutionary faction between the politiques, on the one hand, and the ultras and Hervé, on the other.

There are fertile intimations in all of this pointing toward a re-interpretation of revolutionary syndicalism. One might convinc-ingly argue, given Julliard's description of the leadership crisis, that old-style revolutionary syndicalism with its vision of a producers' society free of capitalists, politicians, and the bourgeoisie was run-ning aground. The ultimate causes, one could legitimately suggest, were the evolving economic and social trends that clearly ran in the face of the syndicalist utopia. Taken together, these trends pointed away from the syndicalist vision of an economically decentralized, stateless, and homogeneous producers' society and toward eco-nomic concentration and centralization, an increase in state power, and a heterogeneous culture where labor was only one among sev-eral competing interest groups. It might be further postulated that the disparity between syndicalist ideology and prevailing social and economic patterns not only formed the basis for the crisis of syndi-calism but was the underlying cause for the factionalization of the syndicalist leadership. If this general explanation is accepted, the real issue in the debate among syndicalist leaders follows logically. Some—Julliard's politiques—worked to bring their ideology in line with developing economic and social realities; others—Julliard's ultras—were scornful of compromise and wanted to make a valiant last-ditch effort to preserve the purity of their cause. Of course, in this kind of historical reconstruction one cannot expect too much of the consciousness of the actors. One should not be surprised to learn that among those forced by circumstances into a revision of their ideology there would be many who, although making the necessary adjustments, would be hesitant to admit, even to them-selves perhaps, that they were one iota less revolutionary.

Julliard, however, remains content with fitting these develop-ments into the old heroic mold. He prefers to take syndicalists at their word and to defend their assertion that they never adulterated the content of revolutionary syndicalism. For Julliard, appearances to the contrary, the crisis of syndicalism did not lead syndicalists to a revision of their doctrine but to a reassertion of its original impetus.

How does Julliard, then, account for the apparent evolution of syndicalist ideology? His argument here is ingenious, if finally unconvincing. Revolutionary syndicalism, Julliard argues, was always something of a misnomer. The leaders of the Confédération générale du travail were never literally revolutionary; that is, they never envisaged the violent overturning of the existing society. What was really "revolutionary" about revolutionary syndicalism was, according to Julliard, method not content; its true revolutionary import was the method of direct action. Syndicalism was "revolutionary" in that it proclaimed the independence of workers—independence from both the state and the socialist parties.

But, what of those syndicalist leaders that clearly and unmistakably talked of revolution in the literal sense? Julliard disposes of them with what amounts to a definitional sleight of hand. One can separate, he maintains, an authentic revolutionary syndicalism represented by the moderate *politiques*—for whom revolutionary syndicalism was never more than the practice of direct action— from an infantile insurrectionism represented by the ultras and Hervé. This latter tendency, having no real connection with authentic syndicalism, Julliard treats somewhat in the manner of an alien virus. Carried largely by Hervé and his disciples, this virus attacked the otherwise healthy body of revolutionary syndicalism, laid it low, in fact, very nearly killed it. But the tried and true syndicalists were able, in the years just before the war, to shake off the disease of Hervéism and, with the rather unsure steps of the recently recovered, moved toward a reassertion of authentic revolutionary syndicalism.[10] In all this, Julliard follows rather closely the explanations given by the *politiques* themselves.

It is against this historiographical backdrop that the conclusions of the following study take on what is hoped will be their significance. First, it will be evident that the crisis of syndicalism, as it emerges in this study, takes on a different hue than in the Dolléans-Julliard main line version. It is argued here that revolutionary syndicalism is a classic case of limited means at the service of unlimited ends. The most important syndicalist leaders were genuine firebrands from other revolutionary movements, mostly anarchism. They wanted to make syndicalism a vehicle for revolution; yet the structure of the movement—decentralized to the point of anarchy —did not give them the wherewithal. In the large, politicized strikes, where the reputation of the Confédération générale du travail was on the line, they failed and failed miserably. The result was a full-blown crisis of confidence. This crisis meant not only that men lacked confidence in leaders but that leaders lacked confidence in each other and themselves.[11]

A second conclusion of this study concerns the significance of the factional division within the Confédération générale du travail outlined by Julliard. It is here maintained that the ultras and Hervéists cannot be so conveniently dismissed as extraneous to "authentic" syndicalism. If at times they did seem infantile, they nevertheless represented a genuine, if frustrated, revolutionary impetus, an impetus that cannot be so conveniently separated from the original conception of revolutionary syndicalism. What happened—as the narrative of this study will make plain—is that the leaders of the movement, faced with a series of demoralizing defeats, began to gradually modify their conception of syndicalism. For some, this meant merely a move toward greater prudence; for others, it meant a considerable theoretical revision of the content of revolutionary syndicalism. This latter tendency, represented by the influential militant Alphonse Merrheim, had, by the eve of the war, pushed syndicalism to a revision that was, in essentials, reformist. Though these "new reformists" predictably rejected the suggestion that they were reformist, they nevertheless tacitly abandoned much that had been the soul of old-style revolutionary syndicalism: the activist minorities, the emphasis on élan, and, most importantly, the revolutionary promise. These new reformists endeavored to convince their fellow syndicalists that the crisis of syndicalism was really a severe case of maladjustment to prevailing industrial and economic trends.[12] Seen in the context of this transformation of syndicalism, the so-called ultras and Hervéists—men whom Julliard places outside the pale of authentic syndicalism—were in reality disenchanted idealists, frustrated with a movement that they interpreted as betraying its revolutionary promise. In sum, it is maintained that the crise du syndicalisme was the manifestation not so much of a movement adrift because of the lure of alien doctrines but of one in the throes of a painful transformation. Those who, quite realistically, had a foreboding of the ultimate results of this transformation were in many ways desperate men. Out of their desperation they urged that all means—not excluding alliances of convenience with other enemies of the Republic—be brought into the battle to ensure that syndicalism remain true to its revolutionary mission.

This leads to the third revision of the traditional view of syndicalism, which claimed that syndicalists knew better than to flirt with reactionaries. The historians of heroic syndicalism have hardly thought to ask the question of whether their doughty warriors could have compromised with royalists; one could not expect them to look for answers.[13] In truth, syndicalist dealings with the Right not only existed but were a source of controversy—some of it quite open—within the movement. Although the number of individuals directly implicated was small, they were important figures in the movement. Moreover, the amount of indirect complicity— those willing to overlook a bit of anti-Semitism for the good of the cause, for example—was much larger. All in all, flirtation with the Action française was tied integrally with the crise du syndicalisme as both cause and effect: not only did royalist intrigues contribute to the deepening crisis, but the crisis itself predisposed certain syndicalists to find a way out of their predicament by a pact with the devil.

One might ask, legitimately enough, on what possible grounds might an alliance between royalism and syndicalism have been sealed. The most common ground, not surprisingly, was calculated self-interest, the age-old game of *politique du pire*. Syndicalist weakness demanded hardheaded realism, which, in turn, suggested that one could not be choosy about one's bedfellows.

But in a few important cases, and, one suspects, also among many of those who saw themselves as realists, there was something more than politique du pire. Both anarchists and revolutionary socialists had witnessed, first, anarchism, then, socialism forsake the cause of revolution. In the aftermath of the Dreyfus affair, extravagant promises made in the heat of battle evaporated. Socialists and Radicals followed their Opportunist elders: the rhetoric of regeneration rather quickly became politics as usual. Charles Péguy, one of the idealistic young Dreyfusards, best expressed the disillusionment that attended the "decomposition of *dreyfusisme*": "It is a great pity, a great sorrow, a great misery, an indefatigable degradation that a generation should have started out in life with such a loud disappointment, such a brutal, such a brutish disenchantment."[14]

To this disenchanted generation wondering how it was that *mystique* was being so rudely converted to *politique*, Charles Maurras had a ready answer: mystique was never more than the hocus-pocus of the adroit politician, the public face of politique. A democracy, by the very logic of its operation, must politicize all issues and deal with none seriously. A generation ago the socialists had promised social revolution, but the very fact that they were democrats ensured that their promises would remain only election slogans. A truly revolutionary program could never be accomplished in a democracy. Therefore, the most genuinely revolutionary program, the one necessary for all others to succeed, was the destruction of democracy.

This was a notion with an ominous future in the twentieth century—the notion that the most fundamental change was not economic but political, that at the source of all problems were the inept and corrupt politicians, that the solution to all problems was a form of government that would not endure them. At about the same time and starting from very different premises, Georges Sorel and his young syndicalist disciples were coming to similar conclusions: the greatest obstacle to the progress of revolutionary syndicalism, they would claim, was not capitalism but democracy.

No single interpretation of the Action française has enjoyed a staying power comparable to that of Dolléans's heroic conception of syndicalism. In fact, perhaps the distinguishing trait of neoroyalist historiography has been the concerted, yet unsatisfying effort to find a niche for the Action française in twentieth–century French history.[15]

The difficulties encountered by René Rémond, the most influential historian of the French Right, are symptomatic.[16] In his otherwise fine study, *The Right Wing in France*, he is clearly at a loss when it comes to the Action française. He convincingly distills the enormous variety of a century of rightist politics into three fundamental tendencies: Legitimist intransigence, Orleanist moderation, and Bonapartist Caesarism. In this schema the Action française, because it presumably did not fit into any of these categories, becomes the attempted synthesis of all three. Although there is some illumination in seeing neoroyalism as the inheritor of Legitimist and Bonapartist legacies, the model is strained to the breaking point when Rémond tries to explain how the Action française incorporates Orleanism. It becomes clear—one suspects to the author himself—that neoroyalism is both something less and something more than a synthesis of nineteenth-century traditions.

A more common temptation has been to view the Action française as a museum piece in the twentieth century. According to Edward Tannenbaum, the neoroyalists were "die-hard reactionaries" and Maurras a curious anachronism in a century that had relegated royalism to the historical junk heap. From these premises it follows that Maurras's argument for a restored monarchy re-creating a social order dead for over a century was naive and therefore could not have been taken seriously.[17]

Yet there is no small danger in making logic rather than history the test in such matters. The historical context is a surer guide as to how influential a thinker was or how seriously his doctrine was taken. Maurras's credentials here are impeccable. Not only was his Action française "the great didactic center of the Right" for over half a century, but his influence went far beyond parties and politics and became an important center of the intellectual and literary life in France.[18] Seen in this light, Tannenbaum's portrait of the neoroyalists as nostalgic "café intellectuals" is certainly misleading.

Whereas both Rémond and Tannenbaum have seen the Action française as looking toward the past, another, more recent interpretation views neoroyalism as the wave of the future. According to Ernst Nolte, Maurras "drove conservatism beyond the limits dividing it from incipient fascism"; the Action française, to Nolte, is unmistakably "early fascism."[19] Nolte's indications are various: Maurras loosed nationalism from its humanitarian moorings, making it "antihumanitarian" and "narcissistic"; he developed the doctrine of the Jew and the foreigner as enemy and scapegoat so prevalent in later fascism; finally, he organized and directed into action those first practitioners of fascist violence, the Camelots du roi.[20] But most important for Nolte is the "metapolitical" undertone of Maurras's thought. Maurras was an articulate enemy of "transcendence"—that very human longing to reach beyond the confining institutional and intellectual frameworks of a historical age toward ultimate fulfillment through a higher unity. "Resistance to transcendence" Nolte sees as the key to understanding not only Maurras but the whole gamut of twentieth-century fascisms.

Undoubtedly, Nolte's concept of "resistance to transcendence" captures an essential, if elusive, component of the fascist mentality. It is a component that has been hinted at and even elaborated upon in other contexts.[21] Reduced to its simplest terms, Nolte's argument asserts that the "emancipatory process"—whether intellectual or social—produces anxiety, which in turn fosters a retreat into more narrowly circumscribed ideas and institutions. Nolte has performed the service of attempting to define this process in global terms and spell out its varied manifestations.[22]

Yet, whatever the value of Nolte's conception of transcendence, few feel very comfortable with his classification of Maurras as a fascist—not historians of the Action française, not those who were lifelong intimates of Maurras, not even many of his avowed enemies. The differences between Maurras's ideas and fascism are more important, it has been claimed, than the similarities. Unlike most fascists, who glorified the irrational, Maurras was a thoroughgoing rationalist, a self-proclaimed disciple of Auguste Comte. Unlike most fascists, whose appetite was for total power, Maurras was a federalist. Against the fairy-tale culture of the blue-eyed and the blond propagated by the Nazis stood Maurras's sensitive appreciation of the cultures of antiquity. Clearly, his elitism was of a different order.

But these differences, although important, do not tell the whole story. Because each fascism is in a sense unique, each could be isolated from the others by its peculiarities, and it could be maintained—by a kind of definitional tour de force, as some have attempted—that generic fascism does not really exist. This is not the purpose here. Fascism, unlike many political movements, was not so much a set of articulated concepts that can be enumerated on a kind of historical checklist as something akin to a religious revival. It had, wherever it existed, a spiritual dimension: a mystique of nation, of blood, and, most importantly, of action. This is the aspect of fascism to which Nolte does not do justice. Not only was fascism a rejection of the forward momentum of liberal society, a "resistance to transcendence," but it possessed, as George Mosse has pointed out, a transcendence of its own.[23] Convinced that contemporary society was mired in decadence, fascism sought the destruction of that society, ideally under the blows of the heroic new elite that would replace it. Energy and frenetic activism were contrasted to bourgeois pacifism and became, in many ways, ends unto themselves. "Fascism," writes Mosse, "did not abolish but instead displaced the revolutionary urge of the epoch."[24]

For a time, in the years just after its founding, Maurras's Action française seemed to offer a movement that was truly revolutionary. The corrupt Republic would be overturned by a willful elite committed to a national renaissance. While the socialist vision, once revolutionary, was being bartered away in the corridors of the Palais-Bourbon, the royalists remained above corruption. The Camelots du roi were to prove that the Action française did not shrink before violence, while Maurras, revealing the seriousness of his mission, brazenly talked of a coup d'état.

Gradually it became apparent, however, that this revolutionary aspect of the Action française was more rhetorical and theatrical than real. If in 1910 one could take Maurras's coup seriously, by 1925 it strained credulity. Increasingly, Maurras's monarchy became a formalistic abstraction, a refuge for tired intellectuals rather than a combat organization. One after another, men of energy impatient for movement left the Action française or, more often, were thrown out.

This portrait of the Action française as revolutionary-turned-reactionary is that drawn by Eugen Weber.[25] He considers that time and circumstance would reveal Maurras, despite his early posture as a radical of the Right, incapable of moving from the word to the deed. Weber's book, combining sympathetic understanding with critical detachment, is the point of departure for this study.

This, however, is not to argue that "early fascism" did not exist in prewar France. The once generally accepted view, promoted largely by French historians, that fascism had no "native roots" in France has been increasingly challenged.[26] From the mid-1880s, disenchantment with the regime deepened as scandals, mediocrity of personnel, and a kind of *immobilisme* began to dispel the mystique once associated with the word "republic." Here and there new men appeared, men with a taste for action and plans of national regeneration through heroic vitalism. There are shades of this in Boulangism and Drumontism, more indication of it in the leagues of the 1890s, but most important during this period were the efforts of Maurice Barrès to articulate and organize a national socialism.[27] This spirit of early fascism lay dormant for a time after the Dreyfus affair. But it was to be revived—this time from the interior of the Action française. The revolutionary aura of the early Action française had the effect of attracting dissidents who, disappointed with everything from Drumontism to anarchism, would be satisfied with no less than the total renovation of society. It is in this context that the campaign to win the workers must be viewed. The winning of the workers became, at once, royalist policy and, at the same time, the special project of a group of Young Turks, men who took the revolutionary pronouncements of the leadership seriously. Using the materials of Maurrassian nationalism and Sorelian syndicalism, these young radicals of the Right worked toward the construction of a national socialism and its incorporation within a royalist framework. Maurras alternately encouraged and discouraged this project, tending always to see its instrumental uses. Already in Maurras's behavior one can discern the inclinations that would make the Action française unambiguously reactionary: a doctrinal rigidity before any innovation and an almost constitutional inability to act in a real crisis. But this is only with the benefit of hindsight; from the prewar perspective the matter was still ambiguous, made all the more so by Maurras's talent for reconciling verbally what in reality was irreconcilable.

Thus, prewar royalism, like its counterpart on the Left, was undergoing a crisis of its own. The *crise du royalisme* was hardly an apparent one: to all appearances the Action française was robust and gaining rather than losing momentum. Yet the leadership struggle with the young radical element was at a critical juncture. At issue was whether the Action française could incorporate a dynamic vision—one that could offer an alternative to the existing society —or whether it would become merely a rallying point for the resistance to change.

The issue of "early fascism" at the Action française raises yet another historiographical problem. Considering that all of the Young Turks who had developed protofascist themes at the Action française claimed to be disciples of Georges Sorel, what then are Sorel's responsibilities in the matter? Could he, more accurately than Maurras, be seen as a legitimate intellectual progenitor of fascism? This question is not made any easier by the fact that in the years just before his death in 1922—years when everyone's ideological cards were being turned up—Sorel remained stubbornly ambivalent. He was fascinated by *both* Lenin and Mussolini. Not surprisingly, later historians have not reached a consensus on Sorel; in fact, time seems only to have intensified the disagreement. No two interpretations of Sorel differ more radically than those of J. L. Talmon and John L. Stanley. Significantly, both were published in the 1970s.[28]

A central pivot in the debate is Sorel's relation to his young disciples, Georges Valois and Edouard Berth. In Talmon's view, Valois used Sorel as a "foundation stone for . . . [his] genuine and full-blooded Fascist philosophy." Valois's later fascism was but an extension, according to Talmon, of the logic of Sorel's revolt against politics, against moderation, and, most critically, against the rationalist heritage of the Enlightenment.[29]

Stanley rejects Talmon's argument on the grounds that the latter emphasizes only the similarities and not the more crucial differences between Sorel's thought and later fascism. Though admitting that Sorel's flirtation with the Action française is Talmon's best argument for connecting him with fascism, Stanley concludes, nevertheless, that these are not sufficient grounds. Not only was the flirtation "short-lived," but Sorel, according to Stanley, remained "reluctant" throughout the whole affair. As for the rest, Stanley maintains, Sorel cannot be blamed for what his disciples said and did.[30]

The tack taken in the present study has been to reconstruct, as meticulously as remaining evidence has allowed, the almost Byzantine interaction among Sorel, his disciples, and the Action française, at both the level of theory and that of practice. This reconstruction tends to confirm Stanley's argument on two important points: Sorel's relations with the Action française were indeed both "brief" and "reluctant"; and it is unfair to view the writings of his disciples, especially Valois's, as mere extensions of Sorel's thought.

Yet it would be far too easy to let the matter drop here. Whereas it might be inappropriate to label Sorel a fascist, there are certain important issues that make the matter less ambiguous than is implied by Stanley. First of all, one cannot ignore the fact that Sorel's enthusiasm for the proletariat was mingled with a profoundly conservative strain, a strain manifested in his sexual puritanism and his nostalgic visions of workshop and society. However much Sorel might have protested the assertion, his vision of the future was heavily mortgaged to the past. Sorel's revolution would restore more than it would liberate.

Further, although it might be naive to simply equate Sorel's thought with that of his disciples, it would be equally misleading to open an unbridgeable gap between the nuanced corpus of Sorel's own writing and the vulgar and derivative "Sorelianism" fashioned by his followers. Sorel himself was both highly flattered by and seriously interested in the writings of the young "Sorelians" despite their blatant racialism and nationalism—flattered and interested, one is tempted to add, in a way that Nietzsche would never have been with the later racial and national "Nietzscheans." Bitterly disappointed with the failure of syndicalists to keep the revolutionary faith, Sorel looked long and hard at the possibilities of a revolution on the Right, a revolution whose sustaining myth and energizing force would be a nationalism of the most bellicose and exclusivist variety. As Sorel pondered the issue—alternately encouraged and disappointed—his young disciples thundered past him and bridged the gap between his own thinking and incipient fascism. In all of this Sorel is unconvincingly cast in the role of the innocent victim, yet another misunderstood teacher betrayed by overardent students.

[2]

Toward a Royalist Syndicalism: The Beginnings

> All true faith is uncompromising, radical, purist;
> hence the true traditionalist is always a revolutionary
> zealot in conflict with pharisaian society, with the
> lukewarm corrupters of the creed. And vice versa;
> the revolutionary's Utopia, which in appearance rep-
> resents a complete break with the past, is always
> modeled on some image of the lost Paradise, of a
> legendary Golden Age. — Arthur Koestler

From the perspective of 1899, the year of the founding of the
Action française, was an alliance between the nationalists and the
working class such a preposterous undertaking? Had not patriotism
since the Revolution of 1789 been a mark of the Parisian popular
classes? During the Boulanger adventure, scarcely a decade before,
had not the working class been susceptible to the general's chau-
vinism? His success, in Paris at least, depended on their votes.[1]

The decade of the 1890s was marked by repeated attempts at
enlisting the Parisian working class in organizations that claimed to
be at once socialist and nationalist. With the new element of anti-
Semitism, it was hoped that the gap could be bridged between
these two principles. For both nationalists and socialists, the enemy
was to be the Jew: as a foreigner for the former, as an exploiter
for the latter. Edouard Drumont's *La France juive* became the inspired text serving the various leagues that sprang up promoting a
nationalist-socialist alliance. Not long after publication of *La France*

juive in 1886, Drumont tried his hand at practical politics. Although his Ligue antisémite ended in failure rather quickly, its organizing principle—the attempt to reach the popular classes with a sentimental anti-Semitism—was widely imitated. Jules Guérin, Gaston Méry, and the marquis de Morès attempted, each in his turn, to drum up working-class support through a militant Drumontism. The nationalist socialists even found their way to the *Revue socialiste* via the anti-Semitic sympathies of its editor, Benoît Malon.

Even more substantial were the efforts of Maurice Barrès and the so-called Left Boulangists during the same decade. The results, though short-lived, were not unimpressive. In the Chamber, Boulangists and socialists found themselves often working in cooperation. In the estimation of at least one scholar of the period, it was not yet unthinkable that a party composed of ex-Boulangists, socialists, anti-Semites, and patriots could have been fashioned and could have found a good deal of support in the working class.[2]

Yet, between the heyday of Boulangist-socialist cooperation and the formation of the Action française, a major political upheaval in the form of the Dreyfus affair dispelled any hopes of a nationalist-socialist alliance. If the lines between socialists and nationalists had been blurred before the affair, they now took on the sharpness of battle lines. For working-class leaders, the anti-Semites and nationalists were now unambiguously the camp of the enemy. *La patrie*, so long the rallying cry of the Left, now definitively passed to the clerics and the army. Thus, the constituency for a nationalist campaign had undergone a radical transformation. When a wave of nationalism swept Paris during the Dreyfus affair, it was a fundamentally different phenomenon than that which had accompanied the Boulangist episode a decade earlier. In Boulanger's great Parisian victory in the by-election of 1889, the backbone of his support had come from working-class districts.[3] In contrast, the nationalism of the late 1890s was rooted in the middle and upper classes. It was the more fashionable *quartiers*, for example, that gave the nationalists their victory in the 1900 municipal elections.[4] Nationalism had gone respectable, and with this respectability it lost enthusiasm for enlisting the working class in a crusade against the Republic.

The Ligue de la patrie française, the great coalition of nationalists formed during the Dreyfus affair, showed itself in no mood to attempt a reconstitution of the Boulangist alliance of extremes against the Center. Its refusal to consider even the pretense of a program of social reform set the tone for the nationalism of the early 1900s.[5]

From its founding, however, the Action française promised to be something more. The stodgy conservatism of the Patrie française was what had led the founders of the Action française to strike off on their own in the first place. Despite their early profession of royalism, none of the original members of the Action française, with the exception of Maurras, were royalists at the time of the founding of the organization. And Maurras's royalism had nothing to do with the person of the pretender or existing royalist organizations; rather, it was concerned with abstract logical deductions about the health of the nation and the institution of monarchy. The conversions Maurras operated on the cofounders of the Action française would have been unthinkable save that his monarchy offered a fresh alternative to what, in their minds, was a hopelessly corrupted Republic. The activist mentality of the young royalists was well represented by Henri Vaugeois, who, along with Maurras, was the moving spirit behind the early Action française. Léon Daudet recalls how Vaugeois, "old extremist radical that he was," preferred converts with leftist credentials to either conservatives or liberals. Vaugeois, Daudet remembers, "cherished the socialist-revolutionary as a dough capable of expanding into an excellent royalist reactionary."[6]

This distinction between supporters of the status quo, be they liberal or conservative, and radical nationalists is indispensable for understanding the early Action française. Abel Manouvriez, a young law student at the time and a rather typical recruit to the Action française, recalls that it was Vaugeois who could reach him.[7] In Manouvriez's words: "Vaugeois, a former university professor, grand-nephew to a member of the 1793 Convention, was in a better position than a man of the Right, a pure *blanc*, to reach and even convince the *radical-patriote* or, if you will, the *socialiste-national* that I was. In his company, I instinctively felt with someone of my *climat*."[8]

Manouvriez's attitude toward the traditional Right, like that of many others who came into the neoroyalist fold before 1914, was hardly sympathetic. For him the regular monarchist clientele—whom he admitted to knowing only vaguely—were suspect. They represented, Manouvriez remembers, "a conservative world, which Drumont had taught me to consider only with distrust." A reading of Vaugeois convinced him that the royalism of the Action française had nothing to do with the traditionalism of the monarchists. He remembers Vaugeois emphasizing, "'We will say it over again and never enough . . . : we are not royalists of regret, we are revolutionary royalists.'" The conversion was made, and the political formulas enunciated by Vaugeois and Maurras were taken up by Manouvriez with the zeal of the converted. "I endowed [these political formulas] with all the seductions of novelty, youth, boldness, and brilliance. Nor was I the only one."[9]

Thierry Maulnier, looking back fondly from the perspective of the 1930s, viewed the early neoroyalists as they undoubtedly had viewed themselves, a "young Right, which was no longer solely the party of old men, great fortunes, and conservative order." He continued: "The phalanxes of the Action française had been, at the turn of the century, the harbingers of this new Right, which was not content anymore to be a party of resistance but intended to be, among others and *above* others, the party of movement."[10]

Yet to be a true party of movement and, at the same time, fly patriotic colors was not an easy task, given the increasingly conservative clientele rallying to nationalism in the wake of the Dreyfus affair. No one could take seriously a party of movement that depended upon Center liberals, Catholics, and the bourgeoisie for its forward momentum. Louis Dimier—himself a fervent Catholic and an early convert to Maurras's royalism—cogently expressed the dilemma of post-Dreyfusard nationalism. "It was a new Boulangism," he wrote, "more aware of its principle than the old, deprived, however, of the participation of one important group, that of the working class, which the socialist leaders had artfully enlisted in the Dreyfusard party."[11] Where could a remedy be found, Dimier asked rhetorically? Only, he answered, in a "bold economic policy that would have placed us in the first rank of those pressing for working-class demands." This "bold economic policy," Dimier reasoned, would put "our monarchy" above the fray of parties and classes and would enable us to reconstitute the "old Boulangist coalition."[12]

It was a course that in time the young royalist organization would attempt to follow. Yet, for several years after its founding, the Action française hesitated. A real opening to the Left—in the form of support for revolutionary syndicalism—came only in the summer of 1908, a full nine years after its founding.

The main stumbling block seemed to be Maurras himself, who, in the immediate wake of the Dreyfus affair, was wary of a "bold economic policy."[13] This wariness is somewhat perplexing in the light of Maurras's early career. He had supported Boulanger. He had kept close ties with Barrès during the nationalist-socialist experimentation of the 1890s. And he had been able to write, as early as 1890, that Drumontism would be fulfilled only when it could win over the socialist masses, "the great blind force, still unemployed."[14] Further, Maurras, who from the beginning was a vocal critic of economic as well as political liberalism, had established a theoretical base from which a royalist social policy could have been readily articulated.

This theoretical base included a number of elements with unlimited potential for a "bold economic policy": a critique of prevailing liberal right-to-work philosophy, based upon Maurras's conviction that work in the modern industrial plant is eminently social; a penetrating analysis of labor's degeneration to the status of a commodity in a free-market society; and, finally, a sympathetic description of how exploited labor can easily be transformed into kindling for political agitation.[15] But whatever the potential latent in Maurras's critique of liberalism, it was left largely undeveloped. Although he maintained that liberal society would certainly decompose given its blatant inadequacies, Maurras blandly assumed that at some point this decomposition would be arrested by the reinstitution of a corporate society where all social groups, including the proletariat, would graciously take up their old stations in the social hierarchy. The man whom Maurras claimed to be his maître in such matters was La Tour du Pin, the conservative champion of Catholic corporatism.

Why did Maurras, who could have few illusions about La Tour du

Pin's attractiveness to the workers, refuse to consider more daring options? How could a man, who had been so innovative in the political revision of royalism, transforming it from a nostalgic code of honor for aging aristocrats to a fighting creed attractive to the young, be so utterly devoid of imagination in social matters?

The answer to this puzzling question seems to lie deep in Maurras's basic approach to politics, economy, and society. "I was and remain convinced," Maurras could write, "that the phenomenon of economics being one thing, the phenomenon of politics is another; it is necessary to first perceive them separately before being able later to study the relations between one and the other. The specificity of political laws, the autonomy of their study, is one of the bases of the maxim 'Politics first,' which is our constant guide."[16] The practical effect of Maurras's distinction was translated succinctly by Maulnier: "With Maurras, the political problem is not solved by the economic revolution, the economic problem is solved by the political revolution: 'Politics first.'"[17]

Thus, social policy received short shrift, because, quite simply, politics were given first priority. It was only later—almost ten years later—when social concerns had forced themselves to the center of the political arena that Maurras, and with him the Action française, reconsidered. When this did occur, the royalists were not without resources. Despite indifference in the highest places, the ingredients for a "bold economic policy" had been developed—but this development was slow and took place far from the real center of power at the Action française. It began when several of Maurras's younger disciples took a keen interest in the evolution of the French labor movement, a movement that was experiencing a period of phenomenal growth in the first years of the twentieth century.

In the wake of the Paris Commune, French labor lay devastated: for nearly a decade after 1871, the organized working class virtually ceased to exist in France. It soon became evident, however, that the roots had not been destroyed. The decade of the 1880s saw a marked revival of the union movement, which was to blossom forth into a full-bodied renaissance during the 1890s. The organized workers, by the end of that decade, had not only thrown off their earlier docility vis-à-vis the Republic, but, even more significantly, they felt strong enough to challenge the tutelage of the socialist parties eager to enlist the syndicalist masses under their banners. By the early twentieth century, French labor had even fashioned a unique ideological alternative, which questioned existing forms of both unionism and socialism. Revolutionary syndicalism, as this alternative was soon labeled, satisfied itself with neither amelioration for its own sake through trade unions nor revolution through political action; syndicalists adamantly rejected amelioration as a goal and politics as a means. Revolutionary syndicalism represented, in the words of a recent and perceptive commentator, "revolutionary action by unions to establish a society based on unions."[18] Its essence was contained in the notion that the workers themselves, unaided by politicians and unfettered by prevailing capitalist forms, could establish a genuine producers' society.

Institutionally, the base of this movement was the *syndicat*. The syndicat was generally much smaller, more local, and more homogeneous than its English counterpart, the trade union. Although the syndicats, by the 1890s, had begun to organize themselves into federations by profession and, usually somewhat later, by industry, they maintained a generous measure of autonomy. Thus, federations typically suffered from a lack of real control over member syndicats. Despite this weakness at the top, federated syndicats had, by the mid-1890s, managed to create a central national organization, the Confédération générale du travail. The new national labor organization suffered in the extreme from the same disease that afflicted most federations: it reigned rather than ruled because it lacked effective means of disciplining member organizations. For several years after its founding, the Confédération générale du travail floundered as little more than a paper organization.

During the 1890s, the syndicalist movement was energized by an impulse that came neither from the growing professional federations nor from the new national confederation but from a third source, the *bourses du travail*. The bourses were a unique French institution. In one sense, the bourse was simply a building donated by the municipality for the use of the workers. It served as a labor exchange, as a meeting place, as a permanent seat for local syndicats, and as an educational and cultural center. But the bourse du travail, in the common parlance of the day, referred to more than a building: the term was used by the general public and the syndicalists alike to designate a particular form of working-class organization. The bourse, used in this wider sense, meant workers organized by region rather than by profession. All the syndicats of a given town, for example, regardless of their professional association, would typically unite to form a local bourse du travail. These bourses, which in the early years were animated by a real esprit de corps and a pronounced sense of worker solidarity, performed many vital functions within the labor movement. The bourse served as a mutual aid society, a propaganda dissemination agency, and, perhaps most importantly, an experimental cell of the working-class society of the future.[19]

It was this last function that the real animator of the bourse movement, Fernand Pelloutier, saw as its central mission. In this context, revolutionary syndicalism—which grew up concurrently with the great flowering of the bourse movement in the late 1890s and the early years of the new century—was seen simply as the first fruit of a specifically working-class culture. Further, the basic institutional framework of this working-class culture of the future was articulated when Pelloutier's dynamic Fédération nationale des bourses du travail formally merged with the Confédération générale du travail in 1902. The result was a reorganized and energized national confederation built upon two separate but equal components: a section of the regionally oriented bourses and a section of the professionally oriented federations.

Beyond a general commitment to revolutionary unionism and an institutional anchor in syndicats, bourses, and professional federations, the specific content of revolutionary syndicalism remained somewhat ill defined. Syndicalist leaders were fond of claiming that revolutionary syndicalism was not a concrete doctrine at all but merely a reflection of the practice of the organized workers. To an extent this was certainly true, but one could hardly avoid the fact that even the practice of the workers was open to various interpretations. Syndicalist leaders, for example, were regularly divided as to the meaning to be attributed to the actions taken by workers. Interpretations varied even more radically once one left the syndicalist movement proper.

From the perspective of this study, two particularly influential interpretations of revolutionary syndicalism are of relevance. A first is that of the anarchists, who came into the syndicalist movement in large numbers during the 1890s and took over many of its most important leadership posts.[20] Through their pamphlets, periodicals, and newspapers, they propagated a version of syndicalism that, not without logic, was often referred to as anarchosyndicalism. A second influential interpretation of revolutionary syndicalism was that promoted by Georges Sorel and his disciples, who, although they had no formal connection with the syndicalist movement per se, were seen by the general reading public, both inside and outside of France, as faithful interpreters of revolutionary syndicalism. Not surprisingly, whereas the anarchists, who were in leadership positions, tended to emphasize more practical and immediate concerns, Sorel was primarily interested in the wider historical and philosophic import of syndicalism.[21]

These two most influential interpretations of syndicalism were by no means mutually exclusive. Both Sorel and the anarchists were consistent and vociferous critics of democracy as it was practiced in the Third Republic. They likewise shared a conviction that working-class participation in electoral politics was detrimental to the true interests of French labor. A revolutionary syndicalism undiluted by participation in republican politics, they both agreed, would be a suitable vehicle for the further development of a specifically working-class culture, one that would contrast favorably with the decadent bourgeois alternative.

These similarities, however, are finally less significant than critical differences separating Sorel and the anarchists. At the center of these differences is a conservative undercurrent in Sorel's thought, often noted as a curiosity but less often analyzed with reference to the corpus of Sorel's writing. A proper understanding of these differences in outlook between Sorel and the anarchists reveals not only how variously the content of revolutionary syndicalism could be interpreted but also how it came to be that the Sorelians were such highly visible figures in the attempted alliance between the royalists and the syndicalists.

A first significant difference between Sorel and the anarchists was on the crucial matter of democracy. The anarchists, as has been noted, were antidemocratic in the sense that they opposed the hierarchical tendencies inherent in most practicing democracies, including the Third Republic. But for Sorel and his *nouvelle école*, as the Sorelian socialists were soon labeled, the attack on democracy was launched on a much broader front. In fact, the word "democracy" as it was employed by the theorists of the nouvelle école was often synonymous with the political heritage of the Enlightenment, especially that characteristic late-eighteenth-century faith in the progressive improvement of humanity. To this, they were adamantly and unequivocally hostile. Their hostility was also directed toward an important corollary of this eighteenth-century creed: that the key to progressive amelioration is to be found in an increased liberation from restraint. According to one of Sorel's most gifted pupils, democracy, used in its broadest sense, is pernicious because it teaches that humanity moves "toward greater and greater liberty [and] that the duty of man is to hasten this progressive liberation."[22] It is here, on the issue of liberation from restraint, that Sorel and his cohort stood foursquare against the anarchists, who, according to Sorelian logic, were the only thoroughgoing democrats because they alone argued for total liberation. Sorel was consistent on this point throughout his long career: not only was liberation from restraint a danger to the morality of the individual, but, more seriously, it was also a danger to the very progress of civilization.

This opposition between Sorel and the anarchists was reflected in their very different attitudes toward syndicalism. The anarchists had liberationist hopes for the working class: the full development of each individual without the moralistic restraints of the past. Sorel, on the other hand, looked to syndicalism as *"a mechanism capable of guaranteeing the development of morality."*[23] His conception of morality was, in contrast to that of the anarchists, traditional. Although he always liked to consider himself an empiricist and could work up a great deal of scorn for those who would claim to prescribe rather than describe reality, his writings betray a stubborn allegiance to a stern moral code.[24] As Irving Louis Horowitz has noted, Sorel "is torn between a confusion of descriptive and prescriptive elements." At the base of Sorel's psychology, Horowitz continues, is not the empirical exploration of human behavior "but an unexplored moral dogmatism. . . . Sorel was captivated by an absolutist theological ethic unhampered by empirical considerations."[25]

This moral dogmatism follows logically from Sorel's deep suspicion—one is tempted to say fear—of the passionate side of man. Whereas the anarchists might argue that a greater degree of instinctual freedom was necessary to the society of the future, Sorel was convinced that increased sexual license could only result in decadence and destruction of the building block of every society, the family.[26]

The close connection between Sorel the moralist, the foe of sexual license, and Sorel the political thinker was fully revealed only with the publication of *Les Illusions du progrès*.[27] The book is an extravagant polemic pitting the pessimistic and morally upright seventeenth century against the flabby optimism of the eighteenth. "One can say," Sorel writes, "that, at the end of the seventeenth century, fear of sin, respect for chastity, and pessimism were disappearing almost at the same time."[28] A degeneration of morality suited to the rise of a pleasure-loving bourgeoisie had set in. This degeneration found its characteristic expression in the writings of the philosophes: democratic dogmas of man's inherent virtue and his potential perfectibility—in short, a theory of natural progress. The equation, for Sorel, was simple. The decline of heroic and ascetic morality equals the rise of democracy. The latter is simply the political expression of the former.[29]

If to Sorel democracy represented degeneration of ethical standards and a threat to the most important societal institution, the family, it also endangered another key institution, the workshop. Like Proudhon, Sorel placed great ethical significance upon man's ultimate fulfillment through work.[30] But, more importantly, to him the workshop was the motive force behind the advance of civilization. The only real progress was concrete technical progress, hard-fought victories over recalcitrant nature.[31] Sorel's view of progress was far removed from the naturalistic theories of the eighteenth century: nature constantly threatened to wash away the puny defenses erected by men to protect themselves. Any relaxation of effort would spell disaster. Men in the workshop had to be keyed, like soldiers in the French revolutionary armies, to sacrifice and heroic deeds.[32]

As with his view of the family, Sorel's ideas about the workshop have an unmistakable air of nostalgia about them.[33] When Sorel spoke of the worker, the model he clearly had in mind is the nineteenth-century artisan. The more contemporary *salarié*, with his characteristic emphasis upon consumptive rather than productive values, was repugnant to Sorel.

Sorel saw democratic values, with their roots in the Enlightenment, as corrosive of the work ethic. The politics of the Left tended to stress remuneration rather than work, instinctual release rather than discipline, and, most offensively to Sorel, a bland confidence that history was on the side of the working class.

From this perspective, the basic conservative undercurrent of Sorel's thought is evident. To be sure, he was a revolutionary—in fact, a revolutionary who candidly looked to violence for its cathartic effect. But his revolution was to revive those virtues of the *ancienne France* that had been swept away in the democratic deluge: devotion to family, traditional sex roles, and the work ethic. It was this deep conservative strain in the thought of Sorel and his disciples, coupled with certain aspects of syndicalist practice, that attracted the attention of the young royalists.

But this conservatism, although basic to Sorel's thought, is not its most conspicuous trait. It was often obscured by Sorel's emphasis on themes generally associated with the Left: sympathy with the working class, emphasis on the necessity of revolutionary change, and, later, the apology for violence. It was also concealed unintentionally by the credulity of many of Sorel's socialist and syndicalist friends overeager to connect Sorel's prodigious erudition with their own cause. Finally, for a time at the turn of the century, it was also obscured by another factor: Sorel's own uncharacteristic enthusiasm. Sorel, rarely given to optimism, was positively exuberant over the renaissance of syndicalism, especially the flourishing bourse movement. Writing to Hubert Lagardelle, a young socialist friend, he exclaimed: "You may well say: 'La Vérité est en marche!'"[34]

Lagardelle was at the time drawing up plans for a new socialist journal, later to become the *Mouvement socialiste*. Sorel was ready with advice: "If you manage to give a shape to these tendencies [those represented by the bourses] in your review, . . . you will have done socialism the greatest service possible."[35]

At first, Lagardelle demurred, hoping that his journal would be above any one faction, that it would function as a critical conscience for the entire socialist movement.[36] But soon his disappointment with the socialists in the Chamber after the Dreyfusard victory led him closer to Sorel's position. Within a few years of its founding, the *Mouvement socialiste* had become the chief exponent of the new doctrine of revolutionary syndicalism, on the one hand, and, on the other, an outspoken critic of the use of democratic means in achieving socialist ends.

René de Marans, a convert to royalism from the ranks of the anti-liberal Catholics, was one of the first among the royalists to publicly express sympathy for the work of the nouvelle école. Writing in 1905, de Marans argued that one could discern two socialisms, one corrupt, an offspring of democratic ideas, the other healthy, a result of the renaissance of syndicalism. The collaborators of the *Mouvement socialiste*, de Marans claimed, were able to distinguish between "what belongs rightfully to socialism and what is democracy's." In practical terms, they identified the increasing incompatibility between the socialism of the political parties and the new "working-class socialism" just becoming aware of itself. The issue between the two was fundamental. Political socialism argued that the social transformation was to be "carried out on the legal ground of the bourgeoisie," whereas the new working-class socialism promised that it would be carried out by the workers themselves, with their own weapons, on their own terrain.[37] The difference between the two socialisms, de Marans maintained, was between direct and indirect action. The former was to be favored, according to de Marans, because it signaled the renaissance of those intermediate groups that had formerly given health to the body politic but had subsequently been smothered by the growth of a centralized and despotic Republic. In his appreciation of syndicalism, Sorel was singled out by de Marans for special praise as a moralist of the first order.[38]

Though de Marans was the first, he was not the only disciple of

Maurras to interest himself in the nouvelle école. Between 1906 and 1908 several articles by Jean Rivain concerning revolutionary syndicalism appeared in the fortnightly *Revue de l'Action française*.[39] Rivain was no ordinary young militant. He had a rare combination of talent, money, and connections. Not only was his mother-in-law, Madame de Courville, highly influential and active on the Action française's behalf, but Rivain's personal wealth allowed him to finance several important royalist projects.[40]

"The Action française, on the one hand," Rivain wrote, "the avant-garde of the revolutionary syndicalist socialists, on the other, are the only ones in France to call themselves antidemocratic." This theme of the revolt of the extremes, the coincidence of revolutionaries of the Left and of the Right—soon to be a common chord of royalist propaganda—was first enunciated by Rivain early in 1907. Rivain, who considered himself a loyal disciple of both Maurras and La Tour du Pin, hoped to demonstrate how revolutionary syndicalism was merely an attempt by a disinherited proletariat to reconstitute its corporate identity. To be sure, admitted Rivain, proletarian behavior and official ideology were far from the corporate ideals expressed in the writings of La Tour du Pin. But the proletariat since the Revolution of 1789 had been a victim: a victim of economic liberalism, of democracy, and of republican education. If syndicalist ideology seemed brutal, it was because the proletariat had been brutalized. "Like all the liberal conquests of the 1789 Revolution," Rivain wrote, "the freedom of work has only consecrated the freedom of the strongest." Because no mutual duties and obligations exist, the workshop has been subjected to this law of the strongest. According to Rivain, "the capitalist having money has strength, . . . [whereas] the worker is reduced to a human commodity."[41]

Given their degraded status, it is not surprising, Rivain argued, that the workers would be susceptible to revolutionary rhetoric. As victims of revolutionary propaganda, workers have adopted much of the revolutionary regalia, even to the point of seeing themselves as an extension of the revolutionary principle. However, careful and objective analysis, Rivain contended, reveals their enterprise to be essentially counterrevolutionary.

In Rivain's opinion, the one apparent counterrevolutionary thrust of the syndicalists was their growing hostility to democracy. This hostility manifested itself most obviously in diatribes against the parliamentary socialists. But attacking the socialists, according to Rivain, was only the first step in a maturation process that would eventually lead syndicalism to exclude all religious, political, and national opinions from the movement. The model that Rivain had in mind was the corporation of the ancien régime, whose concern, he maintained, was exclusively professional.[42]

There was, Rivain contended, an even more important manifestation of the antidemocratic spirit of syndicalism. This was revealed in the very organization of the syndicat itself, which was governed not by a "mindless and sheeplike majority" but by a determined, even violent, minority. In this respect the parallel between the royalists and the syndicalists was to Rivain particularly striking; both placed confidence not in the inert masses but in an aristocracy of energy.[43] In conclusion, Rivain held out the hope that "the development in all its parts of the reaction begun against democracy . . . would take the syndicalists to the doorstep of the Action française."[44]

The early interest of de Marans and Rivain in syndicalism and the nouvelle école might never have gone past a few maverick articles save for an important development within the Action française itself. Rivain was gathering about him a group of very young and talented men, who began to form a rather distinct second generation within the neoroyalist movement. The founders of the Action française—Maurice Pujo, Vaugeois, and Maurras—were all politically active before the turn of the century, whereas Rivain's "second generation" were, for the most part, inexperienced politically.

This second generation claimed to be students of Maurras. They, as much as their master, took seriously the dictum: "Politique d'abord." Yet, unlike Maurras, they developed a genuine interest in social policy. Whatever their motivations—and they seem to have been varied—these young recruits to royalism all sensed that a political revolution, although it should necessarily precede an economic one, would require the support of the working class. They militated, therefore, for something akin to Dimier's "bold economic policy," first within their own small corner of the Action française, and then, when the royalist organization began to adopt certain elements of a more daring social policy, they took the lead in helping to implement it.

The mood of this second generation was in tune with the "generation of 1912" described in a famous *enquête* on France's youth, *Les Jeunes Gens d'aujourd'hui*, by Agathon.[45] The best method for viewing the generation of 1912, claimed Agathon, was by contrasting it with the preceding generation. Born of the defeat of 1870, this earlier generation wallowed in the kind of pessimism best expressed by Ernest Renan: " 'I have no hope. No reasonable man can have hope.' "[46] For this generation, the ideal was the operation of pure intelligence, usually directed toward introspection. Conviction of any kind—be it patriotic, scientific, or theological—was suspect. With neither faith nor hope, the men who came of age in the decade of the 1880s dissipated their energies and, out of a need for self-justification, raised their decadence to the status of a virtue. The effect of this mood Agathon judged to be purely negative, for it led to a debilitating paralysis of the will.[47]

This fin-de-siècle heritage was rejected wholesale by Agathon's "generation of 1912." They proclaimed themselves indifferent to the working of pure intellect and were distrustful of their elders' obsession with the self. Eager to act in the world, they were just as eager for a set of beliefs that would sustain them in their activity and give it direction. Yet, Agathon argued, they did not give themselves over to a naive idealism. Theirs was "an active idealism,"[48] one that set rigorous limits on imaginations. In fact, Agathon finds this realism to be perhaps their most characteristic trait: "Whereas their elders would lose themselves in skeptical cavils, they know that they are *here*, and *here* means that they live in France, at a certain time in its history, and that everything must be considered from this contemporary and French point of view."[49]

Agathon concluded that this spirit of realism expressed itself politically in two ways. The overwhelming majority hoped for some revision of the Republic so as to restore a stronger executive and thus end the domination by a corrupt and indecisive parliament. A small minority, however, were convinced that realism dictated "a nonparliamentary, antidemocratic France, logically organized around the central person of the king."[50] These—the most impassioned of a passionate generation—were described by a young writer, Georges Bernanos, in a letter to a friend: "I admire with all my heart these valiant men of the Action française, these true sons of Gaul, full of good sense and faith, who flinch before no idea, who assert themselves gallantly, define themselves without words. How clear! How trenchant! You believe in it or you don't, but you have to listen to them."[51]

It was this brand of militant realism that characterized the men gathering around Rivain. By early 1907 Rivain had organized a study group, the Cercle Joseph de Maistre.[52] Within a year the members of the group were planning publication of an intellectual forum, which first appeared in April 1908 as the *Revue critique des idées et des livres*.[53] De Marans, now solidly within the royalist fold, and Pierre Gilbert, young poet and brother-in-law of Rivain, joined with the latter to launch the new review. Maurice Barrès, writing from the perspective of 1917, recalled the spirit that animated the project: "These young doctrinaires, men of taste and fire, formed a society of a rare species, an academy, at the same time knowledgeable, sophisticated, and enthusiastic."[54]

The function of the review was to apply the canons of Maurrassian realism to all aspects of French society and culture. Before one could attempt the restoration of the king, the men of the *Revue critique* reasoned, one had to restore the French spirit, redirect national energies from the cul-de-sac of the various romanticisms that had dominated the nineteenth century. The French must rediscover their own heritage.

Politically, of course, this heritage was monarchy, and the *Revue critique* along with other publications of the Action française spent considerable time attacking anything remotely derived from the principles of 1789. The new review also interested itself in cultural matters. Henri Clouard, a literary critic who began his career at the *Revue critique*, later described the dimensions of the cultural project undertaken there. The men around Rivain, according to Clouard, would settle for nothing less than the reform of the "public spirit." They would reeducate public taste, something they saw as sorely in need of reform after the cultural debacle of the fin de siècle.[55]

But in its first years, at least, it was neither the political nor the cultural program of the *Revue critique* that attracted the most attention but rather its social policy. This policy had its starting point in Rivain's earlier studies of the nouvelle école and his interest in the congruences between revolutionary syndicalism and the Action française. The very first issue of the *Revue critique* gave an indication of the degree of attention Rivain's group would lavish on syndicalism.

The editors announced a regular column on syndicalist affairs by Emile Para, a young journalist and a "royalist syndicalist."[56] According to the editors, this association of terms, that is, royalism and syndicalism, was nothing new but rather something that was traditionally monarchist in nature: "The solution of the working-class question by the 'installation of the proletariat' and its organization has been one of the essential postulates of the monarchical doctrine."[57] At present, the editors admitted, relations between syndicalists and royalists were disappointing. But the first necessary step toward reconciliation must be taken.

Para, though relying on themes already articulated by Rivain, had the advantage of a polemical verve absent in the latter.[58] His first column praised the nouvelle école for attempting to rid the working class of its remaining illusions about democracy. Sorel was congratulated for revitalizing Marxism by returning the class struggle to its former primacy in socialist doctrine and exposing the stagnancy of the Marxist parties. It was clear, Para claimed, that syndicalism was moving from a reliance upon democracy to a new self-reliance in the form of direct action.

Along with the editors, Para admitted that the growing negative attitude toward democracy was not as yet matched by a more positive one toward monarchy. But the logic of their situation would lead syndicalists toward the Action française. Syndicalists, Para maintained, although rightly rejecting the politics of electoral parties, were naive in rejecting the reality of the political arena altogether. Direct action that totally ignored political realities would lead to disaster; for, if syndicalism turned its back on politics, the republican politicians would be left a free hand. Whereas they theoretically represented public opinion, the politicians in reality manipulated it. It was becoming apparent, Para continued, that the current press campaign against syndicalism was being led covertly by the politicians and was furthermore only a preparation of public opinion for more drastic things. When the government finally decided to move against syndicalist organizations and arrest their leaders, there would be little public opposition. Thus syndicalists, even though they were as disdainful as the Action française of participation in republican politics, would ultimately see the wisdom of Maurras's dictum: "politics first." They would come to the conclusion that "the working-class problem is above all social and economic, but all that this shows is that a political solution is called for."[59]

The first major obstacle faced by the group at the *Revue critique*, as they no doubt realized, was the sheer difficulty in getting a hearing with syndicalists, who were not in the habit of reading reviews of the Right. The efforts of the royalists to attract attention in syndicalist quarters were given an inestimable boost by the appearance in the second number of an article by Georges Sorel. To be sure, Sorel's article was no direct endorsement of the review itself or of any of its projects, including the wooing of the syndicalists. The article concerned the modernist controversy in the Catholic church and pretended to be no more than the disinterested speculations of an agnostic concerning the broader moral dimensions of the controversy.[60] The content of Sorel's article, however, gave a kind of indirect sanction to the uncompromising style of the Action française, for in it Sorel launched a scathing attack on the moral laxity of those who would sacrifice orthodoxy to adapt the Catholic church to modernity.

The editors of the new review, however, were obviously aware that arguing the logic of a royalist-syndicalist accord—even attracting an occasional article by a syndicalist luminary—was one thing and actively seeking it out was quite another. The latter task was undertaken by a relative newcomer to the Action française, Alfred Georges Gressent, who had assumed the pen name of Georges Valois. With the first number of the *Revue critique*, Valois launched an *enquête* into the attitude of syndicalist militants and intellectuals toward a royalist-syndicalist alliance.

By reliable accounts, Valois was one of the most talented—if not the most talented—convert to the Action française in the prewar years.[61] In the light of the fact that in the next few years the formation of a royalist-syndicalist alliance was to become Valois's personal project, it will be necessary to inquire into the political odyssey that led Valois to the Action française. This odyssey, despite its idiosyncracies, was not an altogether uncommon one among the men who formed the new radical Right in France.

[3]

Toward a Royalist Syndicalism:
Georges Valois

In 1906 the twenty-six-year-old Valois, renegade anarchist and self-proclaimed disciple of Georges Sorel, presented himself at the offices of the Action française. He had already gone to Paul Bourget in a desperate attempt to find a publisher for a highly exotic polemic justifying authority. Bourget sent the young author to Maurras. Not long after, the polemic was published under the auspices of the Action française as *L'Homme qui vient*. It was the start of a long and tumultuous courtship between Valois and the Action française—one that ended some twenty years later when Valois broke with the Action française after having organized France's first fascist movement.[1]

Alfred Georges Gressent was born in Paris in 1878. His own recollections point to the fact that he was the recipient of not one but two educations: one at the knees of his grandparents, the other from the author of *Reflections on Violence*, Georges Sorel. The sequence was not, as one might have expected, tradition and revolt. Both educations, according to Valois, served to reinforce each other, forming the foundation for his "philosophy of authority."

Georges Valois's father died when he was three years old, and his upbringing was entrusted to his grandparents.[2] By his own testimony this upbringing was the most crucial factor in his life. He points out that many of his generation lamented the narrowness of their petit bourgeois origins and achieved maturity only by liberating themselves from its confinements. In contrast, he recalls: "My true liberation dates back to the day when I rediscovered, inscribed in my mind and in my flesh, the living truths that had been transmitted to me by my family."[3]

Valois's earliest memories are of his grandfather's workshop where he was introduced to republican virtues and heroes by a republican "of the heroic epoch." The virtues were both democratic and patriotic: "To live for the people and avenge the injury done to France by the Prussians."[4] But, above all, the young Valois learned that the Republic was on the side of science and progress and was champion of the artisan. These were compatible elements in France after they had ceased to be so elsewhere. The French resisted giving up the notion of the artisan in his workshop as the force behind scientific and technical advance. Valois recalls his grandfather proudly taking him to the Paris exposition of 1889 where republican and technological virtues seemed inseparable. This conjunction was further strengthened by Valois's schoolmasters, who, he remembered, preached "that science is the first property of man, that everything must be done to acquire knowledge of it, that kings, princes, and priests are the enemies of science, and that the greatest glory is to defend the Republic, protectress of science and labor."[5]

Of a somewhat different inclination was his grandmother. "She held to the Decalogue," he recalled, "being neither devout nor even pious."[6] Hers was a peasant legacy: to be honest, to accept one's lot, and above all to work. Valois saw her as the embodiment of the virtues of the *ancienne France*: "When I look for the face of France, a thousand undefined forms rise from the earth and the water, come out of the woods, and melt into the face of a woman whom I recognize and in whose eyes I look for an answer; and there I always read the same commandment, 'Work, my boy, work. . . . Go on, my boy, the day is not over yet.'"[7]

In the workshop of his grandfather, Valois learned the pleasures of craftsmanship—where "one experiences the joys of creation, when one sees a shapeless piece of iron becoming a tool or a rosette."[8] His grandmother's territory, the garden, was the source of even more important revelations. Work was not only joy in creation but, significantly, perseverance over time.

If his grandmother's work ethic had the deepest influence on Valois, his grandfather's politics had the most immediate effect. He recalls, as a schoolboy not yet in his teens, ardently defending the Republic against Boulangism.[9] But the same idealism that inspired his republicanism quickly led him away from the Third Republic. By the mid-1890s he was drinking "long drafts of the young wine that came out of revolutionary vats." His grandfather's passionate defense of the Republic was wasted on the budding revolutionary: "I mentioned Panama: he lowered his head."[10]

Behind his grandfather's republicanism were the principles of 1789, principles that, if carried to their logical end, would call for man's total liberation. From the perspective of the 1890s, Valois reasoned, the only group pressing for this liberation were the anarchists. Accordingly, he became an anarchist. Writing just after World War I, politically his most conservative period, Valois could still say: "The world of anarchy was a world where honest men could venture."[11]

Valois's first contact with anarchism came with a group that met at a café on the rue du Louvre and called itself the Art social. Among those he came to know there were Fernand Pelloutier and Paul Delesalle, both important figures in syndicalist circles. But most importantly, his wanderings among the coteries forming the fin-de-siècle Parisian Left led him to the offices of *L'Humanité nouvelle*.[12] It was here that a small group of French intellectuals, among them Georges Sorel, were attempting seriously to digest and interpret the still novel writings of Marx.

The impact that Georges Sorel must have had on the young Valois can be gauged by a description—written some twenty years later—of a session where the former presided: "Sorel, with the strong head of a winegrower, a clear brow, eyes full of mischievous kindness, could speak for hours without anyone thinking of interrupting him. His general knowledge is prodigious, he knows thoroughly several sciences, he has a philosophical culture, which is, I believe, unique."[13]

Valois was never precise about just what part of this "philosophical culture" was imparted to him during his days at the *Humanité nouvelle*. He did, however, consistently maintain that Sorel was one of the most important influences on his intellectual development.[14] It was Sorel who advised him to study economics. But more importantly still, it was the retired engineer who liberated him from "democratic errors and superstitions."[15]

Considering that Valois is vague about the specifics of Sorel's influence, one cannot in any precise way pin down what he borrowed from the older man. What can be stated with assurance is that Valois began to experience a major shift in political orientation shortly after meeting Sorel. That shift, according to Valois's testimony, took place over a period of several years. It started with a vague uneasiness about anarchist doctrines and ended at the doorstep of the Action française.

By his own account, Valois's political shift was akin to a conversion experience. Several incidents, according to Valois, helped crystallize this change and make it highly personal. Yet the "democratic errors and superstitions," learned at the knee of his master, form a backdrop for all of Valois's subsequent development.

Valois likens his conversion to that of another and more famous Frenchman, Charles Péguy—and not without some justice. Both came to politics very young and idealistic, both threw themselves into the Dreyfusard crusade, both came away disillusioned. Péguy described the cruel disappointment of a young generation of political activists at the rapid degeneration of mystique into politique. Valois was among the disappointed.[16]

It was in the wake of the Dreyfus affair that he, like Péguy, began to feel uncomfortable on the Left. In the 1890s, as Valois saw it, the Left was attractive to those who had political convictions and were ready for personal sacrifice; by 1900 the Left, even the anarchists, had become rather too fashionable. Valois, again not unlike Péguy, prided himself on his humble origins and liked to distinguish between the parasitic rich and the *vrai peuple*. This distinction, Valois felt, was being blurred by the anarchists' newly found popularity, especially among the literary avant-garde where "anarchy made itself very discreet, putting on gloves and jewels." Valois wondered if he was not deceiving himself with an "absurd comedy."[17] Not long afterward, he and his "serious" friends left the anarchist movement. "The origin of our reaction is very simple," Valois wrote; "we loved the *peuple* to which we belonged, and the majority of the anarchists of that period—intellectual bastards—despised them profoundly."[18]

The young Valois, disillusioned with anarchism yet without an alternative commitment, now underwent two formative experiences: a short stint in the military and a year in Russia as a tutor.

Though Valois admits that he began to have certain doubts about anarchist attitudes toward authority from reading Bourget and Barrès, it was only through living in the barracks that a real change occurred. Men did not seem to work for a common cause without some form of constraint. Valois began to accept the necessity of authority. In fact, he admits candidly, "I discovered with stupor that I had a secret admiration for this authority, which gives so much order to the movements of men."[19]

While in military service, Valois further noted that his anarchist friends resented physical labor—something they left for peasants and workers. This was to develop into a central theme for Valois: political intellectuals with their *idées avancées* have no contact, nor do they desire any, with the workshop. They feel labor to be demeaning and have little use for it except to exploit it for their own purposes: "I came to the conclusion that the true working people, deceived in the name of opposite ideas, are the eternal victims of politicians fighting for power."[20]

Sometime in 1902 Valois left Paris for Russia, having received a tutorship with an aristocratic family. The trip had the effect of disillusioning him with another of the cherished beliefs of his Dreyfusard days, internationalism. Valois was obviously impressed by the manners and culture of the family with whom he stayed. He likewise came to appreciate what he was told was the historical role of the Russian nobility—to preserve Western civilization against the thrusts of Asian barbarism. Do away with this nobility, Valois claims, "and the Russian land becomes again a vat where all barbarian ferments are boiling, a vast plain where a nation of peasants, defenseless but for their woods . . . will be a prey to the Asiatic hordes: Europe is open to Genghis Khan, Tamerlane, Attila."[21]

It is clear that Valois's anarchist vision of a universal and harmonious brotherhood was being replaced by the pseudo-Darwinist view of ineluctable struggle. The nation and the social hierarchy within the nation were not the anachronisms that his anarchist friends naively thought—they were necessary, Valois now concluded, for the very survival of civilization.

Valois admits that he did not immediately apply to France this newly found respect for the state and authority. But he was making "progress"—namely, he was moving away from the anarchist suspicion of all forms of authority. He found in the family library the works of "Macaulay, Fustel de Coulanges, and Taine, from whom . . . [he] had been kept by M. Durkheim and M. Seignobos."[22]

Czarist Russia led Valois to yet another volte-face. As a Dreyfusard and an enemy of French anti-Semites, Valois had thought that anti-Semitism in Russia was a fabrication of czarist propaganda. But, upon observation, he came to the conclusion that anti-Semitism was a movement of the masses, the vrai peuple. He discovered that Jews were not internationalists, as he had imagined, but were actually violent nationalists.[23] With their own language and customs, Jews were not a part of Russian culture and society. Even if one could ignore the fantastic plots attributed to the Jews, Valois maintained, one could arrive at the sober truth that "the Jewish people, launched in the midst of nations by their tragic destiny, will always make their own place by disrupting those who welcome them."[24]

Valois recollects his meditation on the Jewish problem on the train back to France. Despite his professed aversion to stories with fantastic plots, he recalls asking himself, somewhere between Warsaw and Berlin, whether the evolution of the world was not toward "a sort of universalism, controlled by the Jews, masters of money."[25]

The final blow to Valois's former ideas and allegiances came soon after his return from Russia. He married and became a father. His anarchist beliefs now took on an air of unreality. Purposely, he isolated himself from the old Parisian political circles, with two notable exceptions—Lucien Jean, a municipal administrator whom Valois had met at the Art social, and Charles Louis-Philippe, a writer of some distinction. Both, significantly, were of the vrai peuple. The literary works of Louis-Philippe, reminiscent of Péguy, are hymns to the working poor of his *vieille province*.[26] Lucien Jean, of more modest literary talent, had, however, a great influence on both Louis-Philippe and Valois.[27] Jean was a critic of anarchism from within and struck what was now a sympathetic chord in Valois, the importance of work. Valois recalls Jean criticizing the anarchists for believing that "when anarchy is achieved, life will be much easier."[28] For Jean, Louis-Philippe, and Valois, work took on an almost religious significance.

The three were no less devoted to that other pillar of the *ancienne France*, family. Valois remembers the words of Jean: "One can discuss forever on all the rest, but man, woman, and child, they form the essential structure of humankind."[29]

Thus, by 1905, Valois had come almost full circle. The influence of Sorel and a series of disillusioning personal experiences, reinforced by his contact with Lucien Jean and Charles Louis-Philippe, had led him back from his anarchist revolt to the *bagage moral* that his grandmother had given him. Family and work were now the twin axes upon which Valois's thoughts were to turn. "Any idea is false," he could write, "that goes against those two facts, which are the foundation of humankind; democracy, socialism, anarchy are valuable only insofar as they are favorable to family and work."[30]

Valois might have added revolutionary syndicalism to the trio of democracy, socialism, and anarchy; for it was syndicalism, as much as the other three, that Valois examined in the light of traditionalist values. Returning from Russia, Valois had obtained a position as secretary at a Parisian publishing house. In line with his Sorelian heritage, Valois promptly became active in the syndicat. He soon was convinced that syndicalism, far from advancing the interests of the workshop, often moved counter to them. Valois was especially disappointed by the lack of interest shown by the workers for the problems of the workshop. Syndicalism interested itself not so much in the organization of work as in the dispossession of the bourgeoisie. The workers "were wondering how they would make a revolution; I was wondering how we would work after the revolution."[31]

Valois's thinking about the postrevolutionary situation led him to a drastic reconsideration of the goals of syndicalism. Reduced to its simplest form, Valois reasoned, syndicalism meant the extension of democracy from the political to the all-important economic realm. In short, the workshop would be democratized: the *patronat* would be abolished, and some form of control by the workers themselves would be established. Socialists, whose primary concern was egalitarianism, looked forward to this, but Valois, who now saw himself as defender of the workshop, was alarmed. He foresaw the post-revolutionary workshop degenerating into a struggle among equals.

This, as he later explained, was a period of great intellectual turmoil for him; he had not yet fitted together the various parts of his intellectual transformation into a coherent whole. His experience in the workshop and in the syndicat, however, had the effect of bringing together his work orientation and his increasing distaste for anarchy in any form, coupled with his correspondingly enhanced respect for authority. One day, he recalls, his editor asked him to prepare a short definition of the word *travail*, and, after paring it down to twenty lines, Valois remembers his shock: "when I reread them [the twenty lines], the excitement having subsided, I was first astounded; I had just formulated for the general economy the law of least effort."[32] Within an hour Valois had written a symbolic representation of his "law of least effort"—the fable of the "man with the whip."

The fable begins with man in a state of barbarism. Early men lived a precarious existence, threatened by both animal enemies and famine. Men's natural laziness, however, prevented them from making provision for the future. When an energetic one among them rose up and tried to convince them to change their ways, they reacted with hostility and plotted his death. Suspecting their plans, the energetic one tied the tail of a tiger to the end of a stick, thereby inventing what for the first time made civilization possible, the whip. Not only was the energetic one able to defend himself, but he constrained his less energetic fellows to work beyond their immediate needs. Men were organized into working units, and, for the first time, the blessings of peace and security were experienced. The man with the whip, for services rendered, demanded only a small "surplus value" from the labor of the others, enough to nourish his sons and raise them to take his place. But the advantages of civilization over barbarism were such that those who first experienced the transition were filled with gratitude toward the man with the whip: "Strike us, master, if you love us; do not give us up lest we should become stray dogs again and give ourselves to animal laziness." Significantly, Valois calls this fable "The Man with the Whip; or, The First Noble; or, The First Capitalist; or, The Originator of Civilization."[33]

With the connection now made between civilization, work, and authority, Valois's conversion was complete. This last insight, which Valois in his autobiography attributes largely to his personal experience, was almost certainly helped along by his reading of Nietzsche. Influence from this quarter was played down by Valois, no doubt because the German philosopher was unacceptable not only to Maurras but to much of the Action française's Catholic support.[34] Yet Valois himself, in less guarded moments, admitted the importance of this influence. Not unlike many young men of his generation, Valois came away not with any real appreciation of Nietzsche but with a few aphorisms, which were garnered from his readings of translations as they were serialized in the *Mercure de France*.[35] They not only served to confirm his growing impatience with anarchism but gave a romantic twist to what he came to see as the necessity of constraint. Superman turned philistine became the man with the whip.

But, if Valois looked to Nietzsche for a solution, the predicament was Sorelian in origin. Valois's anxiety stemmed from what he perceived to be the constant danger of degeneration—a fear that civilization might easily dissolve into chaos. It is this basic theme that underlies *L'Homme qui vient* and, in fact, conditions all Valois's later political theorizing.

The greatest danger to civilization is that life will become too comfortable. If men listen carefully to the instinct of life, they will be able to avoid disaster, but only through vigilance, "by making constant use of energy, by constantly accepting effort, by keeping constantly away from pleasure, which is only enjoyment of a dissipating repose." Thus, according to Valois, "speaks the Instinct of Life."[36]

The problem with man is that by nature he is not inclined to work. Whereas the law of the preservation of the species calls for consistent effort, the individual is motivated by a different law: "*Man is a being whose energy, like all energy, follows the path of least resistance, of least effort."* Civilization, as Valois interprets it, is nothing more than the introduction of constraint to prevent the individual's natural propensity toward indolence from asserting itself: "It is work, the organization of work, that preserves civilization."[37] Thus, the contradiction between man's need to work and his desire to avoid it is the basic problem facing civilization. The solution to the problem—and this is the central theme of *L'Homme qui vient*— entails the restoration of two historical forms of authority, that of the *patron* and that of the *roi.*

The capitalist, for Valois, is simply the man with the whip updated. His authority is justified on the grounds that he is more energetic than his fellows and alone provides the constraint necessary to organize the workshop. Valois's argument for the authority of the king is likewise related to the workshop. By virtue of their superior energy, kings established their rule over a given territory, inducing men to give up the perpetual warfare of each against the other and channeling their energies into work. Over huge geographical areas, under the authority of kings, destructive struggle was replaced by productive cooperation.

Thus, rejecting his earlier commitment to anarchy, Valois came to see two dynamic forces, capitalism and nationalism, pushing civilization to higher levels. Without the constraint they provide, civilization would dissipate. Yet both these forces, so essential to civilization, are under attack by a third force, democracy. Democracy, for Valois, is the antithesis of energy and authority. It is an almost perfect demonstration of the law of least effort. As opposed to an emphasis on producing new wealth through the development of industry, democracy opens an easier route, the exploitation of already existing wealth. Men, who under other regimes would have made their way in industry, now become politicians. Organizing into parties, these politicians struggle with each other for support by promising the enticing prospect of the "Greatest Rest."[38] Under a democracy, the center of national power, the parliament, becomes a mere "assembly of appetites."[39]

Democracy, basing itself as it does on the free association of individuals, is weak, because individuals act in their own interest, not in the greater interest of the nation. Democrats refuse to cooperate in the national effort—and by extension the national war—and instead promote internal conflict by engendering and proliferating feuding parties. In line with the logic of Valois's argument, national wars, because they extend peace and civilization to greater and greater areas, are justifiable, whereas civil wars, representing a retrogression to a prenational epoch, are not.

Valois's argument ends in a curious paradox. Starting from a justification of the most brutal species of individualism, Valois leads the reader to an indictment of individualism itself. The egoism of the man with the whip, which in fact made civilization possible, has now become a historical anachronism. The same energy that men exerted earlier in dominating others must now be channeled toward the benefit of the collectivity. What is wisdom at one historical stage is folly at the next.

But the paradox has further implications. The pure egoism of the man with the whip is forbidden all modern men save one, the king. The energies of the rest of society must be mobilized and at the disposal of the king, who is in a struggle for survival with the heads of other states. This is where, according to Valois, contemporary struggle takes place, at the level of states. The failure of total internal mobilization for this struggle will mean defeat and domination by others.

If one replaces the king with the leader, the fundamental elements of fascism are already quite apparent in *L'Homme qui vient*. The appeal to heroism, the leadership principle, the mobilized masses, the glorification of war, and the primacy of instinct over reason[40]—all these elements, which will later put Valois at the head of France's first fascist party—were already formulated in *L'Homme qui vient*. The only anachronistic element that remains to tie him to traditional conservatism is his commitment to monarchy.[41]

Despite this curious retreat into royalism, the overall spirit of *L'Homme qui vient* is hardly traditional. Perhaps most symptomatically protofascist is Valois's argument against democracy. This argument was being elaborated not only, as one might expect, at the Action française but with increased seriousness on the Left. Up to that time, most socialists had seen democracy, if not as an end in itself, at least as a historical stage more advanced than monarchy.

But the whole thrust of Sorel's most important work was that democracy, far from being a signpost marking historical progression toward socialism, was a fateful retrogression. All the more dangerous, Sorel argued, because democracy, disguised behind platitudes of progress, could ensnare social movements committed to real change. Sorel, in effect, was arguing for a fundamental shift in orientation: the basic problem of contemporary civilization was not economic, as the socialists maintained (that is, the domination of capitalism), but political (that is, the prevalence of democracy). Sorel, and Valois after him, argued that electoral politics was a veritable disease, one that immobilized national life to the point of paralysis. And the solution was not, as the socialists would have it, a war of one class against another but a war against politics itself.[42]

This notion had a career ahead of it. It was later the rallying cry of fascism wherever it occurred in Western Europe. Sorel, unlike the fascists, felt that the problem could be remedied with proletarian violence. Valois, however, was one of the first to come to the conclusion of the latter-day fascists: democratic corruption could only be overcome through the good offices of the heroic leader. The dialectics of *L'Homme qui vient* clearly pointed in this direction; it remained only for the heroic leader to drop the trappings of the legitimate king.

Besides a lingering royalism, another difference can be discerned between the protofascism of *L'Homme qui vient* and later fascism. The principles developed in *L'Homme qui vient* were fashioned to fit a quite different clientele than the lower-middle-class base characteristic of most European fascisms of the interwar years. Valois's bold tones being quite in the spirit of the second-generation neo-royalists at the Action française, he naturally fell in, upon his arrival there, with the young group forming around Rivain. True to his interest in the relationship between work and authority expressed in *L'Homme qui vient*, he was drawn to the earlier studies of de Marans and Rivain on the coincidence between syndicalism and royalism.[43] During 1907, inspired no doubt by discussions at the Cercle Joseph de Maistre, Valois worked to enlarge upon the ideas already set forth by de Marans and Rivain. The result—which can only be described as a premature attempt to construct a working-class variety of fascism—appeared in four installments at the end of

1907 in the *Revue de l'Action française* and later in pamphlet form under the arresting title, *La Révolution sociale ou le roi.*

Valois's point of departure in *La Révolution sociale ou le roi* is the theme developed by de Marans and Rivain: the theory and practice of syndicalism indicate both a sharp break with democratic socialism and correspondingly a movement, however unconscious, toward counterrevolution. Valois saw in the syndicalist emphasis on direct action, as did his two predecessors, the development of a principle fundamentally antagonistic to democracy. But Valois carried the argument an important step forward. Both de Marans and especially Rivain had the unmistakable air of being corporatists —updated corporatists, to be sure, but corporatists nonetheless. Their sympathy for syndicalist trends stopped short of approval of the most basic one, class struggle. Especially in Rivain the tone was almost didactic and the message was clear: syndicalists must give up the notion of class struggle, because royalism implies the willing, one might even say joyful, acceptance of social harmony.

Valois, on the other hand, could hardly conceal the fact that his inspiration was primarily Sorelian.[44] As opposed to the corporatist emphasis on social harmony, Valois developed the Sorelian theme of the virtues of social antagonism, albeit with certain crucial departures from the thought of Sorel. It seemed an obvious attempt to give some badly needed life to neoroyalist social thought by prescribing measured doses of Sorel.

Of course, Valois argued, the form of class struggle promoted by the socialists, the expropriation of the bourgeoisie by the election of a socialist parliamentary majority, is mere duplicity. But removed from politics, in its purest economic sense, the notion of class struggle, Valois maintained, is valuable. He argued that class antagonism serves two beneficial ends. First, it allows the working class to develop its own autonomous forces, rendering it strong enough to defend itself against any attempt at exploitation. Second, it constrains the capitalist to give, "as M. Georges Sorel would have it, the full measure of its capitalist energy."[45] If Rivain admonishes the proletariat, advising them that they must see virtue in corporative institutions, Valois is more concerned that royalists disabuse themselves of their bias against "class spirit":

> Being royalists, we are syndicalists. We are not trying to kill the class spirit. On the contrary we want the working class to have a deeper consciousness of its class interests, so that it will never let itself be duped by the indolent bourgeoisie, and so that it will be able to defend its interests energetically; for we know that working-class action is the best insurance against the degradation of national energy in the present and the future. And we wish the working class to form a block, to achieve its unification and to administer itself freely, without the intervention of politicians or intellectuals, whoever they may be, so that it is able to devote itself exclusively to the defense of its interests, and to oppose any aggression as a homogeneous and irreducible mass that no exploiter of human passion can penetrate. It therefore seems that nothing separates us, royalists, from the syndicalists animated by this class spirit and united, today, by the Confédération du travail.[46]

But, according to Valois, if class spirit is healthy as a means of constraint, it can never be carried to the point of the definitive triumph of one class over another. The most serious error of the syndicalists is the belief that class struggle will result in social revolution and the classless society. At this point Valois recapitulates the arguments developed in *L'Homme qui vient*. A revolution that would destroy the authority both of the state and of the *patron* would be politically and economically absurd, as it would reduce the nation and the workshop to a state of anarchy.

Alongside this argument—which he concedes is theoretical—Valois introduces another. To the Sorelian notion of politician as exploiter, Valois adds the Maurrassian argument of politician and even working-class militant as tools of occult forces, the famous *quatre-états*—Protestants, foreigners, Freemasons, and especially Jews. For the young Valois, seeking explanations for his disappointment with the Left in the wake of the Dreyfus affair, the conspiracy of "Gold" against "Blood," which Maurras developed in *L'Avenir de l'intelligence*,[47] seemed to have an appeal. Maurras explained why the mystique of the Dreyfusard crusade turned so quickly into politique: it had never been mystique in the first place, only mystification by French Jewry anxious to enlist the working class for its own purposes. Such an operation could have been successful only if one assumed that Jews had connections within the working-class movement.

This is a theme that Valois seized upon. The whole argument of *La Révolution sociale ou le roi* converges on this point: the infiltration of working-class organizations by Jews. This infiltration is most pronounced, Valois asserted, within the ranks of the socialist party, whose journals and politicians are openly financed by Jews. But it has now also reached the syndicalist movement, and, Valois asserts, certain syndicalists themselves have begun to speak out against it.[48]

Because the Republic is incompatible with the existence of syndicalism, and a social revolution will bring only the domination of the Jews, Valois came, by a process of elimination, to the king. Unlike the politician, who depends on the electoral game, the king is above politics. His only concern is the nation and its strength vis-à-vis other nations. To maximize this strength, the king "is directly concerned that the people, by this I mean all the wage earners, remain healthy, robust, and energetic, and not be exploited by the masters of industry; for, if the people are exploited, they lose their strength, and so does the nation."[49]

Unlike the Republic, where the proletariat is represented by bourgeois politicians, the king will call upon delegates directly from worker organizations: "The King must therefore not only favor but also promote the total organizational development of the working class, calling on what gives it its most rigorously working-class character: *the class spirit*."[50]

La Révolution sociale ou le roi, as already noted, was directed, at least in part, toward royalists. It attempted to demonstrate that a royalist could have nothing to fear from the *esprit de classe* that animated the syndicalist movement. Valois could realistically hope to reach this royalist audience through the *Revue de l'Action française*. But the problem was how to reach militant workers, an audience not likely to be reading either the *Revue de l'Action française* or the *Revue critique*. In an attempt to overcome this obstacle, Valois and the group at the *Revue critique* planned to run in their review an on-going enquête into the attitude of syndicalist militants toward a syndicalist-royalist alliance. A copy of Valois's *La Révolution sociale ou le roi* was to be sent out to leading syndicalists along with a series of questions concerning the feasibility of Valois's thesis.

With the launching of the enquête, the concept of monarchical syndicalism, first suggested by Rivain and de Marans and developed by Valois, was assured at least a test run. Further, the pledge made in the first issue of the *Revue critique*, that even beyond the enquête there would be continued exploration of the possibilities of a new social policy, seemed to indicate that the young royalists were serious in their commitment. Beyond this, however, another opportunity presented itself. Almost simultaneously with the appearance of the *Revue critique*, the Action française began publication of a daily newspaper. This, more than any other single factor, lifted the Action française out of the anonymity of the world of Parisian political sects and into the national limelight. The *Revue critique* group could not have been insensitive to the possibilities of the daily *Action française* in their plans to reach the working class. This, however, would require convincing the royalist leadership that an opening toward the Left would be a fruitful enterprise.

From Theory to Practice: 1908

> The Republic says to the worker: "You are hungry. Here is a priest. Eat and drink!" "I would rather have," the worker answers, "bread in sufficient quantity and a place to retire in my old age." The Republic then takes a gun and blows out his brains.
>
> Rivarol [Léon Daudet]

As in most matters at the Action française, Charles Maurras had his way.[1] For the first few years, the social question was no more than an afterthought to the main royalist preoccupation, the building of a political organization. Yet, by about 1906, social problems pushed to the foreground. From 1906 until the eve of the First World War, France witnessed an outbreak of violent social clashes not only between employers and employees but, more seriously, between strikers and government troops. The *question sociale*, as the whole set of issues surrounding this social unrest came to be known, developed into the major focus of French politics.[2] Under these circumstances, even an organization that claimed the primacy of the political could ill afford to ignore the social question. The royalist leaders were not quick to accept this. Between 1906, the year in which Georges Valois presented himself at the Action française, and mid-1908, the royalists vacillated among several different approaches to the social question.

The first of these, which could be termed the corporatist approach, was represented at the Action française by Firmin Bacconnier and the abbé de Pascal. The abbé wrote regular columns for the *Action française* throughout the prewar period and taught courses at the Institut d'Action française where, aptly, he held the Chaire La Tour du Pin. Corporatism for de Pascal was inseparable from Christian ethics. The ideal that liberalism held out of a "free and conscious being" was to de Pascal a moral outrage. "Conscious of what?" the abbé asked. "Of his infinite misery and his infinite needs," he answered. And again: "Free from what and to do what? Free, in his isolation, to vegetate and die of starvation, exploited by other beings . . . conscious of their unregulated power and free to give full satisfaction to their appetites."[3] With those who upset the corporatist harmony, de Pascal was severe. Unlike Valois, he could not, however, understand how beneficial results might come from class friction: "It is impossible," he reasoned, "to bring order out of revolutionary principles destined to create disorder."[4]

Bacconnier, a typographer converted to royalism by Maurras, was also an avowed disciple of La Tour du Pin but of a more activist frame of mind. He was determined not only to propagandize but to organize workers on behalf of a corporatist social order and a royalist political one. Following Maurras, he maintained that revolutionary syndicalism was healthy insofar as it was a revolt against democracy. But it was as yet incomplete because it spent its entire force on a defense of class, neglecting the overriding importance of profession. Class interests were legitimate, Bacconnier admitted, yet he also cautioned that the "organ of class interest, the *syndicat*," must find its proper place within the larger corporatist framework. Outside of the corporatist order, according to Bacconnier, the syndicat could only be a force for anarchy, "an agent of civil war."[5]

As might be expected, Bacconnier took social hierarchy seriously: men of "humble condition" like himself owed a certain deference to those of a more exalted station. According to the police, the royalists in the pretender's entourage "appreciated in him that he did not mean to treat them as equals, . . . but that, on the contrary, very humbly, [he] asked for their guidance and magnified the distance that separated him, a man of low birth, from them."[6] Even though this deference was not calculated to win converts among the more militant workers, it had its effect among the royalists. The duc d'Orléans himself encouraged Bacconnier to reorganize the small royalist-worker group that he had earlier formed. The result—no doubt with benefit of royalist subsidy—was the *Accord social*.[7] Bacconnier's style apparently also suited Maurras. First Bacconnier's articles, and later the announcements of his Accord social, became regular fare in the *Action française*.

Whatever Bacconnier and de Pascal lacked in appeal for the working class, they at least had the virtue of being ideologically in tune with the neoroyalists' professed corporatism. This was more than could be said of another intermediary in whom the Action française became interested, Pierre Biétry. It was not Biétry's ideology, however, that first attracted the attention of the Action française but the prospect that he was capable of organizing workers in significant numbers.

The Fédération des jaunes de France, headed by Biétry, boasted a membership that, had it been accurate, would have made it a serious rival of the Confédération générale du travail.[8] It was Biétry's intention to make the Jaunes into an attractive ideological alternative to revolutionary syndicalism. Workers would be emancipated not by revolution and expropriation but by becoming property owners themselves. The institution of property, according to Biétry, was not the evil the revolutionaries made it out to be; the real problem was its limited access. Extension of the benefits of property ownership was a touchstone of the Jaunes' propaganda attack: "Long live the worker emancipated by property." This Biétry mixed with a violent attack on socialism: "We are, above all, antisocialist." The political strike, internationalism, expropriation were all destructive to the idea of the worker as *co-propriétaire*.[9]

Biétry's prestige peaked in 1906 when he succeeded in winning election to the Chamber of Deputies from Brest. Any suspicions that still lingered seemingly evaporated; nationalists and conservatives alike saw in Biétry a "national savior." There was no shortage of offers of support—both moral and financial—and almost the entire rightist press united behind him. According to the police, among the offers "the most pressing and at the same time the most generous" were those of the Action française.[10]

Royalist collaboration with Biétry, however, did not await his electoral victory. It was Biétry who first approached the Action française in leaner days before his success at the polls.[11] It was arranged that he would speak in a hall provided by the royalists and attended by many of their sympathizers. The impression made by Biétry was quite favorable, and an agreement between Biétry and the Action française was reached.[12] A measure of the confidence placed in Biétry by the Action française as of 1905 is indicated by the fact that he delivered lectures at the prestigious Institut d'Action française.[13]

Thus, as the year 1906 began, the Action française had two social policy options open to it. Apparently, the fact that they were contradictory was not of great concern as they were pursued simultaneously. The contradictions, however, lost their importance before the fact that both policies proved inadequate.

The corporatist option, represented by de Pascal and Bacconnier, was handicapped not only by the limited appeal of corporatism among the workers but by the personalities of the two men themselves. De Pascal could make no pretense of reaching a popular audience; his esoteric and didactic tone could interest only the already converted. Bacconnier, who set his sights higher, had some degree of success in moving from intellectual principles to the actual organization of workers. While the royalist squad of young toughs, the Camelots du roi, was still in the early stages of recruitment in late 1908 and through 1909, the few dozen men that Bacconnier's Accord social could bring to the streets in support of an Action française demonstration were important to the royalists.[14] But Bacconnier's humility before social hierarchy as well as his basic conservatism were limiting factors. His Accord social, judged by its numbers at least, remained more nearly a study circle than a social movement. The Action française, though it did not hesitate to use Bacconnier when he served its purposes, could not long have held hopes of reaching the working class via the Accord social.

Biétry and his Jaunes seemed a more promising prospect. Not only was the Fédération des jaunes organized on a national basis, but Biétry's election to the Chamber gave him an important propaganda forum. Yet royalist hopes in Biétry proved to be short-lived. In November 1907, a police report indicated that the Action française and Drumont's *Libre Parole* had both pressed and had succeeded in convincing the pretender, the duc d'Orléans, to end the subvention doled out to Biétry's federation.[15] An explanation was offered in another police report. It noted that the Action française was not happy with the fact that Biétry was making the rounds of the various royalist organizations, "eating a little at every manger and stopping at none."[16] But what was worse than mere disloyalty, as later police reports make clear, the Action française had come to view Biétry as something of a bluff.[17]

The police themselves had come to this conclusion some years earlier. According to a report of 1904, Biétry's method was predictable. He would search out discontented workers in a certain area and organize them into an independent syndicat. At the first meeting of the newly formed syndicat, local nationalists would be called to pack the hall. If the operation succeeded, Biétry would promptly visit the employer to demand subsidy. Besides employers, various rightist organizations would also be approached on the basis of Biétry's "influence" within the labor movement and the salubrious effect of his antisocialist ideology upon workers.[18] The Action française, in their eagerness to use Biétry, was perhaps the injured party.[19]

At the very same time that Bacconnier and Biétry were being tried and found wanting, the new approach of the *Revue critique* group was gaining momentum. The virtues they possessed presented a refreshing contrast: they combined a dynamism lacking in Bacconnier with a trustworthiness absent in Biétry.

Georges Valois, almost as soon as he came into contact with the second-generation neoroyalists, became the dynamic force behind the group's efforts. He seemed perfectly suited to lead the kind of "bold economic policy" that, Louis Dimier hoped, would harness the energies of the popular classes and make the Action française into a mass movement. Dimier, in fact, contended that Valois alone was fit for such a role. He was the only one among royalist militants who knew the syndicalist movement from inside.[20] He was the only one with any real interest in economics. But most important, according to Dimier, was his force of character. "He was a hardworking man," Dimier could write, "firm in his decisions and with a trenchant will. He was of the people, he had their pride, their fighting spirit and their distrust. [He was] gifted with a subtle intelligence and a great clear-sightedness."[21]

Nevertheless, Valois lacked one important requisite for success in the Action française—the appreciation of Charles Maurras. The convert from anarchism, from the very first day it seems, aroused Maurras's suspicions. First, there was the matter of the Nietzschean overtones of *L'Homme qui vient*. Maurras detested Nietzsche.[22] Second, and more significantly, there was the question of the very Sorelian conception of the virtues of class antagonism developed by Valois in *La Révolution sociale ou le roi*. Maurras was quite explicit about what he liked and disliked in Sorel. If one took away, Maurras explained, all of the doctrines of the Action française borrowed from the past, one would be left with a single precept, the *coup de force*. This, he maintained, is equivalent to "violence" in the theories of Sorel. The Action française was therefore in accord with Sorel on the necessity of violence. But there was an important difference. For royalists, violence was a means to an end: it could be justified on the grounds that the victor can dictate social peace. For Sorel, violence was justified not for the end it serves but for its inherent cathartic virtues; it found its own reward in class struggle. Maurras concluded that Sorel's theory of violence was "the *coup de force* without the public salvation that legitimizes it."[23]

In the very first encounter between Valois and Maurras, in 1906, Valois's Sorelianism was called into question. Maurras recommended that Valois familiarize himself with the works of La Tour du Pin. Valois persisted in presenting his "own views on the organization of work," views that even before his contact with de Marans and Rivain anticipated *La Révolution sociale ou le roi*. Valois reminded Maurras that Sorel had demonstrated "that a passionately revolutionary working class can give the bourgeoisie the opportunity to regain its historical mission." Valois, however, cautioned Maurras that this rejuvenation of the bourgeoisie could only be accomplished if the latter were prevented from using the power of the state against the working class. In order to ensure that this abuse of state power would not occur, Valois proposed using the monarch as a "permanent arbiter"—not a dictator, Valois emphasized, but merely an arbiter standing "above classes in conflict, even at war, to force them all into respecting the rules of the game."[24]

The notion of a society with "classes in conflict, even at war," was one hardly designed to sit well with Maurras. Despite Valois's recollection that Maurras was "without prejudice on the question," Maurras nevertheless ventured the opinion that Valois's theories did not seem to him to be "organic" enough. Rather than a horizontal conception of society, which makes of "the nation a structure of superimposed layers with no communication with the top," Maurras suggested a vertical model where contact between the state and different social groups would be direct.[25]

The amount of enmity displayed in this first encounter is difficult to determine,[26] although it seems that from the very beginning Maurras had made up his mind about Valois. Dimier is succinct: "Maurras did not like him, nor did he Maurras."[27]

However, the two men, at least before 1914, never came into open conflict. Maurras's strategy seemed to be to keep Valois under surveillance and away from any position of real power, all the while using his ideas, albeit in modified form.[28] Because of his experience with a publishing house, Valois was able to take charge of the royalists' press, the Nouvelle Librairie nationale. But this came only in 1912.[29] Meanwhile, his columns seldom appeared in the daily *Action française*, the real center of activity in the royalist organization.

Despite these strained relations between Valois and Maurras, the idea of an accord between royalists and syndicalists made its way, during the first half of 1908, from the small group at the *Revue critique* to the pages of the *Action française*. By the late summer of 1908, the daily *Action française* not only publicized a social policy very similar to the one developed at the *Revue critique* but attempted to get a hearing in working-class circles through a rather unprecedented gesture of solidarity with striking workers. During the bloody confrontation between the government and strikers at Villeneuve–Saint Georges, the *Action française* rather blatantly took the side of the workers. This gesture was to be only the first step. It marked the opening stage of a campaign to win worker support that was to occupy a prominent place in royalist activities right down to 1914.

How this opening toward revolutionary syndicalism became official royalist policy—especially in the light of the relationship between Maurras and Valois, its most forceful proponent—is unclear. The most significant factor, however, seems to have been pure expediency: the Action française, committed as it was to restoring monarchy "by all means possible," could not resist the opportunities presented by heightened tensions between the syndicalist movement and the French government. These tensions grew steadily worse after 1906, until by mid-1908 there was virtual civil war between militants of the Confédération générale du travail and the Clemenceau ministry.

From the perspective of the organized working class, the Clemenceau ministry—which lasted from the fall of 1906 to the summer of 1909—was marked by the alternation of extravagant hopes and cruel disappointments. The hopes stemmed from the widespread belief that, with the passage of the Law of Separation in 1905, social reform would replace anticlericalism as the dominant concern of the Dreyfusard coalition of Left republicans, Radicals, and Socialists. Two events nourished these hopes in the spring of 1906. First came the great electoral victory of the Left. As a result, the strength of the Dreyfusard coalition was increased by a margin of some sixty seats in the Chamber of Deputies. This victory, interpreted by many as a mandate for further reform, was capped by the Clemenceau ministry's declaration of policy, which, according to one commentator, was "the most radical manifesto produced by any incoming government before the Popular Front."[30] It boldly proclaimed that it would work for an extensive program of social reform: a reduced workday, workers' pensions, a new law defining the status of civil servants, the introduction of a progressive income tax, and the creation of a special ministry of labor to better deal with the problems of the working class.

But shortly after the new ministry had been installed, the enactment of this ambitious program of reform was endangered by repeated confrontations between Clemenceau and organized labor. These confrontations became increasingly bitter and soon degenerated into pitched battles between government troops and strikers. Not surprisingly, as a result of this highly charged atmosphere, most of the promised reforms were never enacted. In fact, the legacy of the Clemenceau ministry stood in stark contrast with the great expectations of the spring of 1906: a total of 104 years in prison sentences, 667 workers wounded, 20 dead, and some 392 dismissals.[31]

One could, of course, argue that a collision between an avowedly revolutionary Confédération générale du travail and a preponderantly Radical ministry was inevitable. As had been pointed out on numerous occasions by contemporaries, what was involved was not a mere clash of personalities but a confrontation between radically different conceptions of society. The leading syndicalists envisioned not only a collectivist society as an end but class struggle as the necessary means. Further, their notion of class struggle was not mediated, as it was for many socialists, by the acceptance of the democratic electoral arena and the provisional necessity of the state. The syndicalists, at least those who claimed to speak for the movement in 1906, had little use for either parliament or state. The society of the future would be administered by federated trade unions.

The Radicals, on the other hand, were hostile to both collectivism and class struggle. Most Radicals remained individualists of an unrepentant variety and found their solidarity not in the socialist idea of class but in the Jacobin idea of nation. Their social radicalism, such as it was by 1906, manifested itself in a kind of old-style populism. The "little man"—be he worker, peasant, schoolteacher, or shopkeeper—needed to be protected from the machinations of the rich and powerful. To that end reform legislation, which would regulate abuses, was not inconsistent with Radicalism. In fact, it was necessary to preserve society from the disintegrating effects of pure laissez-faire. This conviction of the necessity of a modicum of social reform, although it separated most Radicals from their more conservative republican brethren, who still advocated a more classical form of economic liberalism, hardly allowed them to feel comfortable with parliamentary socialists, let alone revolutionary syndicalists.[32]

Given this rather sharp cleavage between the social vision of the Radicals and that of the syndicalists, one could have hardly expected relations between the two to be without friction. Yet some accommodation was certainly not out of the question, and, in fact, it had been achieved in practice during the previous ministries of

Waldeck-Rousseau and Combes. The crucial middlemen in this accommodation were those parliamentary socialists, led by Jean Jaurès, who argued that the price of a minimum program of social reform was Radical-Socialist cooperation within the Chamber and live-and-let-live between Left parliamentarians and syndicalists outside of it. The fragility of this coalition was fully perceived by Jaurès, and his considerable oratorical agility was required to keep it together. To the syndicalists he argued the unsatisfying logic of half-a-loaf victories; to the Radicals he urged measured evasions in response to the often intemperate pronouncements of the Confédération générale du travail; to both he preached the necessity of what others were calling shabby compromise. The alternative to an accommodation, Jaurès insisted, was the disintegration of the Left bloc and the onslaught of a vengeful clerical reaction.

By mid-1906, however, Jaurès's oratorical powers and political acumen notwithstanding, the Dreyfusard coalition was clearly coming undone. A first indication of impending dissolution came as early as 1904 when those forces in the Socialist party that had criticized Radical-Socialist cooperation from the first rallied to score a great victory. The scene was the International Socialist Congress held in Amsterdam. Here Jaurès's long-time antagonist within the socialist movement, Jules Guesde, succeeded in equating Jaurès's parliamentary tactics with Eduard Bernstein's theoretical critique of orthodox Marxism. With the help of the German Social Democrats, Guesde was able to put the weight of the Second International behind an uncompromising rejection of bloc politics: the blurring of the lines between "bourgeois" and "proletarian" parties stood condemned. Further, as a result of a decision of the Amsterdam congress concerning socialist unity, the French socialist movement was directed to unite and form a single party. The resulting Parti socialiste, section française de l'internationale ouvrière, not only condemned class collaboration in the abstract but disbanded what had been the main vehicle of Radical-Socialist cooperation in the Chamber, the Délégation des gauches. Many Jauressian socialists in the new party were unwilling to consider the defeat as definitive; informal cooperation, they argued, would replace a formal steering committee. But no one could deny that the Dreyfusard coalition had been dealt a serious blow.

A second force acting to dissolve the Dreyfusard alliance was also very much in evidence by 1906—the increasing militancy of the French labor movement, manifested especially in the behavior of the Confédération générale du travail. For almost two years, the main thrust of syndicalist energies had been monopolized by a campaign for the eight-hour day. The climax of the campaign was to come on 1 May 1906 when workers, utilizing the technique of direct action, would simply take what their employers had refused to give. Either by an unlimited strike or by a work stoppage after the eighth hour, the individual unions would realize an eight-hour day. It soon became clear that the agitated rallies, the revolutionary posters, and the tone of the labor press testified to the fact that the confederation not only had done its work well but also had created a mood that went beyond the issue of the length of the workday. The Parisian bourgeoisie, clearly unnerved as the appointed day approached, were taunted by the militants of the Confédération générale du travail. From the Paris bourse du travail a huge banner defiantly proclaimed: "Starting 1 May 1906 we will be working 8 hours a day only." Fashionable Paris prepared for the worst: many locked themselves in with a stock of food in anticipation of a *journée d'émeute*—or perhaps several.

Georges Clemenceau, at the time minister of the interior but soon to head his own government,[33] was not reticent about his position. In an audience with the leaders of the Confédération générale du travail on the eve of 1 May, Clemenceau not only was candid concerning the prospect of a *journée* but characterized what would become the policy of his ministry toward revolutionary syndicalism: "You are behind a barricade, I am in front of it. Your means of action is disorder. My duty is to restore order. My part is [therefore] to go against your efforts. The best for each of us is to accept this fact."[34] If the organized workers had any doubts about the minister of interior's single-mindedness, they were soon dispelled. The morning of 1 May found Paris flooded with government troops; the same day, several leaders of the Confédération générale du travail were arrested on charges of conspiring with the reactionaries against the Republic.[35]

This leads to an examination of the third force that, along with the socialist rejection of collaboration with Radicals and the in-

creased syndicalist militancy, led to the disintegration of the Dreyfusard alliance: the person of Georges Clemenceau. Clemenceau's
responsibilities in this matter, as with much else in his life, are
controversial. Certainly it would be admitted, at a minimum, by
even his defenders that finesse was never Clemenceau's strong suit.
His celebrated surliness and his conspicuous deficiency in the diplomatic arts made him particularly unsuited to the task of keeping
syndicalists, Socialists, and Left republicans working with some degree of cooperation.

But the case that has been brought against Clemenceau is more
serious than that of character unsuitability. From the very beginning, the Left charged Clemenceau with Machiavellian duplicity, an
accusation that has been repeated in many historical accounts.[36]
He not only presided over the disintegration of the Dreyfusard
alliance, his opponents argued, he actually orchestrated it. Realizing
that political tactics dictated a majority farther to the right than had
been the case under earlier Radical cabinets, Clemenceau decided
that the best way to build a solid centrist clientele would be to
present himself as a man of order, unafraid to take repressive mea-
sures against the syndicalists. Thus, the brutal confrontations of the
next few years—if one accepts this thesis—were not unfortunate
accidents but the results of calculated policy.

Clemenceau, of course, has had his defenders. Most recently,
David Robin Watson has taken issue with the characterization of
Clemenceau as a "Machiavellian" and "a man of blood."[37] Rather,
he deserves to be characterized, according to Watson, as a sincere reformist who desired nothing more than "the transformation of France into a genuinely liberal, democratic, and egalitarian
society."[38] Clemenceau, Watson explains, felt that the necessary
precondition of this transformation, if it was to be achieved within
the framework of a parliamentary democracy, was the strict maintenance of public order. Thus, according to Watson, Clemenceau's
concern for public order, which, Watson admits, had high priority
during Clemenceau's ministry, must be seen in the context of his
deeper commitment to social reform.

There are, however, serious problems with Watson's defense of
Clemenceau. In the process of explaining how Clemenceau was
able to maintain the requisite public order, Watson's narrative be-

gins to sound not unlike that of Clemenceau's critics. By the time Watson arrives at an explanation of Clemenceau's dealings with the Confédération générale du travail in the crucial year of 1908, he is openly admitting what he had set out to disprove some pages earlier—that Clemenceau had not only "shown himself capable of Machiavellian tactics" but revealed a certain "cynicism" in pushing the Confédération générale du travail toward a confrontation.[39]

Whether it was a question of outright cynicism or a more simple lack of tact, Clemenceau's difficulties with the syndicalists began almost from the time he took office and continued throughout his two-year ministry. Given the ideological gulf between syndicalists and Radicals, issues with potential for conflict were numerous, and seemingly few of them were avoided.

It is also true that the Confédération générale du travail, for its part, made no attempt at being conciliatory. It took every occasion to proclaim its commitment to total revolution, to argue against any compromise, to malign republican institutions, and to attack the government in the most unrestrained terms.[40] Further, a number of leading syndicalist militants gave every indication that they not only wanted but were prepared for a showdown with the Clemenceau government, a showdown in which the long-feted and much-discussed general strike would finally be unveiled.

There was, however, one important difference separating the two sides. The syndicalists were much the weaker party and had little real chance in an all-out contest of strength with the government. This was something that the syndicalist leaders either knew or should have known and the Clemenceau ministry, thanks to its effective network of police spies, was certainly in a position to know.

The tension between the Clemenceau ministry and the Confédération générale du travail came to a head in the summer of 1908. Early in May of that year, a strike broke out in several important sand quarries on the banks of the Seine just south of Paris between Villeneuve–Saint–Georges and Corbeil. The demands of the strikers were not unusual: higher wages, reduced hours, increased pay for overtime and hazardous work. The real issue at stake, however, was more critical. Success of the strike meant recognition of the syndicat by the owner; failure meant collapse of the syndicat. Because of the importance of the issue involved, effective leadership of the strike strategy passed into the hands of the more experienced, and often more radical, Paris leaders. The first serious incident occurred on 2 June 1908 at Vigneux, not far from Draveil. The police, attempting to protect some scabs, tried to force entry into the temporary headquarters of the strikers; the latter offered resistance, and in the ensuing melee the police fired. The toll: two strikers dead; ten more seriously wounded. Jacques Julliard's verdict is that the police were certainly provoked but that, just as certainly, they overreacted.[41] More importantly, he saw such an incident as an almost logical consequence of the ministry's hostile attitude toward the working class, combined with a tacit approval of overenthusiasm on the part of the police.

This last theme was taken up by the syndicalist leaders, who wasted no time in attributing ultimate responsibility for the events of 2 June. Within hours of the incident, Paris was covered with placards with the provocative caption: "GOVERNMENT OF ASSASSINS."[42]

During the next few days, the confrontation between the Clemenceau ministry and the syndicalists intensified. On 6 June a huge rally to protest the incident at Vigneux was held in Paris, and a general strike was voted to be the only proper response to the government provocation. Clemenceau further escalated tension on 11 June with a defiant speech in the Chamber. The construction workers' federation, the national industrial federation most directly involved, responded with the declaration of a twenty-hour strike in all affiliated syndicats to go into effect at a time to be determined by its executive committee.[43] Toward the end of June the Paris dailies were buzzing with speculations concerning the imminent general strike.[44]

Behind tough public pronouncements, a familiar division was developing within the revolutionary syndicalist leadership between the more militant and the more prudent, in Julliard's words, the *violents* and the *politiques*. The former were persuaded that the government's challenge had to be met and that the general strike, voted in principle at the 6 June rally, had to be implemented at all costs. But the politiques, led by the confederation's secretary-general, Victor Griffuelhes, contended that those syndicats and federations most critical to the success of a general strike—public transport, electricity, and gas—could not be depended upon to follow a strike order.[45] Julliard describes the strategy of the politiques, whose advice, it seems, prevailed at both the Confédération générale du travail and at the construction workers' federation: "[Both] play a subtle game: they do not want to look as if they are slowing down the movement, yet they are mainly preoccupied with preventing an incident that would force them into carrying out their threats. A difficult task. It is like walking around a powder mill with a burning candle in one's hand while trying to prevent an explosion."[46]

Were the leaders of the Action française able to perceive what was apparent to both the préfet de police and the secretary-general of the Confédération générale du travail—that talk of general strike was something of a bluff? It is not at all clear. What does seem clear, however, is that they knew that whatever its strengths or weaknesses syndicalism was headed on a collision course with the Republic. They no doubt felt that this collision, when it did come, would present certain opportunities for them. At any rate, it was about this time that the Action française decided to launch an all-out campaign in support of the syndicalists. A long police report documented this crucial turn and attempted an explanation.

Sometime in late June or early July, according to the report, there was a conversation over dinner between Firmin Bacconnier and Charles Maurras. The president of the Accord social tried to impress upon his counterpart at the Action française the critical role that workers could play in royalist plans. Once the king was restored, Bacconnier argued, the present clientèle of the Action française—old royalists, bourgeois, students—would each have an important role to play. But for the job of restoration itself this clientele would be of little use—for this the Action française would have need of the working class. Maurras, the police informant reasoned, saw through this rather transparent ploy of Bacconnier to get support for his organization but took over Bacconnier's idea of using the workers for royalist ends.[47]

The circumstance of this change seems a bit contrived—a sudden flash of inspiration over dinner witnessed by a police agent. More unlikely still is that Bacconnier needed to enlighten Maurras on either the limitations of existing royalist support or on the pos-

sibilities of a working-class alliance. But as to the logic behind the
decision to support syndicalism, the report seems sound. Taken as a
whole, the police reports of 1908 indicate that the Action française
was anxious to move from theoretical pronouncements to action in
the streets. Because it lacked sufficient force on its own as yet,
it eagerly sought out allies. But it was becoming all too obvious
that these allies were not to be found in the neoroyalists' natural
milieu—the traditional and nationalist Right.

By 1908 the ranks of the traditional royalists were a dry well for
the Action française. To be sure, the Action française had made
a few celebrated conversions among the *vieux royalistes*—those
whose loyalty to the pretender predated the founding of the Action
française; its success, however, was limited. In mid-June 1908 the
police noted that the new-style royalists had given up recruitment
efforts in the old royalist organizations. The "old royalists" were,
according to an informer, "too chic to risk themselves in street
fighting."[48] Added to this obvious difference in political style was
another, of perhaps even more consequence: both the Action française and the older royalist groups were competing for subsidies
from the pretender, the duc d'Orléans. The fact that the upstarts
around Maurras received a handsome share of the available funds
did not sit well with the older royalists.[49]

More promising, it would have seemed, were what remained of
the nationalist leagues of Dreyfusard days. Their spirit was certainly
more akin to that of the Action française. Here, it is true, the
Action française had more initial success, most notably the adhesion of Léon Daudet.[50] But by 1908 those who remained
unconvinced by neoroyalism were increasingly distrustful of
the Action française. The police noted that at the Patrie française,
Paul Déroulède's Ligue des patriotes, and Jacques Piou's Action
libérale there was an unwillingness to mix with the Action française;
not only were the neoroyalists dictatorial and violent in dealing
with all opposition, but after any joint effort they claimed all the
credit.[51] Besides, the nationalist leagues, to all appearances, were
settling in for a comfortable middle age.

Whatever the reasons, there can be no doubt that beginning in
early July neoroyalist policy took a decisive turn. The indications
are numerous. Emile Para, who had only occasionally contributed

articles to the daily *Action française*, was recruited from the *Revue critique* to write a special column concerned with working-class problems. Orders went out to provincial sections of the Action française to "keep up with the workers' movement, and to fear neither discussions nor going to syndicalist meetings."[52] Members of the staff of the *Action française* were sent to working-class areas to expound the social program of the monarchy, a program now containing large doses of Valois's polemic, *La Révolution sociale ou le roi*.[53] The meetings of the Accord social were given prominent play in the daily, and several students attached to the Action française were sent to Bacconnier, enabling him to expand his lecture circuit. The daily *Action française*, which before July was circulated largely in the more fashionable *quartiers*, now found its way into the working-class areas.[54]

In the midst of this flurry of activity at the Action française, the lingering strike crisis took a definite turn. On 27 July several arrests were made after an incident involving syndicalists and police. The construction workers' federation, already heavily committed to action should another provocation occur, announced that the twenty-four-hour general strike, already proclaimed, would take effect on 30 July for all affiliates of the federation. It further called for a demonstration on the same day at Draveil-Vigneux. The reaction of the government was by then predictable. Armed troops would "protect order."

On the afternoon of 30 July a familiar scenario unfolded. Government troops responded to scattered shots from the massed strikers with cavalry charges. The strikers repaired to nearby Villeneuve–Saint–Georges and awaited the troops behind hastily constructed barricades, while the troops in their turn met the challenge with an armed assault. The toll for this second *journée*: four workers dead, and a great number of workers and troops wounded.[55]

It has since been contended—most recently and most carefully by Jacques Julliard—that the government's responsibility in this affair was heavy. At least one and perhaps two of those arrested for provocation in the crucial incident of 27 July were police informers. One of them, Lucien Métivier, had had a personal interview with Clemenceau himself only a few months prior to his arrest. Julliard admits that there is no conclusive proof that Métivier was acting as an agent provocateur; but the very fact that the government kept him under arrest, knowing both of his past connection with the police and that his continued detention would stimulate the strikers' outrage, is enough to implicate the ministry.[56]

If, in retrospect, it seems that the ministry bears an important share of the responsibility for the events at Villeneuve–Saint–Georges, contemporaries judged the matter differently. With the exception of *L'Humanité*, organ of the Socialist party, almost the entire Parisian press was hostile to the strikers. As the details of the day at Villeneuve–Saint–Georges reached Paris, the press moved beyond mere condemnation and began calling for government action against the Confédération générale du travail. Typical was the reaction of *Le Temps*, which claimed that the Confédération générale du travail was no longer a "corporative" organization. It was "purely insurrectionary," and, *Le Temps* concluded, it had to "be dealt with as such."[57]

Despite its mounting campaign in favor of the syndicalists, it is unlikely that many of the readers of the *Action française* were fully prepared for the royalists' response to the events of Villeneuve–Saint–Georges. The responsibility for the dead and wounded, according to Maurras's lead editorial, lay not with the strikers or the Confédération générale du travail but with the republican prefect whose "lack of courage, sang-froid, and tactical sense" led to the collision between troops and strikers. Even more directly responsible was Clemenceau himself, whom Maurras compared provocatively with Thiers. For this "criminal head" the events of 30 July were no mistake of judgment: "This slaughter was not the result of a misunderstanding or of a mistake. It cannot be ascribed to an error of calculation. He wanted it. He aimed at it."[58]

Maurras took the occasion of this latest crisis between government and strikers to expound fully the new Action française initiative toward the working class.[59] The bourgeoisie, according to Maurras, thinks that the "working-class question" is simply one of money, of reform. It fails to see that the real problem is the worker's total lack of security—he depends on a wage, but what of tomorrow? One must attend to one's own affairs, the bourgeoisie righteously maintains, but this means nothing to a worker, who has no control over his own future. His only security is to organize and to strike. "Do not ask him why," Maurras concluded; "that is his affair, that is his war. Yes. The war of the classes will be born every time that one class talks of the duty of the others, instead of examining if it is doing its own."[60] Although Maurras stopped short of Valois's enthusiasm for class struggle as a sign of healthy social dynamics, his tone was nevertheless a departure from the more common rightist tack of preaching to the proletariat the virtues of social harmony.

Beyond this criticism of the bourgeoisie, Maurras went to what he considered the source of the problem—liberalism. Lacking any principle of responsibility, liberalism has cut the worker off from society: "He [the worker] is without 'title' and without 'state.' He is a savage, he is a nomad. One suffers with him what he suffers. But even more than he, society suffers. One has understood the working-class question when one has seen that there it lies."[61]

The solution to the social problem, according to Maurras, requires the reincorporation of the working class into society. Under a republican form of government, however, this cannot possibly take place. Exploitation of the social problem is the lifeblood of republican politics. Without the cycle of incitement and repression, the Clemenceaus, the Briands, the Piquarts, the Vivianis could not have made their way. Thus, the social problem is in reality a political problem, or at least its solution would entail a change of regime. The current revolt of syndicalism is a symptom that the working class is becoming aware of this; the bourgeoisie, however, has remained obtuse: "Educated, cultivated, with ample leisure for thinking, the bourgeois could not spell out what the worker deciphers every day: the names of their common enemy: politics! democracy!"[62] Nothing Maurras wrote was, strictly speaking, a theoretical departure from his professed corporatism.[63] But an important strategic difference now separated Maurras from old-style corporatists. If Maurras is still an advocate of social peace for the future, he is now a rather vocal apologist for political revolution in the present. Proletarian violence, although not a virtue in itself, is implicitly condoned if it is directed against the Republic.

Meanwhile, immediately following the latest incident at Villeneuve–Saint–Georges, the struggle between the government and the Confédération générale du travail reached a climax. Both sides played their last cards: the government sent out an arrest order for the leaders of the confederation; the syndicalists, for their part, declared a one-day general strike in all federations for 3 August. The government proved much the stronger party. With their leaders in jail, the working class failed to rally, and the long-awaited general strike proved to be an embarrassing failure. The sand quarry workers returned to work the following day, defeated.[64]

During this time of crisis for the syndicalists, royalist support continued firm. The front page of their daily was preoccupied with the defense of the syndicalists and attacks on the Republic. Maurras condemned the arrest of the syndicalist leaders, claiming that the government was trying to take over the Confédération générale du travail. Those conservatives who applaud this move, Maurras commented—knowing full well that he was directly indicting many of his own subscribers—"understand nothing."[65] What is more, Maurras seemed to take a certain relish in the growing isolation brought about by royalist support of the syndicalists: "So the Confédération générale du travail is wrong; it is syndicalism that, from one end of the Parisian press to the other, having been dealt blows, is now dealt reprimands; Opportunists, Radicals, nationalists, conservatives, they all chide the organized worker, the organization of the working class! In the midst of this heartrending unanimity, there is but one exception: the royalists. And we are proud of it."[66]

By 4 August, the general strike a failure and the sand quarries set to resume operations, the worst of the crisis seemed over. According to the royalists, however, it was just the beginning. With their usual flair for the dramatic, the staff of the *Action française* seized upon a symbolic incident, which they claimed would prove the present difficulties only a prelude. In a short paragraph in boldface type, the *Action française* noted the hanging of a huge bust of Marianne, symbol of the Republic, from the Paris bourse du travail on the afternoon of 3 August. For the next few days, the royalists occupied themselves with interpreting the significance of this event.

Despite the feigned indifference of the Parisian press, explained Maurras, the date of 3 August 1908 will be remembered as the most significant date since 14 July 1789. For a long time, Maurras continued, the Action française had predicted the revolt of the workers against the Republic. The progress of dissatisfaction on the Left had been noted early by Jean Rivain and Georges Valois. But 3 August marked the first open manifestation of hostility. All those around the world, who mistakenly see France only as a symbol of revolution, can take notice: "To be a Frenchman does not anymore mean to be a liberal, a democrat, an agitator, or a friend of the Jews."[67] The liberal press is trying to conceal the import of 3 August, but the Action française will spread the word:

France, Europe, the world will hear the reasons and the causes of a great new event: the rupture of democracy and syndicalism, the separation of the Republic and the proletariat. . . . Then, friends of Europe and of the world, in order to celebrate this first great symptom of the French Counter-revolution manifested on the third of August, one cry is in order, a cry of synthesis and reconstruction: Long live the King of France![68]

First Response on the Left

The second-generation royalists at the *Revue critique* had won a major victory within the Action française: their project for a royalist-syndicalist alliance was, by August 1908, being promoted from the front pages of the *Action française*. Less encouraging, however, were the results of the *enquête* promoted by Valois in the *Revue critique* and sent directly to the syndicalists themselves.[1] Valois had solicited reactions on two basic questions. First, was syndicalism compatible with the existing Republic? Second, could syndicalism coexist comfortably with a restored monarchy? Responses to the enquête were published in the *Revue critique* starting with the first issue in April 1908 and continuing through the spring of 1909.

A first disappointment came with the response from the *Mouvement socialiste*. De Marans, Rivain, and Valois had all singled out the intellectuals at the *Mouvement socialiste* as leaders of the antidemocratic revolt gathering strength on the Left, which suggested important parallels with royalist thought. Georges Sorel, whose response was the first to appear, was brusque. He explained that one fact prevented him from even considering the questions posed by Valois: the massacre of 30,000 men by the royalist-dominated Assembly in 1871. Valois retorted that the responsibility lay not with the royalist Assembly but with Thiers. Sorel, in a second letter, was still reticent. Even if Valois was correct, Sorel wrote, the widely shared assumption among the working class of royalist complicity precluded any discussion of the matter.[2]

Valois was further disappointed that neither Hubert Lagardelle nor Edouard Berth, the young disciples of Sorel at the *Mouvement socialiste*, had even taken the trouble to respond. Lagardelle later recalled that when the editors of the journal received Valois's letter they were surprised and felt Valois's request to be "extravagant." Neither Berth nor the others at the *Mouvement socialiste*, according to Lagardelle, thought it useful to respond: "So far were we from suspecting that our denouncing of democracy could be turned into a defense of monarchy that we thought it a waste of time to protest against a harmless paradox."[3] Nevertheless, Lagardelle continued, "out of caution" it was decided that Robert Louzon should send a short note expressing the negative reaction at the *Mouvement socialiste* to Valois's enquête.

Louzon's note, published in the *Revue critique* in May 1908, went, unlike Sorel's, to the heart of the matter. Louzon recalled Marx's argument: a republic, because it excluded the mediating role of a monarch, was the ideal ground for the final struggle between capital and labor. This was borne out in practice, Louzon argued; one could observe that revolutionary syndicalism was most advanced under republican regimes.

Valois, in a long response to Louzon, was at his polemical best. He pitted Sorel against Marx. The problem with Marx, according to Valois, was that he did not have enough empirical evidence concerning democracy from which to work. On the other hand, Valois maintained, Sorel was a careful observer of the Third Republic and was able to demonstrate how democracy could be extremely dangerous to the workers' movement, steering it away from revolutionary goals by the offer of a state-protected trade unionism. Valois concluded with a counterthrust. Did Louzon believe that the Republic would foster class struggle and bring about the social revolution? Or was Louzon, in fact, really still interested in social revolution?[4]

Even less encouraging than the reaction of the *Mouvement socialiste* was that of Valois's old allies within the anarchist movement. From the staff of the *Libertaire*, an anarchist suggested that if monarchy had any current appeal it was only a matter of perspective: "Monarchy is superb under the Republic just as the latter was very beautiful under the Empire."[5] Jean Grave, editor of *Les Temps nouveaux*, was less polite: "It [monarchy] is well buried, and one must have fossilized brains to hope that this crumbling ruin can be restored."[6] Valois was quick to dismiss these negative reactions among the anarchists by claiming that they were not in a position to speak from a working-class point of view but only as defenders of the "bourgeois déclassés."[7] The reader of the enquête was left to ponder why the opinion of the anarchists had been solicited in the first place.

The responses that Valois undoubtedly awaited most anxiously were those of the workers themselves. All told, seven letters from workers were published as part of the enquête.[8] Though generally more cordial than the responses of the intellectuals at either the *Mouvement socialiste* or the anarchist publications, they nevertheless indicated that the workers were by no means ready to embrace the idea of monarchy. This unfavorable disposition was best expressed by Isidore Bonin, president of the woodcutters' syndicat in Avallon (Yonne), who claimed that a restored monarchy could have no appeal for workers because "it would be only a survival from a past reminding us too much of the slavery and serfdom of the ancien régime."[9]

If workers had not yet developed positive association toward the idea of monarchy, Valois's enquête was at least able to document varying degrees of disenchantment with the Republic. According to one syndicalist, an agricultural worker, the rural proletariat, although still "firmly attached to the republican principle," was clearly disappointed with republican practice.[10] Raoul Lenoir, president of the federation of metal casters, expressed his disgust for the "republican plutocracy," which he claimed was "at the peak of its Pantagruelian digestion."[11] Emile Janvion, president of the municipal employees' syndicat and a leading Parisian militant, noted that workers under an English monarch and a German emperor were better off than French workers. The latter, continued Janvion, must resort to holding their congresses on foreign soil, because they are forbidden "in France by the Republic of the Rights of Man and of 'liberty of opinions.'"[12]

Except for this compensating bit of antirepublican rhetoric, Valois's enquête led, it seemed, only to a kind of public admission of what was already obvious to many—workers were, at best, indifferent to monarchy. Yet there were some who remained unconvinced that Valois's efforts were futile. Not that anyone was seriously worried about mass conversions to royalism among the working class; but would there be certain syndicalist leaders, given their recent humiliation, willing to play the royalist game out of desperation and revenge? Would the workers, who since the Dreyfusard crusade rallied behind the Republic when the forces of reaction threatened, now stand indifferent? Or worse, would they be willing to join forces with reaction, at least temporarily, in the face of a common enemy in the form of the Republic?

Among those posing such importunate questions were the police and important segments of the republican press. As early as August 1908 talk of conspiracy between royalists and syndicalists began making their rounds in the press. The *Petit Provençal* reported that rumors were circulating in Paris to the effect that the Action française had to find a safe place to hide its correspondence. The royalists, the Marseille daily continued, feared that a police search would reveal their collusion with the syndicalists.[13] The prestigious *Indépendance belge* announced that word had reached it, although conclusive proof was still lacking, that the Confédération générale du travail had received "important sums of money" from the royalists.[14] Henry Bérenger's *Action*, priding itself on being the advance wing of the Radicals, attacked the royalists for conspiring "in the shadow." Unnerved by the specter of an attack on the Republic from both the Right and the Left, *L'Action* put the workers on guard: agitation against the Republic would benefit only the conspirators of the Right.

The staff of the *Action française* seemed to relish the notoriety. They conscientiously reported accusations of conspiracy, often quoting them at length.[15] Though they denied being party to any technical conspiracy, they hardly seemed intent upon laying suspicions to rest. "The 'entente' [between royalists and syndicalists] exists," wrote a royalist, "it lies in the nature of things, in the harmony between the syndical and the monarchical forms, and in the lack of harmony between the republican and the corporate forms: it is not necessary to give 'subsidies' to the circle to prevent it from sympathizing with the square."[16]

By the summer of 1908 conspiracy rumors were also rife among police agents at both the national Sûreté générale and the Parisian Préfecture de police. At the height of the Villeneuve–Saint-

Georges affair, the mood of the police was characterized by intense suspicion. Police apprehensions were heightened by the fact that a journalist from the *Action française* had been wounded in the melee and rather pointedly identified himself with the strikers rather than the press. Further, Emile Para, another royalist journalist, had been implicated by a police agent in the hanging of Marianne from the bourse du travail.[17]

Most of these suspicions, however, were laid to rest within a few days when agents reported that all royalist overtures were being cold-shouldered by the syndicalists. In fact, throughout the fall of 1908, the royalists were cast by police spies in the role of the unrequited suitor. Despite a valiant campaign by the Action française to gain the release of syndicalists imprisoned in the wake of the Villeneuve–Saint–Georges affair, the men at the Confédération générale du travail remained steadfastly indifferent. A police report of late September 1908 noted that among syndicalists "no one, not even the lawyers, wants to take the responsibility of talking with royalist journalists, even in the interest of the accused."[18]

For the most part, throughout the remainder of 1908 and into 1909, police agents seemed convinced that the Action française had misjudged the syndicalists in calculating that they could gain the latter's confidence. Yet certain agents—at this point still a minority—began to have their doubts. One, reporting in October 1908, observed that the daily *Action française* now circulated among the working class and, without offering anything definite in the way of evidence, surmised that "those who believe in the existence of a link between the Confédération générale du travail and the Action française are in a good position to demonstrate it."[19] Another agent concurred, claiming that certain syndicalist militants no longer conceal their sympathy for the Action française; he concluded that "a thousand little observations confirm the certitude that some relations exist between the main syndicalist and antimilitarist leaders . . . and the neoroyalists."[20]

What is most striking about these contradictory reports of late 1908 and early 1909 is their impressionistic quality, their lack of precision. The various agents, it seems, were speculating on the basis of very fragmentary information. At this stage only one set of reports was more precise, suggesting that the agent had gained access to information within the Action française.[21]

One of these more substantial reports describes a state of indecision at the Action française concerning the proper tactic to adopt toward a scheduled syndicalist rally for the syndicalists still in prison. There was, according to the report, general agreement among the royalists as to the desired end: ideally, the rally should move from the concrete issue of the prisoners to become an antirepublican demonstration. But opinions differed as to the means to achieve this end. One faction was convinced that a royalist representative should be sent to make a statement before the assembled syndicalists denouncing the Republic. Proponents of this tack agreed with its detractors that it could easily backfire and turn antiroyalist rather than antirepublican; to prevent this, they proposed that a proroyalist *équipe*—a group of young toughs—be sent in support of the orator. A second faction, headed by Vaugeois, deemed this approach too transparent.[22] The attack on the Republic, the second group argued, should come from a syndicalist leader himself, adding significantly that there were many among the militants at the Confédération générale du travail who would not refuse "to lend themselves or, more exactly, to hire themselves out" to the Action française.[23]

A second report by the same agent affirms that Vaugeois's idea was accepted, although unfortunately the agent does not indicate whether a syndicalist was found to implement the plan. He does disclose that the royalists had tried but did not succeed in recruiting an équipe. Importantly, the report stresses that the Action française had not given up on the idea of direct intervention with royalist orators backed by "these teams of so-called workers or wage earners." The royalists, the informant concludes, were currently working on the difficult task of building these équipes.[24]

These reports of November 1908 are significant because they describe two lines of strategy that, though at first posed as mutually exclusive, were to become complementary components of a single policy. One can be precise as to when the direct method was ready to be tested in practice: on 26 March 1909 Léon Daudet, accompanied by an équipe of Camelots du roi, began a highly promoted circuit of meetings in working-class areas.[25] It is not possible to determine with such precision when indirect method was first initiated, but it seems likely that as early as mid-September 1908 the Action française had made contact with an important syndicalist militant.

Only in the light of later events is one led to believe that one other police report of the fall of 1908 had uncovered something substantial. This report, one that was not followed up at the time, was from an agent at the Sûreté. He claimed that the royalists had established relations with "some workers' syndicats and even subsidized them."[26] He continued that among those who were willing to act as intermediaries between royalists and the syndicats a certain Emile Janvion, "a former employee at the Préfecture de la Seine and former editor of *L'Aurore*, would not be the least active."[27] Emile Janvion, as events were to prove, became a major axis upon which royalists hopes for an alliance with the Left were to turn. Not only did Janvion later sponsor a newspaper where dissident syndicalists were regularly treated to rather thinly disguised royalist propaganda, but he also became a vital link in the chain that would connect, the Action française hoped, the virulent royalist anti-Semitic campaign with a latent, yet widespread, anti-Semitism among the workers. But this is to anticipate events. What first attracted the Action française to Janvion, and what convinced them that he was serviceable, was his deep involvement in the rather serious factional disputes dividing the syndicalist movement. This infighting, fanned by the debacle of Villeneuve–Saint–Georges, had, by late 1908, ignited a major crisis within the syndicalist movement. Because the royalists calculated that this crisis could, if properly exploited, serve them as an entry into the Confédération générale du travail, it will be necessary to both inquire into the nature of the crisis and ascertain the degree of Janvion's complicity.

Edouard Dolléans, in his pioneering history of the syndicalist movement, argues that by the end of 1908 revolutionary syndicalism had lost its original momentum. The *temps héroiques* were succeeded by a more prosaic age, one of internal crisis, of intense personal rivalries, and of gradual reorientation.[28] But in fact the crisis that overtook the movement was simply an intensification of problems that had been papered over in more heroic times. Henri Dubief has stressed the "incoherence" of the majority resolutions passed at the Amiens congress of 1906, resolutions that the syndicalists came to regard as the charter of their movement.[29] These resolutions were worded to avoid the major issue that was dividing not only syndicalists but almost every other European socialist movement at the time—the issue of reform or revolution. But soon enough this problem was to split syndicalists into warring factions.

The struggle between reformists and revolutionaries, especially as it intensified after 1908, has been examined by the historians of pre-1914 syndicalism. Though in pure numbers the majority of the rank and file were probably reformists, the revolutionaries, one brief period excepted, maintained a precarious control of the Confédération générale du travail throughout the prewar years. They managed this largely through a voting system where all federations, regardless of size, were represented equally. The largest federations were thus put on an equal footing with the smaller, more numerous, and often more radical federations. Schemes for proportional representation of federations, which would have given over control of the movement to the reformists, were, not surprisingly, regularly defeated at congresses controlled by revolutionaries. The "crisis," the term applied by the syndicalists themselves to the troubles that paralyzed their movement, was openly manifested in this often violent confrontation between reformists and revolutionaries.

But this reformist-revolutionary dichotomy had a still more subtle manifestation. Within the faction that called itself revolutionary, there was also, behind public pronouncements, an "incoherence." This tension within the camp of the revolutionaries has been observed by certain historians of syndicalism but, in this writer's judgment, never sufficiently analyzed. As has already been noted, Jacques Julliard uses the categories *politiques* and *ultras* to describe this factionalism. The ultras, according to Julliard, saw their primary role as one of agitation: the most important task of syndicalist leadership was to keep the worker from falling prey to the illusion that concessions were the end-all of syndicalism. The prototype of the ultra was Georges Yvetot, the outspoken antimilitarist and successor to Pelloutier as secretary of the Fédération des bourses.

Not surprisingly, the arrival at a strike scene of leading militants like Yvetot was seen as a prelude to an escalation of violence.[30]

This tendency, however, increasingly found opposition from a second group at the Confédération générale du travail, a group designated by Julliard as the *politiques*. The latter fully realized that agitation of a strike and subsequent victory for the strikers could indeed lead to a growth in revolutionary awareness. But they also realized, Julliard claims, that agitation without careful calculation of the possibilities and limitations of the particular situation could lead to defeat and discouragement. This realization led to a growing caution on the part of many of the leaders of revolutionary syndicalism, most notably those with the greatest direct responsibility.

The development of this prudence has been variously interpreted. For Julliard, who is quite open in his admiration for the *politiques*, it represents no break with their professed commitment to revolution. The *politiques* adapted and revised this revolutionary commitment, Julliard admits, but for this "[t]hey are no less revolutionary, they are only more consistent."[31] But this manner of mincing words obscures recognition of an important development, one that Julliard's own careful research points to: the *politiques*, although giving continued lip service to the rhetoric of revolution, were in practice becoming reformist.

Another recent historian of syndicalism, F. F. Ridley, describes this evolution, especially as it occurred in the important cases of Victor Griffuelhes and Emile Pouget.[32] Early in the movement, both tended to emphasize the importance of ultimate revolutionary goals, minimizing the importance of more immediate reforms. But by 1908 Griffuelhes was looking back upon this earlier period as "romantic," whereas Pouget "came near suggesting . . . that the expropriation of the capitalists, which, after all, was to be the core of the revolution, would take place as the gradual by-product of everyday activities—a doctrine not far removed from the *évolution révolutionnaire* of the reformists such as Jaurès."[33]

Set in this context, the struggle within the "revolutionary" faction was more than just a tension between the more and the less prudent. It was another dimension of the reformist-revolutionary struggle, a struggle no less brutal and no less important simply because both sides subscribed to the same theoretical pronouncements. These "incoherences"—both within the movement as a whole and within the revolutionary faction itself—account for the severity of the *crise du syndicalisme*. For the issue at stake was a serious one. Were the French syndicats to become, with the majority of their American, English, and German counterparts, largely professional organizations accepting and working through the existing political structures? Or were they to maintain their radical character and insist that the most important task was the destruction of these structures and their replacement by a "free association of producers"? The politiques—if one looks at what they did rather than what they said—were moving away from their earlier revolutionary commitment.

Emile Janvion was a prominent spokesman for the ultra position when he was first contacted by the Action française. Like many another syndicalist, Janvion was active in anarchist circles before gravitating toward the workers' movement. He had toured the provinces on a speaking circuit with Louise Michel, worked to involve the anarchists in the Dreyfusard cause, and edited the short-lived anarchist newspaper, *L'Ennemi du peuple*.[34] In 1904, by virtue of his status as a low-grade *fonctionnaire* in the municipal civil service, he came into contact with a newly formed municipal workers' syndicat. The transition from anarchism to syndicalism was complete when Janvion joined the syndicat and shortly thereafter was appointed delegate to the federation of municipal workers. His superiors in municipal services were increasingly displeased with his double career, especially after Janvion had embarked upon a vigorous campaign for the right of fonctionnaires to organize and adhere to the Confédération générale du travail. His "aggressive and indisciplined tone" led, first, to a forfeiture of three days' salary and finally, in April 1907, to his dismissal. The immediate occasion for this dismissal came when Janvion signed an especially violent placard sponsored by the Confédération générale du travail.[35]

If Janvion's career as a civil servant was thus abruptly terminated, prospects for a second career, that of a syndicalist leader, were never more promising.[36] He had risen rapidly through the syndicalist hierarchy, and at the time of his dismissal he was representing his federation on the *comité confédéral* of the Confédération générale du travail. The obvious political overtones surrounding his case made him something of a celebrity within the syndicalist movement.[37]

Through 1907 and 1908 Janvion kept a high profile. Following his dismissal, he began a series of speaking engagements in support of the right of civil servants to unionize. His savage invectives, particularly those directed against the Clemenceau government, earned him a reputation as something of a firebrand. Addressing a syndicalist gathering in Moulins, he grew so violent in his attacks that a police officer in attendance issued a citation, charging him with outrages against the government.[38] As his flair for the theatrical made for good newspaper copy, Janvion's attacks on the government were savored by the anti-Clemenceau segments of the "bourgeois" and reactionary press. Typical was an incident in the Chamber of Deputies where Janvion, from his place in the gallery, interrupted a speech by Clemenceau, claiming that the prime minister had once contributed money to a cause that he was currently attacking from the tribune. The nationalist *Patrie* and Drumont's *Libre Parole* joined in congratulating Janvion.[39]

Not surprisingly, within the Confédération générale du travail Janvion became one of the leading spokesmen for the ultra position, often publicly criticizing the policies of the more moderate *politiques*. In August 1907, *Le Matin*, one of the large circulation Parisian dailies, published a revealing inquiry: "Without the Parliament or against it? Where syndicalism is going; divergences in the C.G.T." In the article, Emile Pouget argued the position of the *politiques*. Syndicalism, he wrote, is an organization not of opinions but of interests; as such, it must remain above divisive political issues. But this, according to Pouget, does not require that one attack those outside of the movement who do involve themselves in politics, most notably the politicians themselves. The proper stance for a syndicalist is to mind the store and ignore the political arena.[40]

Janvion attacked Pouget's notion of the *syndicat* as a mere professional interest group. If Pouget were to have his way, Janvion reasoned, it would make of syndicalism "a bundle of muscles and guts, an organism with neither ideal nor fire."[41] Syndicalists, Janvion argued, must be ready to fight for their vision of the future society, an organization of free producers, because the parliamentary socialists are in the process of enlisting the working class in a campaign to build a very different kind of society, one based on the capture of the public powers. Janvion favored resolving the "incoherence" of the Amiens resolutions by a frank revision. Neutrality toward politics is a half measure; syndicalists must stand up against the socialist parliamentarians and affirm that "the syndicat is a weapon of revolutionary struggle, which must now be used for the attack." To ignore politics is not enough: the syndicat "must be used *against* politics," against parliamentarism.[42] Thus, the ultras represented more than mere impulsiveness, as Julliard suggests; they saw their function as preserving and advancing the revolutionary content of syndicalism.

Moreover, the struggle between the ultras and the politiques was not confined to the syndicalist movement; it had ramifications outside the movement per se and, within a short time, affected the broad spectrum of the French Left. That this was the case was due largely to the influence of a single man, Gustave Hervé, whose enormous popular repute on the revolutionary Left the ultras had the good fortune of enlisting in their cause.

Hervé, a former history *professeur*, had, by 1905, established himself as the enfant terrible of the prewar French Left by his virulent attacks on patriotism and his conviction that the proper place for those who call themselves revolutionaries was in the streets. Hervé has not been treated kindly by French historians of the Left. Alfred Rosmer, himself a militant leader, summarized what has become the consensus view: "Hervéism, in spite of its insurrectionism expressed mostly by a verbal violence, in spite of the real influence that it had for a while on good working-class activists, created in fact but a temporary and superficial agitation. Demagogy and adventurism. Nothing will be left of it."[43]

Yet, however short-lived his influence, the impact of Hervéism between 1906 and the war was little short of remarkable. One commentator has called Hervé's newspaper, *La Guerre sociale*, "the most effective propaganda sheet in France."[44] Certainly, no syndicalist publication could match its popularity. In 1910 the *Guerre sociale* could boast a circulation of about 60,000 copies compared to 8,500 for the *Voix du peuple*, the official voice of the Confédération générale du travail.[45] But Hervéism was more than a newspaper. Hervé also ran a publishing house, he was an important figure in the Socialist party, and he and his lieutenants had organized a rather formidable insurrectionary network. Clandestine Hervéist groups operated not only in each of Paris's twenty arrondissements but also in the major provincial cities. Police repeatedly implicated the Hervéists in fomenting wildcat strikes, in aiding deserters from military service, and even in manufacturing explosives and using them to sabotage government equipment.[46]

Hervé, moreover, was not only a frenetic activist; he was also an organizer. His deepest aspiration was to channel all revolutionary energy—be it socialist, anarchist, or syndicalist—into a single "insurrectionary committee." Though no formal organization ever came into being, Hervé, for a few short years at least, became de facto leader of the French revolutionary Left, wielding enormous, if informal, power.[47] From the point of view of many Socialist party regulars, this power was insidious, because it threatened recognized lines of authority and raised the specter—always disturbing to self-proclaimed revolutionaries—of "enemies to the Left." Thus, many members of the newly united Socialist party were profoundly, and often vocally, irritated by the phenomenon of Hervéism. But even more serious was the impact of Hervé on syndicalism. Here, Hervé's message that the greatest danger to any revolutionary was cooptation struck a responsive chord. Julliard, who makes little effort to conceal his distaste for Hervé, admits grudgingly that during this period he "truly fascinate[d] the C.G.T."[48] Pierre Monatte, a contemporary syndicalist leader and enemy of Hervé, went as far as claiming that for several years syndicalist doctrine and Hervé's insurrectionism appeared to be synonymous.[49]

Given Hervé's conception of his role as the watchdog of revolutionary élan, it is hardly surprising that, by the spring of 1908, Hervé was admonishing the *politiques* in much the same fashion as Janvion. After a quiet 1 May, Hervé, in a lead editorial, charged that syndicalists were becoming as timid as socialists. Certain syndicalists give the excuse that they do not have sufficient numbers as yet for bold action, when what is really needed, Hervé claimed, is not increased numbers but a dose of temerity. Or, he asked provocatively, is the working class afraid of the police? One does not make revolution, according to Hervé, "through strokes of cleverness, by maneuvering, quibbling, or putting one's flag in one's pocket, any more than by going to the polls. . . . To uncover the layers of prejudice and error fed by the great capitalist press to the overworked, ignorant, and enslaved masses of the proletariat, something else is needed. Revolutions are prepared and made only with passion, enthusiasm, and audacity."[50]

Janvion had a ready answer as to why these latter qualities no longer characterized syndicalist leadership. Like not a few other disillusioned revolutionaries, Janvion succumbed to the temptation of seeing behind every failure the long thread of conspiracy. Starting in late May 1908, Janvion began a series of articles in the *Guerre sociale* entitled "The Masonic Peril in Syndicalism."[51] "Judeo-Radical capitalism" is now, Janvion maintained, securely in power. It has owed its success largely to the credulity of the workers, who were duped into supporting it in the name of higher truths during the Dreyfus affair. But recently this ruling elite has run into difficulties. Since the separation of church and state and the subsequent decline of the obsession with anticlericalism, those in charge have run out of diversions for the masses. Coupled with this, the ruling elite has had to face the rise of a syndicalist movement committed to the destruction of the existing order. But the rulers are not without resources. Freemasonry, the undercover agency created to perform the bidding of the Judeo-Radical dynasty, is currently charged with the infiltration, diversion, and ultimately, the control of the syndicalist movement.[52] This is accomplished largely by recruiting the unsuspecting, though ambitious, working-class leaders into the Freemasonry. Janvion claimed to have in his possession the names of over thirty important militants who, while preaching in their syndicats the virtues of class struggle, were, in their lodges, practicing class collaboration. Their complicity was no less dangerous, Janvion argued, for the fact that it was unconscious.[53]

Meanwhile, the struggle between the ultras and the politiques intensified through the summer of 1908. As early as May an informer described the antagonism between Janvion and the Griffuelhes-Pouget faction. Janvion "speaks very badly" of Griffuelhes and Pouget, treating them as opportunists. Pouget, for his part, is grouping partisans to resist an assault, which he is sure will be launched by Janvion at the syndicalist congress set for October 1908 in Marseille.[54]

The hostility between Pouget and Janvion came to a head, according to another report, in early June while the *comité confédéral* of the Confédération générale du travail was composing a manifesto in response to the 2 June incident at Vigneux. Janvion, always ready to stoke the coals, pressed for a blunt statement charging Clemenceau with having given the order to push the strikers into a "bloody conflict." Clemenceau's strategy, Janvion wanted the confederation to charge publicly, was to create deliberately an incident that would put him back in the good graces of the reactionaries. Pouget retorted that he was not going to be the author of such "insanities," and, if the others supported Janvion, he would withdraw from the project altogether. Janvion, the report concluded, "insisted no longer."[55]

Ironically, the debacle of Villeneuve–Saint–Georges dealt the politiques a near fatal blow. Although one could argue that it was pressure from the ultras that forced the Confédération générale du travail to call, first, for the demonstration of 30 July and, then, the general strike of 3 August, it was nevertheless the politiques, who, however hesitantly, took the actual decisions. Griffuelhes and Pouget, the two with the most direct responsibility, found themselves in jail during the Marseille congress. With the politiques thus weakened, not only the reformists but also the ultras renewed their attack. At the congress itself, the politiques, with the aid of the ultras, were able to beat back the reformist bid to take over the movement. The reformists' old war-horse, proportional representation, was once again defeated.[56] But the politiques were less successful in dealing with pressure from the ultras and were forced to compromise on a critical issue—the highly explosive resolution on antimilitarism.

The politiques, in preparing the motion on antimilitarism, wanted something strong enough to allow them to continue their antimilitary propaganda but not so extreme as to reduce their already precarious majority. The ultras had other plans. They had already published in the *Guerre sociale* a tough antipatriotic proposal, which was referred to disparagingly by the politiques as the "G.S. motion." A compromise measure was finally attempted, but the draft that went before the congress was hardly compromising: it declared "that in case of a war between the powers the workers will respond to the declaration of war with a declaration of a general revolutionary strike."[57]

The impact upon the congress was predictable. The reformists were enraged. Louis Niel, shortly to become the reformist candidate for secretary-general, argued that this brand of extreme antipatriotic rhetoric could only ensure that the Confédération générale du travail would remain a movement attractive to a small minority of workers. In response, Janvion reintoned his by-now familiar refrain: "I would rather have no syndicalism than this syndicalism without ideal, without fire, a mere grouping of interests and intestines, comparable to a friendly association of prison wardens, cops, or *jaunes*."[58] Though the measure passed, it had the effect of pushing the syndicalist movement even deeper into crisis.

The ultras, it now seemed to many, were defining the policy of the Confédération générale du travail. *La Guerre sociale*, jubilant over its victory at the congress, did little to discourage this view. A headline interpreted the Marseille congress for its readers: "The C.G.T. accentuates its revolutionary tendency. It declares itself in favor of the general strike in case of a war. The debacle of the Guesdist-reformist equilibrium coalition."[59]

The actual situation among the revolutionaries who controlled the Confédération générale du travail was growing more confused daily. Rather than the ultras defining policy, as their enemies claimed, no one faction was any longer making policy. The internecine warfare within the revolutionary faction had resulted in an almost complete breakdown of the ability to make policy.[60]

The release of Griffuelhes and Pouget from jail shortly after the Marseille congress offered the hope that with their leadership the politiques could once again establish peace within the revolutionary camp. But the ultras could no longer be placated. A police informer reported in mid December a "serious thing": the reformists in their struggle against those in control of the Confédération générale du travail had enlisted the support of numerous ultras.[61] The latter were now apparently set on overturning the politiques at any cost. Albert Lévy, treasurer of the confederation and ultra, launched charges that Griffuelhes had misused the confederation's fund. Although the real problem seemed to lie with Griffuelhes's lack of talent as a bookkeeper rather than with his lack of honesty,[62] the ultras were not above using the issue to unseat the secretary general.

By January 1909 the fight between Lévy and Griffuelhes had become extremely vicious and personal. Janvion and Yvetot were, according to the police, the "unchallenged leaders" of the ultras, whereas Alphonse Merrheim and Alexandre Luquet led the politiques. As a result of this unrestrained factional feud among the revolutionaries, the reformists were able to gain—for the first time since the founding of the organization—control of the Confédération générale du travail. In February 1909, thanks to the combined votes of ultras and reformists, Louis Niel became secretary-general of the confederation.[63]

It is thus clear that the Confédération générale du travail was, by late 1908, in total disarray—a disarray that by early 1909 verged on paralysis. It is also clear from police reports that Janvion's part in this crisis was not insignificant. The question remains: to what extent was Janvion the royalists' man, and, correspondingly, what role did the Action française play in the struggle between the ultras and the politiques?

One might theorize that the Action française was intent upon destroying the Confédération générale du travail, and their strategy was, through Janvion, to aid the most reckless faction. Janvion, in this scenario, would be an agent of the royalists' sabotage. This theory, however, does not take the Action française seriously enough. It assumes that as "conservatives" the royalists had as their real goal the prevention of further victories by the Left. But, as Eugen Weber has argued, it is misleading to view the pre-1914 Action française as conservative; it was "revolutionary" in the sense that it was serious about overturning the existing order by a frontal attack, a coup d'état.[64] That the Action française became conservative in the 1920s is not a good enough reason—although an easy temptation—for assuming that it was also conservative before the war. A reading of the prewar *Action française* reveals how large a part the preparation for the anticipated coup played in royalist thinking.[65]

The most plausible explanation of why the royalist leaders took such pains with the syndicalist campaign is to be found in the strategic importance of the working class. What would be the attitude of the workers should the Republic be threatened? The leaders of the Action française could not have been ignorant of the lesson of the Dreyfusard years: the nationalist upsurge, so promising at the beginning, faltered when the workers rallied to the Republic. At a minimum, the Action française needed the indifference of the working class in case of a royalist opportunity for a coup. But the Action française certainly hoped for more than indifference. It counted on help in the form of a vigorous revolutionary and antirepublican movement on the Left.[66] All the better if this movement emphasized many of the same themes as the Action française's.

In this respect Janvion was ideal. He was incontestably for a revolutionary Confédération générale du travail. His attacks on the Republic were appreciated early at the Action française.[67] His offensive against Freemasonry was an even greater source of delight to the royalists.[68] By January 1909 the earlier isolated report that Janvion had made contact with the Action française was confirmed by other reports. Police noted six to eight visits to the Action française within a two-month period.[69] Later in the same month, an informer indicated that Janvion was now ready to play "the game of the royalist orator," although without any admission of royalist affiliation.[70]

But what was the exact nature of the relationship between Janvion and the Action française in late 1908 and early 1909? Did he become something of a royalist agent, merely taking instructions and reporting back information? Or was the relationship more of a cooperative venture, both the royalists and the ultra Janvion displaying the guile not uncommon in serious conspirators against the state?

The first option is at least plausible. Janvion was dismissed from his post at the Préfecture in 1907 and was not reinstated until 1913.[71] By his own admission he never accepted a position as a paid official in the syndicalist movement.[72] There is no indication as to how Janvion supported a newspaper that he later founded unless one accepts police reports that he was accepting royalist funds.

Yet, there are indications—though no solid evidence—that he was not simply the hired man of the Action française.[73] Janvion, just two days before the first police report of his collaboration with the royalists, had given the daily *Action française* an interview. In it he had suggested that the latest defeat for the Confédération générale du travail was merely the last bitter fruit of the Dreyfusard alliance. Although still claiming to believe in the innocence of Dreyfus, Janvion, not unlike many another disillusioned Dreyfusard, felt that the "Dreyfusard revolution" had had a disastrous effect upon the revolutionary Left. It had introduced a "gangrene" into the movement by its collaboration with the bourgeoisie, the Freemasonry, the Jews, and the Protestants.

Janvion, however, was not alone in feeling bitter. Gustave Hervé, within a few days of the Janvion interview, reiterated the same theme: "Ahoy! Dreyfusard bourgeois! What do you think of all that [the Villeneuve–Saint–Georges affair and its aftermath]? Since it's not one of yours this time, an officer millionaire, but just plain workers, you are not interested anymore, are you? The C.G.T. was good enough to protect the bourgeois, whether Jewish, Protestant, or Freemason, against the anti-Semite and clerical wave that threatened you! Now that the danger is over, now that you don't need the revolutionaries anymore, they are good enough to be thrown to the dogs and the judges."[74]

By the end of the year—the Action française now capturing headlines with its antics at the Sorbonne—the *Guerre sociale* spelled out more fully the implications of its disgust with its old Dreyfusard allies. The beleaguered Republic argument, according to Hervé, would no longer find takers among the revolutionaries. Let the royalists, Hervé continued, "pull up Marianne's skirts and give her a good spanking in front of everybody, and if we show up, it will only be to laugh. Gone are the days when we would take revenge on the nationalists for the insult inflicted on President Loubet's hat! Finie la comédie! La saison des poires est passée!"[75] Rather than attack the nationalists, as in former times, the revolutionaries, Hervé continued, can take lessons from the royalists and borrow "some of . . . [their] combative spirit, some of . . . [their] audacity."[76]

By February the staff of the *Guerre sociale* had carried their logic one step further. Will we, of the revolutionary Left, come to the aid of the Republic menaced by the royalists? Will we, of the revolutionary Left, regroup in the old Dreyfusard columns, once again lured by the promise of the bourgeois arrivistes? "No, no, a thousand times no!" wrote an Hervéist. "Far from considering helping the Radicals save Marianne, it would be better to start thinking of the possibility of participating in her strangulation. Once the regime is overthrown, we could then see how to make the best of the situation for revolutionary socialism."[77]

One could argue that certain elements on the Left, including Janvion and his friends at the *Guerre sociale*, had taken a decisive turn. They were convinced that the time had come to end the unholy alliance between revolutionaries and progressives and to sever the ties that had bound them together since Dreyfusard days: loyalty to the Republic and hatred for reactionaries. In the interest of bringing down the Republic, the time had come for even unholier alliances.

Meanwhile, at the Action française Charles Maurras could afford to be coy. In response to the *Guerre sociale*'s offer to help overturn the Republic, he wrote: "We would not have dared to say it so crudely. But such is the evidence. And here is our response— revolutionary socialism is much less a threat for country, religion, and order than the consortium Clemenceau-Fallières-Briand."[78]

[6]

The Royalist Offensive:
The Low Road

The years 1909 and 1910 were to be years of redoubled effort for the Action française in its campaign to lure the working class. This effort can be traced along two broad fronts. The royalists, on one front, worked toward some kind of an alliance with syndicalist intellectuals, especially that most influential of syndicalist intellectuals, Georges Sorel. Progress here was slow, and visible results came only in 1910 (see chapter 7). On a second front, at the level of working-class militants, feverish royalist activity continued throughout 1909 and most of 1910. Royalist strategy here was directed toward increasing syndicalist alienation from the Republic, wrecking whatever was left of the old Dreyfusard alliance, and showing the Action française as a useful ally in the struggles of the working class. In this broad strategy, the royalists employed both tactical alternatives debated within the Action française late in 1908.[1] One option, that of infiltrating the syndicalist movement through the good offices of a cooperative working-class militant, was enjoying some degree of success by 1909. Not only was Emile Janvion, the militant in question, able to promote neoroyalist themes at large syndicalist rallies, but, more importantly, by late 1909 he had founded a biweekly newspaper that began to take on appearances of a royalist beachhead within the syndicalist movement. The other option, that of a direct royalist dialogue with the syndicalists, was, at the very same time, being given an extensive trial run. This latter option engaged the full attentions of the most celebrated convert to royalism in the prewar years, Léon Daudet.

From the very beginning, despite his impeccably bourgeois credentials as son of a noted literary figure, Léon Daudet was the logical choice to bring the royalist message to the unfamiliar terrain of the working-class *quartiers*. He was a force behind the organizing and launching of the daily *Action française*, and his talent as a rough-and-tumble satirist was a critical factor in its success. Daudet, according to Eugen Weber, "was Maurras's complement: where Maurras explained dispassionately and logically, the sanguine Daudet seduced by his fire and verve, providing a body for what had so far been only a doctrine."[2] This "fire and verve" was apparent not only in Daudet the journalist but in Daudet the public speaker. And his oratorical weapons were peculiarly suited to the task at hand: savage irony seasoned with outright character defamation.

Whereas Maurras was the prototype of the sequestered ascetic, a monk for his politics, Daudet was the gregarious bon vivant. One sensed with him not so much political convictions as politicized emotions. The most intense of these—with the possible exception of patriotism—was anti-Semitism. Weber, true to the spirit of the man, labels his anti-Semitism a "complex sentiment, partly inherited, partly rationalized, partly opportunistic."[3] But beneath it all, it would seem, was an undifferentiated emotional response. This emotional quality revealed itself in the frequent anti-Semitic diatribes in the daily *Action française*: nearly always his descriptions were caricatures, yet caricatures so vivid that the reader suspects that they lived in Daudet's mind.

Daudet's first worker rally was scheduled for late March 1909, and, from the amount of advance billing given, it was clear that the worker alliance was now a top royalist priority. The format of the rallies was to be that of the *réunion contradictoire*, a public debate. First, Bernard de Vésins, a young officer as well as an effective royalist speaker, would introduce Daudet, who in turn would give the essentials of "royalist syndicalism"; then the floor would be open to questions and rebuttals. The tone of the new royalist venture was set by Daudet's first presentation.

We will start, exclaimed Daudet, by stating what we royalists are not; from this, what we are will emerge. We are not conservatives! They only want to preserve the status quo. We are not liberals! They only *speak* of liberty. And we are not against syndicalism! Our enemy is the Jew. Further, we are not politicians! It is among them that the Jews can buy their stooges: Jaurès, Millerand, Briand! All politicians—Right, Left, and Center—are parasites that must be destroyed. Destroy the regime and the country will live! This leads to what we are: true revolutionaries. "The revolution does not frighten us."[4]

The first meeting was held in a working-class area near the place d'Italie with attendance at somewhere between 200 and 500.[5] The royalists were taking no chances with their first foray outside of their home turf, the *quartiers chics*. Not only were de Vésins and Daudet accompanied by an *équipe* of Camelots du roi, but, according to the police, nine-tenths of the audience were connected directly or indirectly with the Action française.[6]

According to the police, this first royalist effort could not be counted a success. But the same report indicated that there was no discouragement at the Action française. They apparently were prepared for an uphill struggle. De Vésins took heart from the fact that there had been no attempt at preventing or disrupting the meeting. Further, de Vésins noted, royalists and workers were already in accord on one central point: antirepublicanism. "The rest," he concluded, "will come in its own good time."[7]

But as to the effect of this tack on the working class, as of 1909 at least, there can be no doubt that it fell short of royalist expectations. By midsummer the police no longer seemed greatly troubled by Daudet's réunions contradictoires, even though they were no longer so heavily packed with royalist sympathizers. A report of early July concluded that the result of Daudet's rallies was not "bien fameux." The problem, according to the police, was that the presence of the Camelots du roi prevented any really spontaneous discussion. At one midsummer rally, an agent claimed, had it not been for the Camelots Daudet "would have been outrageously booed."[8] But, like de Vésins, Daudet was not easily discouraged. He was convinced that it was not enough for royalists to write and talk among their own numbers in favor of a worker alliance. He was likewise convinced that clandestine connections with certain revolutionaries were insufficient, because, alone, they inevitably fostered an air of conspiracy and would lead to both sides being compromised. Face-to-face exchanges, Daudet therefore maintained, could not be avoided. If the workers were not, as of yet, ready to come to the Action française, the royalists would be obliged to actively attempt the pursuit of the workers.

Part of Daudet's rationale behind the réunions contradictoires was that they would give an opportunity for the revolutionary Left to see firsthand that the ranks of the Action française were not manned—whatever certain socialist politicians might charge—by the foppish and dissolute sons of the aristocracy and haute bourgeoisie. The Action française boasted that, especially with personnel of the Camelots du roi, one could appreciate the genuinely popular taproots of the neoroyalist appeal and how this popular clientele contrasted starkly with the conventional image of the royalists. Judging from the police reports of 1909, however, the humble social background of many of the Camelots was not immediately impressive to the organized worker, at least insofar as this was manifested at Daudet's réunions contradictoires. But it did pay handsome dividends in other, rather unexpected quarters. By the beginning of 1909 almost the entire staff of Hervé's *Guerre sociale* had served, or was presently serving, sentences in the Republic's political prison, La Santé. Hervé and his talented entourage, conceiving of themselves as organizers of the coming revolution, became the self-appointed teachers and protectors of the numerous workers who were temporarily incarcerated following their activities in strikes or demonstrations. At the same time, some of the recently organized Camelots du roi, fresh from their first encounters with gendarmes of the Republic, found themselves in the intimate company of the antirepublicans of the Left.

La Santé provided for the royalists something they could never have provided for themselves—a common ground where they could meet, exchange ideas, and even form personal friendships with the men of the Left. For this La Santé was ideally suited, as it was much more a halfway house for political insurgents than a jail.

Here, amidst relatively comfortable surroundings and a good measure of convivial camaraderie, one could map strategy for future insurgencies at one's leisure.[9]

In May 1909 the readers of the *Action française* learned how well imprisoned royalists and revolutionaries of the Left were getting on. Eugène Merle, Miguel Almereyda, and Victor Méric—known best to Parisians for their vitriolic antipatriotism and their allegations against the honor of the French army—were described in glowing terms. They were, according to the royalist daily, ardent men of fine character. Further, and for the royalists the highest form of praise, they were "irremediably French."[10] The government, the *Action française* charged, put royalists and revolutionaries together hoping they would kill each other off. Despite certain differences, each found the other of the "same temperament," each gained an important measure of esteem for the other. Victor Méric, recalling fondly "a season at La Santé," confirmed this from the side of the revolutionaries. With only one exception, Méric remembered the royalists as "congenial." But more important than a mutual affection, the two groups, royalists and revolutionaries, developed a mutual respect. The image, promoted by some leftist politicos, of the Camelots as the "spoiled children" of the rich was, Méric claims, dispelled for the revolutionaries. Although Méric recalled that there were "a few genuine sons of the fleur-de-lis, who were proud of the 'de' before their names, . . . the bulk of the troop [of Camelots] was made of stalwarts of the shopkeeping class and scions of janitors."[11] Méric was also disabused of another item of leftist conventional wisdom: that partisans of rightist movements were dandified milksops. His reeducation was furthered by his acquaintance with men of the caliber of Marius Plateau, a Camelot leader. Méric remembered that, although Plateau was "very pious, never forgetting his Catholic duties, he talked about one thing only, and that was 'beating someone up.' For him, beating someone up was a complete program. With all this," Méric concluded, "he was extraordinarily strong and certainly very courageous."[12]

The fraternal spirit that developed at La Santé between these prewar radicals of the extreme Left and Right was even admitted by the generally unfriendly syndicalist daily, *La Révolution*. "All this little world," the readers of the *Révolution* were told, "royalists, revolutionaries, journalists, demonstrators, Camelots, workers, live together in a fraternal hodgepodge. Days are spent in lively discussions. At mealtime, the royalists toast to the Revolution, . . . which must, according to them, bring back the King. The revolutionaries, very civilly, toast the King, . . . who will bring them the Revolution."[13]

This prison confraternity, admitted so freely by leaguers of both the Left and the Right, was not calculated to still the persistent rumors of conspiracy circulating in the republican press. But how much conspiring was actually going on at this stage between royalists and Hervéists? Had the royalists been able to convince the men of the *Guerre sociale* that they and their Camelots could be valuable allies in forthcoming antirepublican struggles? Méric admits that royalist intentions, at least, were unmistakable: their goal was "to cajole us and win us over."[14] That the royalists succeeded in these designs, Méric not surprisingly denies. He recalls the boast of Maurice Pujo to the pretender, circulating in the spring of 1909, that the revolutionaries were "on our side." His sardonic rejoinder: "Tu parles!"[15] But one would not expect that Méric would have admitted to having been taken in by the royalists, especially in the light of a later wartime episode when several ex-members of the *Guerre sociale* and the royalists were party to a vicious feud.[16] More impressive than what Méric denied is what he admitted: "We were on very cordial terms with the royalists," he wrote. "We both considered ourselves victims of Clemenceau's arbitrariness. We were leading, though on different grounds and with opposite aims, the same struggle against a regime that they termed 'republican' and we termed 'bourgeois.'"[17]

Could Maurras have expected more than this as an interim report on the progress of what he once called the *entente naturelle* between syndicalists and royalists? This "season at La Santé," a season highlighted by royalists and revolutionaries taking turns proposing toasts to the demise of their captors, not only made fine copy for the *Action française* but demonstrated—and not without a touch of levity—what the royalists had been predicting and the revolutionaries threatening. The Dreyfusard coalition of the parliamentary and revolutionary Left for the defense of the Republic had been dissolved, and in its place was the specter of a new coalition—

an antirepublican bloc for tactical cooperation in bringing down the Republic.

While royalist direct efforts to open a dialogue with the revolutionary Left were being actively pursued by Daudet and the Camelots du roi, Emile Janvion continued to be the focus of more discreet royalist initiatives. This discretion, at least from the perspective of 1909 and 1910, seemed to be less ambiguously successful than the more overt royalist operations.

One sure measure of this success was Janvion's ability to present to large popular audiences a rather thinly disguised version of the royalist pitch to the working class. In April of 1909, for example, at a huge protest rally attended by some 10,000, Janvion took up a favorite royalist theme: workers should not be frightened by the specter of reaction. Janvion pointed out to his auditors that syndicalists have often been accused, because of their vigorous antiparliamentarism, of playing the "game of reaction." That should not bother them unduly. "The Republic in danger?" Janvion asked. "That is all the same to us! The reactionaries do not worry us. . . . We don't have to bother about the form of government." Janvion also included his anti-Masonic tirade—being concurrently echoed in the daily *Action française*—and concluded with the suggestion that workers had more freedom in monarchical England than in republican France.[18]

At another public rally, a few months later, Janvion proved himself serviceable in the royalist cause in yet another way. At this rally, which brought together the various factions of the Left to demand the release of comrades serving time in republican prisons, Janvion was the presiding official. Conveniently, Janvion saw fit to recognize Léon Daudet, who had come to ask that the names of royalist prisoners be associated with those of the Left. Daudet's tack was not unfamiliar: he attempted to shift royalist-worker relations from the impasse of antipatriotism to the open field of anti-Semitism. "If we [neoroyalists]," Daudet vowed, "ever see the Jewish saber raised, the saber that we refuse to recognize as French, . . . on that day, we royalists, will be at your side, on the same side of the barricade."[19]

Thus Janvion, whether as direct emissary of the Action française or whether as stalking-horse for leading royalist personalities, had proved himself a considerable asset. Yet his true potential to the royalists could be fully appreciated only toward the end of 1909 when he announced his plan to launch a biweekly newspaper. This newspaper, christened *Terre libre*, was conceived as a kind of watchdog of the syndicalist movement, which, according to Janvion, was the constant prey of "politicians, parties, and occult sects."[20] The staff of *Terre libre* was ideally suited for its watchdog duties: the most vituperative of the socialist, anarchist, and syndicalist movements were represented.

Leading Janvion's cast of frondeurs was his old companion from anarchist days, the mysterious Georges Darien.[21] One had to resist, according to Darien's unflinching logic, all that is illusion, including the favorite illusion of the revolutionary Left, the *peuple*. The oppressed—those in whom tyranny has not sparked the fires of revolt—deserve as much as their oppressors to become objects of hatred.[22]

From the syndicalist movement came two important and well-known firebrands: Benoît Broutchoux, longtime leader of the revolutionary faction within the miners' union, and a secretary from the metalworkers' federation, Marius Blanchard.[23] Both were frontline ultras, exasperated by the drift of the Confédération générale du travail toward reformism and full of venom toward those they considered responsible.

But Janvion's staff, curiously enough, was not made up exclusively of men of the Left. It also included Marius Riquier, a royalist, contributor to the *Revue critique*, and intimate of Georges Valois. A common mood united Riquier with the rest of the staff at *Terre libre*. It was a mood of toughness, the same brand of hard-nosed realism upon which the young generation at the *Revue critique* prided itself. Ideals were the wares of politicians sold at a discount before elections and during times of crisis. The proletariat, Riquier wrote in *Terre libre*, has been bombarded with "big words," words calculated to humble them: "Science, Evolution, Solidarity, Progress, Affinities." Through bitter experience, however, the proletariat has become wary. They have heard "big words" juxtaposed with massacres of workers by soldiers of the Republic: "Hysterical aspirations toward the Ideal, vehement invocations to Justice, prophetic hymns to the glory of Truth, all that which made up the content of the *Dreyfusard mystique*, all that seems too cruelly ironic today."[24]

Riquier went even farther. Within anarchism itself, he claimed, there was an unhealthy propensity toward unbounded idealism unchecked by experience: anarchists want a society totally free, one with no lines of authority; yet everywhere one finds hierarchy, organization, and authority. Rules are made, and rebels are punished. Is this just, asked Riquier? "Yes, after all," he answered, "because it is natural; by that I mean that it is in keeping with the secret instinct of individuals and with the most profound social necessities; even though it is possible to overthrow a regime and rebel against a society, it is vain and grotesque to revolt against the very conditions of life."[25]

Were the revolutionaries of *Terre libre* willing to admit Riquier's attack on the logic of these first principles? In their disillusionment with the "optimistic and humanitarian *nuées*," were they willing to follow the path from anarchy to authority sketched out by Valois? Clearly Riquier was presenting, rewarmed yet unmistakable, the pessimistic naturalism of *L'Homme qui vient*, and it is apparent that many at *Terre libre* were echoing his sentiments. Janvion's columns, especially, reveal the extent to which debunking revolutionary shibboleths could serve to bridge the gap between the extreme Left and the extreme Right.

It could, of course, be argued that taking Janvion and the men of *Terre libre* seriously is unwarranted in the light of the fact that they were accepting royalist funds. They were not only receiving royalist money, but, one might add, they were receiving it covertly. Thus the argument could be made that Janvion was merely saying what he was paid to say: he had in effect become a royalist tool.

Seeing Janvion in this light, however, raises more problems than it solves. If Janvion was not convinced of the value of the ideas that he was expressing, the question arises as to why he would devote such considerable time and energy to a marginal operation like *Terre libre*. There was unanimity among police agents that royalist funds were in extremely limited supply, and the amounts that came Janvion's way might have kept his newspaper afloat but could have hardly provided Janvion with a large living.

Further, the issue of covert funds is less incriminating than it might seem at first glance. True, Janvion never announced publicly that the royalists were contributing financially to *Terre libre*. But he made increasingly little effort to conceal evidence of collusion with the Action française. Janvion openly proclaimed that keeping connections with royalists working to overthrow the Republic was a lesser evil than cooperation with those who would continually involve the working class in its defense. The inclusion of Marius Riquier—a declared royalist and friend of Georges Valois—on the staff of *Terre libre* was a blatant advertisement of the kind of company Janvion was keeping. If all of Janvion's cards were not on the table, enough of them were, so as to leave little doubt as to those that remained in his hand.

If it is to be maintained that Janvion needs to be taken seriously, there remains then the difficult question of the "evolution" of Janvion's ideas. Many of the themes that found their way to the pages of *Terre libre* were familiar to the readers of the *Action française* and the *Revue critique*. Once again, one might argue that the paymasters were calling the shots: the royalists were in effect renting space in a newspaper circulating in syndicalist circles. This argument, however, would overlook the important fact that most of the themes taken up by *Terre libre* were themes that Janvion had been emphasizing before he had come into contact with the Action française. In this context, the royalists were not so much paying Janvion to say what they wanted to hear but paying him because he had said it already—and was likely to go on saying it.

An obvious example of this is the anti-Masonic theme. Anti-Masonism was daily fare in the *Action française*, but Janvion's conception of a Masonic conspiracy to destroy syndicalism predated the founding of the royalist newspaper. Of course, with the benefit of a regular forum, Janvion could afford to be more methodical: a special column in *Terre libre* devoted itself to Masonic "news." This column was something of a running progress report on how the Masonry was faring in its campaign to divert the working class from its true goals. The report took on the air of an exposé, giving names of Masons who were involved in this or that working-class publication, this or that working-class organization. A typical ploy used by Janvion would be to publish an intercepted letter from a socialist

Mason to another Mason, a *patron*, where both parties employed the informal *tu* and the Masonic *frère*.

Likewise, the antirepublican and antisocialist diatribes, which became regular features in *Terre libre*, antedated Janvion's connection with the royalists. The manner in which the Republic was handling working-class discontent simply gave Janvion more ammunition. He continuously mocked the pretension that the Republic is somehow an advanced social form, one step ahead of what preceded it. "To be the victim," Janvion wrote, "of the bullets of a dictator, of an emperor, or of a king, what a shame for civilization! But to fall under the tricolored bullets of a Gallifet, of a Clemenceau, of a Briand, shouting 'Long Live the Republic!,' what an advantageous difference!"[26]

A less obvious instance of Janvion's consistency was the issue of antimilitarism. From the pages of *Terre libre* Janvion argued that propaganda against war was so much "humanitarian sentimentalism." What was needed, Janvion contended, was the disarray of war as a spur to revolution.[27] Although Janvion had given the argument a revolutionary twist, it must have seemed as though he was playing the royalist game, for nothing was more distasteful to the ultrapatriotic Action française than the antimilitary propaganda of the syndicalists. Yet even here Janvion's attitude can be traced back to before his first contact with the royalists. As early as 1904, at an antimilitary congress, Janvion warned against a "sentimental" antiwar position.[28]

The whole issue of Janvion's consistency—and by implication his relations with the Action française—was raised publicly over the most controversial of all the themes developed in *Terre libre*, anti-Semitism. In the first issues of *Terre libre*, anti-Semitism was present but low keyed; the prefix "Judeo," for example, was used as a mild slur. By early 1910, it had become more strident. *Terre libre* chastised those on the Left who would criticize an individual Jew but fail to make a racial inference: "Such is the power of Jewish gold that even now one cannot say the word *youpin* without being taken for a *calotin*."[29]

By early March, Janvion was on the defensive. Someone on the staff of the *Libertaire*, an anarchist review with which Janvion had been associated, had referred to him as "Janvion of old, who had not yet become the anti-Semitic demagogue of today."[30] Janvion was irate, although not so much over the charge that he was anti-Semitic as over the accusation that he had changed. More than ten years earlier, Janvion claimed, he had warned of the Jewish "danger." His awareness of this danger, he argued, came in the midst of the Dreyfus affair.

The affair was formative for Janvion in much the same way it had been formative for Valois. How was it, Janvion asked as Valois had asked, that mystique had been converted so abruptly and so completely into politique? How could such enormous stores of idealistic energy, the fervor of a potentially revolutionary generation, have been so easily channeled into the most vulgar genre of electoral politics? Janvion felt impelled—and he was not alone among embittered twentieth-century would-be revolutionaries—to search out an answer in conspiracy. Surely, Janvion reasoned, the canalization of such a full-blooded species of revolutionary energy could have been accomplished only with deliberate calculation and consummate political skill.

This was a theme that obsessed Janvion. On numerous occasions he recalled the effervescence of the early days of the Dreyfus affair and his high hopes as a young anarchist. At first, he remembered, there was a feeling that Dreyfus, as a bourgeois, was not the concern of anarchists. But soon events had overtaken them. There was, he recalled, action in the streets and "revolutionary powder in the air."[31] Consequently, we joined in the fight hoping to spread our doctrines. He remembers being sent personally to Algeria to combat the ideas of Drumont.[32]

For a time, as Janvion recounted it, the affair had possessed extraordinary revolutionary potential. Very soon, however, it was ingeniously defused of this potential by the clever politicians and the ever-scheming Jews. The politicians, for their part, saw the affair as a mystification with the inherent power to catapult them into high political office. "Clemenceau, Briand, Millerand, Viviani," explained Janvion, "have been the beautiful results of this work: 'Light!' 'Truth!' 'Justice!'—the three metaphysical wheels of the Dreyfusard tricycle—are housed today by the ministry."[33] The Jew, meanwhile, no less scheming than the politician, according to Janvion, used the affair to protect his privileged position. Under the pretext of fighting the privileges of the *calotte*,[34] Catholic clericalism, the Jew has managed to hide the abuses of his own sect. Whereas a right-minded man of the Left is scandalized by the calotte, the same man, Janvion argued, has had to "come to terms with the gang of reactionaries, via the synagogue, and the lodges; they compromise with the whole gang of *republican and socialist swindlers*."[35] Any Jew, therefore, who does not forsake the exclusiveness of his religion, according to Janvion, is on a par with the calotte. He makes himself a racist, a believer in the "aristocracy of his race," and, therefore, "this judaizing *youpin* is our enemy just like the clericalizing *calotin* or the Freemason indulging in the affectations of his rite or the petty calculations of his political ambitions."[36]

Thus, Janvion came to what he claimed was merely evenhandedness in identifying the reactionary enemy: all those who were not outright revolutionaries were part of what should be considered an undifferentiated reaction. According to this logic, Jews were no better than Catholics, socialist politicians no better than nationalist politicians, and republicans no better than monarchists. The great Dreyfusard betrayal had come about when the revolutionary Left had fallen under the illusion that Jews, socialist politicians, and republicans were somehow a lesser evil, were somehow less objectively reactionary, simply because they waved the banner of progressivism.

Janvion, however, did not rest content here. Despite his oft-repeated claim that the reaction was an undifferentiated evil, he himself began to differentiate. He now claimed that those forces that called themselves "progressive" were in reality a greater rather than a lesser evil, because they won their victories not in open and honest battle but through cunning, ruse, and cooptation. From this perspective, Janvion argued, the debacle of the revolutionary forces in the wake of the affair was fully explicable. It was a case of a conspiracy operated by the false friends of the revolutionary Left during the heat of the Dreyfusard struggle, who had more to gain from the manipulation of revolutionary symbols than from their realization.

This style of conspiratorial rationalization, which played no small part in the psychological appeal of many forms of radical polemicizing on both the radical Right and the radical Left in prewar France, could serve a dual function. On the one hand, it could offer aid and comfort to those whose simplistic fantasies did not superimpose well when projected onto a complex reality, whereas, on the other hand, it could offer them an escape route by pointing the way to a precarious conspiratorial footbridge across the political spectrum. Janvion, carrying his conspiratorial logic to its end, could argue that the royalists, open and forthright reactionaries that they were, could prove trustworthy allies in the battle to the death with the real enemy, the covert reactionaries, who hide their true colors under the flag of progressivism.

The readers of *Terre libre* were soon treated to the final product of Janvion's conspiratorial odyssey. Whereas *Terre libre* fell short of an open avowal of the Action française, its message was hardly obscure. Every opportunity was seized to demonstrate how in "monarchies," like England and Germany, workers fared better than in republican France.[37] The Camelots du roi were portrayed as the unsung heroes in the fight against republican despotism.[38] Further, it could not have escaped notice that *Terre libre*'s campaign against assorted "humanitarian *nuées*" paralleled, down to the very phraseology, those of the publications of the Action française.

The most ominous of Janvion's attacks on the *nuées* were made, however, not in *Terre libre* but in the *Action française* itself. In an interview given in early June 1910, he spoke of "rather new ideas" circulating in certain syndicalist quarters about future worker demonstrations. Rather than holding large, amorphous rallies for distant causes, syndicalists were contemplating a new form of action, which would be carried out by an organization that would have the advantage of being small, energetic, and disciplined. "With this organization," Janvion wrote, "the working class would have in Paris a troop of two thousand militants, always ready to march and to carry away the masses. This is more than is necessary for a well-calculated coup."[39] For those who missed the implication, the royalists wrote between the lines: the proletariat was abandoning the old socialist version of the revolution as a mass uprising and was being converted to Maurras's idea of the organized coup. The

Acion française quoted Riquier—to whom they refer as a young "syndicalist writer"—on the new idea: "For sure, it is less picturesque and less melodramatic, but more efficient and safer."[40]

That Janvion could speak of 2,000 organized militants in mid-1910 was little more than braggadocio. There is no indication that the "new ideas" had passed the discussion stage. As to *Terre libre* itself, it was still the publication of a maverick sect. Its circulation, even taking Janvion's own estimate, was hardly encouraging.[41] Furthermore, as might have been anticipated, Janvion had to suffer the silence of the politiques at the Confédération générale du travail. A publication such as *Terre libre*, if it was to thrive, could only do so with the aid of controversy, and the politiques, despite adequate provocation, refused to provide it.[42]

Yet, despite these initial handicaps, *Terre libre* could at least count on one factor that would not fail to work in its favor. This was the disarray, confusion, and bitter infighting that characterized the syndicalist movement throughout 1909 and 1910. The various factions of the movement, now in almost open battle, threatened to destroy what effectiveness the French labor movement had possessed. This was fertile ground for Janvion's propaganda.

The situation within the Confédération générale du travail had been degenerating steadily since mid-1908: the shock of Villeneuve–Saint–Georges, the ultra coup at the Marseille congress, and the public charges that Griffuelhes, secretary-general of the confederation, had misused the organization's funds followed one another in rapid succession.[43] The replacement of Griffuelhes by Louis Niel, a leading reformist, as secretary-general in February 1909 proved to be only an invitation to further turmoil. With a mutual enmity toward the politiques as the only binding agent, the ad hoc coalition of reformists and ultras that had put Niel into office was an inherently unstable one. Niel maintained himself in office, if the police are to be believed, only with the continued support of the ultras.[44] No one was very surprised at the brevity of Niel's tenure in office. The precipitating event that brought Niel down was the failure of an important postal strike in the late spring of 1909, another humiliating defeat for the Confédération générale du travail. By the end of May 1909, the various factions of the Confédération générale du travail were once more set to do battle. This time there was talk of scission, talk to which Griffuelhes himself gave credence in a newspaper interview.[45]

For most of June, according to police reports, there was an open scramble for control of the Confédération générale du travail. The ultras and the reformists hoped, once again, to block the Griffuelhes-Pouget faction from recapturing the pivotal office of secretary-general. Police reports mention at least two ultras in the running for the post: Marius Blanchard,[46] a secretary of the powerful metalworkers' federation, and Emile Janvion, both of *Terre libre*. According to one agent, the latter had "a serious chance"; not only would he have the support of the ultras, the agent reasoned, but also many of the reformists would be behind him because of his reputation as the archenemy of Pouget.[47] A later report by the same agent confirmed Janvion's seriousness as a candidate.[48]

However threatening the ultra-reformist challenge continued to be, it was not, it soon became evident, strong enough to prevent the politiques from recapturing the office they had so long held. By early July, Léon Jouhaux, a politique and protégé of Griffuelhes, was installed as secretary-general. The election of Jouhaux, with benefit of hindsight, marks a last significant turning point: never again were the ultras strong enough to challenge the leadership of the Confédération générale du travail. They were gradually reduced to perpetual opposition, an opposition that was sometimes vocal—indeed, as will be seen, it even threatened on occasions to disrupt the workers' movement—but one that receded from the center of power at the Confédération générale du travail. Meanwhile, under Jouhaux's leadership, the confederation moved steadily away from a revolutionary syndicalist orientation and toward an accommodation with the Republic. The caution practiced by the politiques and apologized for as tactical necessity came to be promoted under Léon Jouhaux as doctrinal virtue. But this transformation of France's leading labor organization did not run its course smoothly. The commitment to a radical transformation of society through the revolutionary violence of the militant worker, with its defiant antimilitarism and uncompromising and apocalyptic mentality, died hard. In the hands of Janvion and certain of his ultra friends, sensing no doubt that their cause was lost, this commitment moved from stubborn defense to a scurrilous rearguard warfare against the Confédération générale du travail.

As royalist initiatives toward the working class moved forward during 1909 and early 1910, their chief architect, Georges Valois, was kept safely from public view. Except for an occasional article or interview, Valois's name was not featured in the columns of the *Action française*. The reason, if one is to believe Louis Dimier's testimony, was Maurras's continued distrust of the young convert from anarchism.[49] Although Valois's public exposure remained limited, his private activities on behalf of the projected worker alliance were apparently given free rein. His knowledge of syndicalism and connections within the syndicalist movement were at something of a premium at the Action française.

As police reports indicate, it was Valois who was the intermediary between Janvion and the royalists: the money that kept *Terre libre* in business came from the political bureau of the pretender through Valois to Janvion.[50] Valois's relations with Marius Riquier, the most outspoken of the royalist defenders at *Terre libre*, were close.[51] But Valois's plans ran farther than *Terre libre*. Rather persistently, he worked to bring his message to the most prestigious of all syndicalist publications, the *Mouvement socialiste*. Here articles by the most influential syndicalist militants were published side by side with those of the brightest of the young intellectuals who had been drawn into the syndicalist movement. Here, also, was the most cherished prize of all, Valois's old mentor, Georges Sorel. If Janvion and his *Terre libre* were to be the low road to the militant syndicalist leadership, Georges Sorel and his friends at the *Mouvement socialiste* would be the high road.

[7]

The Royalist Offensive: The High Road

It has become part of conventional wisdom in the history of French labor to dismiss Georges Sorel as having had no real influence on the course of revolutionary syndicalism. Edouard Dolléans and Maxime Leroy, two of the most sympathetic historians of syndicalism, did much to correct the prevailing contemporary view, which made Sorel's name synonymous with revolutionary syndicalism. Leroy liked to recall Griffuelhes's remark, when questioned about the influence of Sorel: "I [only] read Alexandre Dumas."[1]

As early as 1911, another perspicacious analyst of revolutionary syndicalism, Gaétan Pirou, noted the gulf between Sorel's small coterie of intellectuals and the workaday syndicalist militants. The latter, Pirou observed, tended to think in terms of economic self-interest and liberation from the strictures of bourgeois morality. They envisioned a society of new wealth and new freedom. The vision of the theoreticians was considerably more somber: wealth and freedom were not the cure but the disease. Syndicated workers were valuable precisely because they were poor and adhered to traditional moral codes.[2]

All of this was a healthy corrective to seeing Sorel and his intellectual disciples as founders and directors of revolutionary syndicalism. Yet it tends to obscure several important facts. First, it makes the distinction between militants and theoreticians rather more absolute than it actually was. For the provincial worker-militant, who alternated between the workshop and the union hall, syndicalist theory was obviously not a pressing concern. The top Parisian militants, the leaders of the Confédération générale du travail, were less plausibly the "simple militants" that they often liked to project. Whereas much of their time was spent on the practical business of running an increasingly large bureaucracy, they were hardly unaware of the ongoing discussion of the broader import of their movement. In fact, they were, on occasion, impassioned participants themselves. It becomes difficult, for example, to see a great divide between the *Mouvement socialiste* and the *Vie ouvrière*, the former run by "theoreticians," the latter by "militants." The truth is that at the highest levels the line between pure theory and pure practice becomes difficult to appreciate.

A second problem connected with the revisionism regarding Sorel's influence is that it went entirely too far. That Sorel was, especially at the early stages, more influenced by syndicalist practice than vice versa was admitted by Sorel himself. With the publication of *L'Avenir socialiste des syndicats* and *Reflections on Violence*, however, Sorel was recognized as the most important interpreter of the syndicalist movement by the militants themselves. Testimony to this is given by Paul Delesalle, who was both a friend of Sorel and, as *secrétaire-adjoint* of the Fédération des bourses, one of the most important syndicalist leaders.[3]

The *Mouvement socialiste*, Paul Delesalle maintained, was more than a journal for intellectuals. It offered a large and open forum where militants of different persuasions might argue their cases. According to Delesalle, some of the "best militants of syndicalism have become assiduous collaborators." As to Sorel, Delesalle vigorously denies the allegation that he was virtually unknown to the leading militants. He was widely read and discussed by militants, including—Delesalle goes out of his way to point out—Griffuelhes.[4] Besides being familiar with his writings, a number of militants knew Sorel personally through informal Sunday meetings hosted by Lagardelle.[5] Whatever they might argue after the fact, syndicalist militants were not only fully aware of the prestige associated with the name of Georges Sorel but willing, when it could be arranged, to exploit it for their own purposes.[6]

The reason for the subsequent downgrading of the importance

of Sorel is not difficult to understand. Sorel's enthusiasm for revolutionary syndicalism proved to be remarkably short-lived. Before his *Reflections on Violence* was even in book form, Sorel was privately expressing serious misgivings about the syndicalist movement. It was not long before these misgivings were to take the form of public criticism. This was taken by the militants as a betrayal, and a betrayal never to be forgiven.

As early as 1906, in fact, Sorel had begun to see signs of moral degeneration within the syndicalist movement. In the wake of the first open conflict with Clemenceau, Pouget and Griffuelhes had accepted space in *L'Humanité* to make their case known to the public. Sorel was furious at this "outright act of desertion." He wrote to Lagardelle that he was afraid that syndicalists, out of despair, would make themselves into opportunists. He went as far as suggesting that Lagardelle give up publishing the *Mouvement socialiste*: "If I am not mistaken, there is nothing else to do but to *disappear honorably*; it is better to disappear in the name of principles than to die of a prolonged starvation."[7]

By 1908 his disenchantment had become definitive. Sorel was convinced that the conflict between Clemenceau and the syndicalists, raised to the level of open warfare after Villeneuve–Saint–Georges, was being orchestrated by Jean Jaurès: the politicians had wormed their way to the inner councils of syndicalism and were capable of manipulating the movement for their own purposes. Charges that Clemenceau had consciously planned the massacre at Villeneuve–Saint–Georges, which were making the rounds in leftist publications, infuriated Sorel. He was certain that the charges were contrived, a bit of demagogy designed to bring unwitting syndicalists into a socialist-led anti-Clemenceau coalition. His real worry was that syndicalists, once in a working alliance with socialists, would lose their independence and with it their capacity to fight what Sorel conceived to be the real enemy—parliamentary democracy. The virtue of the *Mouvement socialiste*, from Sorel's point of view, had been that it had long fought against the incursion of the democratic politician. Now, Sorel warned, this virtue was in danger of being compromised, and it was necessary to take a firmer stand.[8]

When it became apparent that the editor of the *Mouvement social-*

iste was not heeding his advice, Sorel played his trump: "Today," he wrote to Lagardelle in late October 1908, "I am firmly resolved to withdraw *immediately* from a review that is an accomplice in the maneuvers that have just caused the descent of the Confédération générale du travail into the Jaurès-Combes swamp."[9] Though Sorel did not hold to his threat just yet, he continued, as his correspondence with Lagardelle reveals, the attempt to turn the latter around by every means that could be mustered, not excluding outright boorishness.[10] He again urged Lagardelle to stop publishing the *Mouvement socialiste*. As there was no hope for syndicalism, at least in the near future, he should gracefully bow out. "When the movement picks up momentum again by itself," Sorel wrote to Lagardelle, "you could come back, having kept your strength and not burdened by the chain of all the errors now being committed by syndicalists in the tow of politicians."[11] Lagardelle was not understating the case when, in an introduction written some years later, he concluded that "Sorel's thought has very much evolved since *L'Avenir socialiste des syndicats*."[12]

The evolution of Sorel's thought, to the surprise of many of his friends, including Hubert Lagardelle, was not simply away from syndicalism. In early September 1908 he wrote his lifelong friend, Benedetto Croce, that he was publishing an article on religious modernism in the *Revue critique*, an article that he would not reedit, he added, lest someone attack him for writing in a royalist publication.[13] Sorel's explanation for letting his article be used in the first place was brief: "These young people [of the *Revue critique*] are very intelligent. As they continually quote my books, I could not refuse such a collaboration."[14] But it was not solely the adulation of the young nationalists at the *Revue critique* that had led Sorel to contribute his article. The evolution of his ideas had prepared him, by the fall of 1908, for the appreciation of a new force in French life, the revival of nationalism.

Sorel has been called, and indeed he has called himself, a historical pessimist. Much of his hostility toward the Enlightenment, his favorite whipping boy, flows from its connection with the rise of a theory of natural progress. Decadence, not progress, was considered natural by Sorel. The universe—the social as well as the physical universe—was running down.[15] What brought Sorel back from the brink of despair was his belief in the possibility of regeneration through the exertion of the one force capable of struggling against dissolution, the human will. At certain historical junctures, through heroic, almost superhuman, efforts, men could turn back the tide of dissolution. Thus Sorel, although not so optimistic as to subscribe to a theory of progress, was not so pessimistic as to deny the possibility of a renaissance.[16]

But a renaissance, for Sorel, was no fortuitous event. The tremendous energies it required, as well as the will to discipline those energies, were not easy commodities. A renaissance was not to be looked for among those of comfortable circumstance; the poor and the downtrodden were better prospects. Sorel's long infatuation with the working class was based on just this paradoxical appreciation of their oppressed status.[17] Signs that workers were willing to ameliorate their status by compromise rather than struggle were, to Sorel, tantamount to betrayal of their mission. Yet, just as prospects for a working-class renaissance had begun to dim, Sorel thought that he detected a glimmer of hope from another quarter.

The best source on Sorel as he passed through his so-called nationalist phase is Jean Variot, a nationalist himself and Sorel's confidant.[18] In one of Variot's earliest transcriptions of a conversation with Sorel, in November 1908, the defender of proletarian violence was represented as having already come to an appreciation of the value of nationalism. A nation, no less than a class, could reap the benefits of being the injured party, Sorel argued. He recalled Prussia after its defeat at the hands of Napoleon at Jena. "Adversity, for nations," he concluded, "is often a source of energy; it calls for self-examination. It gathers up their forces."[19]

Like Prussia of the early nineteenth century, contemporary France had experienced its share of "adversity": first, the crushing military defeat at Sedan; then, the Dreyfus affair, which Sorel had come to view as a spiritual defeat. By the turn of the century, a nationalist renaissance had been a real possibility in France, for nationalism possessed "marvelous opportunities." It could have, Sorel maintained, consolidated all the energies latent in patriotism and replaced "an idiotic Boulangism by a well-considered action," which would have defeated the "scheming" of the Dreyfusards.[20]

If nationalism had so far failed its mission, despite its promise, the cause of this failure was not, according to Sorel, difficult to explain: "The mediocrity of the nationalist personnel is the true cause of this debacle." The Dreyfusards, clever in politics if in nothing else, were easily able to clear the field of nationalist opposition. Meanwhile, all of Europe "was rubbing its hands in anticipation of the downfall of French nationalism." But just as the "debacle" seemed complete, "an unexpected event took place." This event, Sorel argued, "is the creation of the only serious nationalist movement that has ever existed in France: the group of those who follow Maurras, the people of the Action française. This movement must be closely studied. It is not led by a man ignorant of the great human tides. Maurras has studied the political life of the world. He knows that there is a proletariat with a 'historical life.'" Sorel, refusing to speculate as to whether Maurras can actually bring about a restoration, claimed that this question is not what truly interested him. "What I am interested in," Sorel asserted, "is that he stands up in front of the colorless and reactionary bourgeoisie, shaming it for having been defeated and trying to give it a doctrine."[21]

That Sorel could become concerned with the collective fate of the nation, that he would look hopefully to the Action française, was not the simple result of his disappointment with syndicalist leaders. The experience of the Dreyfus affair and its aftermath was as great a formative influence on Sorel as it was on his student, Georges Valois. For years he had railed against the opportunists, who had been the political beneficiaries of the Dreyfusard victory. But only in 1909 did he produce a serious attempt to come to grips with the results of the affair. *La Révolution dreyfusienne*, as even Sorel's defenders have admitted, is not one of his better works: it is mean spirited and, at times, simple minded.[22] Clearly, Sorel's anger got the better of him. But beneath this anger one can discern the dimensions of a genuine concern. The Dreyfus affair, Sorel contended, beyond the aesthetic offense of being cheap public melodrama, had had serious repercussions on French society.

The affair, according to Sorel, had had the effect of destroying what remained of aristocratic influence in public life, an influence that had guaranteed some semblance of social authority. "It seems to me," Sorel argued, "that political theoreticians have not been enough aware that the institutions of modern liberalism require that power belong to an aristocracy with enough intelligence to call forth those men whose capabilities honor the country." The Dreyfus affair, as Sorel now saw it, had destroyed this "aristocracy of intelligence" and in doing so perpetrated "the ruin of the social structure that made possible a tolerable operation of the parliamentary regime." In the wake of the affair, a gang of venal and lowborn politicians had replaced the "aristocracy of intelligence," and thus the national parliament, Sorel contended, had become a springboard for demagogues and electoral jobbers.[23]

Not only did the Dreyfus affair have the effect of disinheriting the only elite capable of governing, it also corrupted the means by which they might govern—France's historic legal system. The anticlerical campaign staged by Dreyfusards in the wake of their victory, as Sorel saw it, could have been carried out only by a flagrant disregard or manipulation of laws protecting Catholics. As a result, Sorel argued, "our minds have become used to attaching very little importance to the *guarantee of law*, without which there is no liberty."[24] The victory of the democrats had been total. The Dreyfusard revolution had not only swept before it the nationalist opposition but, more importantly, Sorel argued, the social and juridical framework of the nation.[25]

Sorel, as his conversations with Variot revealed, did not concern himself only with the internal damage done by the victorious Dreyfusards. In the realm of international relations, he maintained that a nation could prosper only if men of sufficient independence and authority were free to conduct what he termed the *grande politique*. The scope of the grande politique was, for Sorel, necessarily almost unlimited: "The spirit of utopia—we could call it the spirit of disorder within and the foreign diplomatic combination without—represents the enemy."[26] Sorel had apparently come to feel that the position of France was dangerously vulnerable. Nations, he warned, would do well to contemplate the myth of Achilles' heel, for it "is perhaps but a proud image of the life of nations; they are formed by a series of great sacrifices and sometimes die for having neglected blows against a vulnerable spot."[27]

One cannot but suspect that Sorel's newly found concern with the grande politique had been directly inspired by his reading of

Charles Maurras. His pronouncements on the subject were delivered, according to Variot, on 16 June 1909. Just a few weeks later, Sorel wrote a cordial letter to Maurras, which began:

I have just read your second edition of *L'Enquête sur la monarchie*. It seems certain to me that your criticism of contemporary experience justifies well what you wanted to prove: "In modern France, traditional monarchy would be the only institution capable of achieving the vast tasks assigned by the present theoreticians of the State to the government of a great country." . . . I have been surprised, for a long time, by the folly of contemporary authors, who ask of democracy to accomplish a work that can be tackled only by monarchies filled with the sentiment of their mission.[28]

By the summer of 1909 Sorel's attitude toward the Action française was marked by both interest and incredulity. His incredulity was not so much about the institution of monarchy itself as the power of the royalists to bring about a restoration. The issue of monarchy to the side, what encouraged Sorel was the vigorous attack launched by the royalists against the Republic and the "too mediocre individuals" who ran it—the *mufles*, as Sorel had christened them.[29] In July 1909, in the Italian review *Divenire sociale*, Sorel gave first public recognition of his admiration for the Action française. Here, interest and incredulity were mixed but in rather unequal portions: "Maurras's friends will probably not succeed in their enterprise of monarchical restoration; but they will do the country a great service by giving it back a feeling for intellectual values; a feeling that has been lost. . . . No social group but the Action française was up to fulfilling a role that requires both scholarly knowledge and faith. It was certainly not the Socialist party that could have acted against the domination of the *mufles*."[30]

To help organize the "total war against the mufles" became, for the next few years, a consuming interest with Sorel. Because a nationalist renaissance seemed the most propitious means to that end, Sorel kept a vigilant eye for additional recruits willing to fight the mufles. Early in 1910 Sorel became excited over just such a prospect. Charles Péguy, like himself a "Dreyfusard of the first hour," had just published the first installment of a projected epic dealing with Joan of Arc. Péguy, who had already separated himself from the Left Dreyfusards by his criticism of antipatriotism, was now on his way, it seemed, toward an affirmation of Catholicism. In a long review article appearing, significantly, in the *Action française*, Sorel warned against appreciating Péguy's work, entitled *Le Mystère de la charité de Jeanne d'Arc*, from simply a literary point of view: "For . . . this magnificent work is destined to occupy a prominent place in the general history of our country; twenty years from now, the name of Péguy will be inseparable from the renaissance of French patriotism." Péguy's work spelled, for Sorel, the end of the unchallenged reign of the Dreyfusards. "Today," Sorel wrote, "the farce is over: to the astonishment of other countries, the reasonable patriotism of the true France is now reappearing. And here comes an old Dreyfusard claiming for patriotic ideas the right to direct contemporary thought."[31]

The extravagant hopes placed by Sorel upon Péguy can be understood from several perspectives. Most important for Sorel was the moral weight carried by Péguy: his integrity was already becoming legendary.[32] His former impassioned defense of Dreyfus and his independent socialist leanings separated his patriotism from that of the self-interested conservatives. Around his review, the *Cahiers de la quinzaine*, gathered some of the most talented of the young French literati. Daniel Halévy, Julien Benda, and Romain Rolland published early, important works there. Clearly, Péguy, along with his *Cahiers*, would have been a boon to the nationalist coalition, which Sorel was hoping would coalesce. Péguy would be an ideal complement to the Action française, whose appeal was narrowed by its monarchism. Sorel even fostered hopes of publishing in the *Cahiers*, according to Variot, "a certain number of his studies on the possible relations between a pure Marxism and a reasoned nationalism."[33] Although Sorel might be skeptical of workers rallying to the king, Valois's idea of a national syndicalism had obviously captured his imagination.[34]

But as events were soon to prove, Sorel misjudged the direction of Péguy's thought. For one thing, Péguy did not intend that his private religious feelings be put to the uses that Sorel had in mind.[35] For another, although Péguy might have detested as much as Sorel did the political exploitation of the Dreyfus affair, he was not about to fight shoulder to shoulder with anti-Dreyfusards of Maurras's ilk. His regrets about the Dreyfus affair, as he made all too plain in his "Notre Jeunesse" of late 1910, were regrets about the behavior of others, not misgivings about his own conduct. At the *Cahiers*, Péguy assured his readers, Dreyfusard mystique remained pure and intact.

Sorel was now clearly discouraged. His break with the *Mouvement socialiste* and revolutionary syndicalism was a matter of public record by the spring of 1910.[36] The *Cahiers de la quinzaine*, as Sorel was slowly becoming aware, was not going to be an alternative forum. He hesitated to take the next step—open collaboration with the royalists, a collaboration that the royalists were now assiduously courting.

His attitude at this point was paradoxical. There was no doubt in his mind that when his article on Péguy appeared in the *Action française* he would be accused of complicity with royalism. "One will not fail to see there," Sorel wrote privately, "an act of adhesion to the 'Reaction'; Lagardelle's friends, who speak everywhere against me, would be happy to know that I met a few people of the Action française; one knows everything in Paris."[37]

The reaction to Sorel's newly found respect for nationalism, when it did come, was much what Sorel had anticipated, although perhaps more cruelly ironic. "I am told," wrote one commentator, "that peevish minds would suspect him [Sorel], falsely no doubt, of having very recently embroidered the French fleur-de-lis and the sacré-coeur on the syndicalist banner."[38] Despite his premonitions, Sorel was overwrought with indignation. Taking his case to the front page of the *Action française*, he charged that he was being maligned only because his *Révolution dreyfusienne* had hit a raw nerve with the old Dreyfusard crowd. They injure me, Sorel claimed, even though I did not touch on the issue of the guilt or innocence of Dreyfus. Perhaps, Sorel menaced witlessly, I should write "a pamphlet on the reasons for believing in the treason of M. Alfred Dreyfus."[39] This hypersensitivity to the accusation of having sold out to the reactionaries was a constant preoccupation with Sorel, and one that in the end led him to break all relations with the Action française.

But not just yet. In fact, at about the same time that Sorel was railing against those who were unfair to him, he was moving toward an even closer collaboration with certain royalists connected with the Action française—more specifically those "very intelligent young men" about whom he had written to Croce. Sorel had been won over to the idea of a joint syndicalist-nationalist review. The inspiration behind this project was Valois. The task of winning over Sorel had been made easier by Sorel's most faithful disciple and trusted friend, Edouard Berth.[40]

As one who had been converted early to syndicalism through Sorel's influence, Berth joined the staff of Lagardelle's *Mouvement socialiste* and became one of the mainstays of the *nouvelle école*. As a prose stylist and systematizer of ideas, he surpassed his master. Under Berth's pen, many of Sorel's hesitant and often disorganized ideas became forceful and systematic. But Sorel always refused to see Berth as just a student; he maintained that the younger man was a profound thinker in his own right, one of the most "prominent men of our time."[41] Certainly, Sorel exaggerated Berth's profundity, but his talent as a first-rate polemicist and interpreter of intellectual trends did make him a valuable asset to the *Mouvement socialiste*. Along with his mentor, Berth had by 1910 become estranged from the journal that he had done so much to promote, and he was intrigued, even more than Sorel, by Georges Valois and the Action française—though not nearly so intimidated as Sorel was by what people might say.[42]

In the early part of 1910 Berth had written an article—considerably longer than Sorel's—on Péguy's *Jeanne d'Arc* and was looking for a publisher. Sorel was ready with advice: "Valois would ask nothing better than to have it published in the *Revue critique* . . . ; but I deem it dangerous for you to commit yourself totally to Valois's friends; you certainly will be able to have it published (somewhat shortened) by the *Nouvelle Revue française*."[43] When this latter project did not materialize, Sorel was considerably less hostile to the idea of the *Revue critique*, but he advised Berth that, if he had to have recourse to the royalist publication, he had best use a pseudonym. The article was never published in the *Revue critique*,[44] but within a month Valois had convinced Berth of the wisdom of active participation in a new review where ground could be broken in syndicalist-nationalist collaboration.

All agreed that Sorel had to participate for the project to succeed; but he was difficult to bring around. In addition to his habitual fear of criticism, he was in a poor state of health.[45] Yet he accepted the offer to direct the review, to be called *La Cité française*. His motives are not easy to discern. Undoubtedly, he still hoped for great things from a nationalist revival; the *Cité française* would give it impetus. From a less selfless point of view, it would be a place where he could continue to publish his work, a serious consideration in the wake of his abandonment of his old friends, both syndicalist and Dreyfusard.[46] Finally, and most importantly if one is to take Sorel's own word, there was the solicitude that he felt for his young disciple. "I accepted," Sorel wrote to Croce, "on the condition that Berth be codirector; this way, if the enterprise succeeds, I will be able to withdraw and leave Berth in a prominent position. Socialist literature, so far, has not brought him luck; he must come out of this deadlock to assert his talent, and he will be able to do so as director of a review."[47]

Under Sorel's directorship, the staff of the *Cité française*—which included Valois, Berth, Variot, and Pierre Gilbert—enunciated its guiding principles. An aggressively nationalistic declaration was drawn up. In it the staff of the *Cité française* laid the framework for a new French national community, a mission hitherto impossible because of the various "European" ideologies that had dominated the last century. Thus, "the first task of the *Cité française*," the declaration read, will be the liberation "of French intelligence" from the thrall of alien ideologies. The most pressing concern in this respect was democracy. Though the founders of the *Cité française* represent diverse points of view, the declaration continued, they are all agreed on the cardinal point "that if the questions posed in the modern world are to be resolved in a sense favorable to civilization, it is absolutely necessary to destroy democratic institutions."[48]

Behind democratic institutions, so detrimental to the health of France, were the ideas that fostered the democratic spirit. These, too, would be challenged: "One will therefore fight against the false science that has served to justify democratic ideas, against the economic systems that are designed by their inventors to besot the working classes, against the work of false historians who reduce history to a democratic genesis. Lastly, one will denounce the crimes of these anarchists of literature, who, under the pretense of novel or theater and for the pleasure of degenerate bourgeois, have spread the lowest moral values."[49]

The same themes were reiterated in even more vitriolic form by Sorel in a lead article for the first number of the *Cité française*. His syndicalist defenders, who found it impossible to believe that the author of *Reflections on Violence* could subscribe to nationalist doctrines, were disarmed. All nations, Sorel admitted, produced exceptional men, "but France is probably the country in which superior intellects have been best combined, at various epochs, to form classical groups; this is the reason why French civilization has occupied such an eminent position in history, as so many writers have proclaimed many a time." This civilization, according to Sorel, fragile product of past genius, can be preserved only with a heroic exertion of will. "What is called decadence," according to Sorel, "is nothing else but the awakening of powers, whose vulgar, barbaric, or absurd manifestations had been momentarily hidden by an artificial order imposed by genius. Thus the true is very unstable in our country, whereas our bad instinct perpetually engenders the false."[50]

To "stabilize" truth, Sorel recommended the solution preached by Maurras for years—a return to classical taste. Against the dangerous meanderings of the unrestrained spirit, the good sense and orderliness of the classical model offer a healthy alternative. Sorel made it clear that he was not just opting for a new literary fashion: "The present crisis is more of metaphysical than of literary interest."[51]

It seemed as though the *Cité française* would not only be a personal coup for Valois but an important step forward in the royalist efforts to attract the working class. Two of the leading figures from the staff of the highly regarded *Mouvement socialiste* had come to see the wisdom of Maurras's *entente naturelle*. Yet, just as the first number of the new review was to be sent out, the project collapsed. The problems that ended this first open attempt at syndicalist-nationalist collaboration were more personal than philosophic.

Sorel, as has been seen, always acted with great hesitancy, only following Berth's lead. Not long after accepting the directorship, he wrote wearily to Berth: "I am very frightened by the work that the review is going to mean for me . . . ; I wonder how we are going to be able to do it: for a long time, we will have only mediocre collaborators, and readers will be expecting much better things than we will be able to give them."[52] Could those "very intelligent young men" have grown mediocre in so short a time? It is more likely that Sorel's recurrent fear for his reputation once again surfaced.

Originally, Valois was careful lest it should seem to Sorel that the *Cité française* was a tool of the Action française. Variot, Sorel's friend and confidant, was included on the staff, along with Berth, in order to lay to rest Sorel's fear of a royalist preponderance. As time went on, however, Valois became less cautious. A power struggle between Valois and Variot developed, and Variot offered to resolve the issue by quitting the project. Sorel would not hear of it and left in a huff, blaming Valois.[53]

Despite the failure of the *Cité française* to materialize, rumors that Sorel was fraternizing with the men of the Action française were now in the open. Hubert Lagardelle, who was publishing a collection of his writings, felt the need to separate the frequently antidemocratic tone of the *Mouvement socialiste* from the spirit animating the *Cité française*: "We meant to criticize democracy, not to suppress it, but to go beyond it."[54] He also felt obliged to state his position vis-à-vis the Action française:

I will not dwell on the most incredible confusion, which has been created by the neoroyalists of the *Action française*. From our criticism of democracy, they have simply concluded that syndicalism led to monarchy. But I am sorry to say that M. Maurras with his high culture will not succeed in proving the complicity of syndicalism and monarchy.

If one raises as an objection the recent agreement of Georges Sorel, followed by Edouard Berth, with the friends of the *Action française*, I will answer that two swallows do not make a spring.[55]

These were brave words by Lagardelle, but Berth and especially Sorel were of more importance to the *Mouvement socialiste* than Lagardelle either would or could admit. With their departure, the journal went into a steady decline.

By the end of 1910, because of attacks from all sides, Sorel felt the need to defend himself publicly. In an open letter to his Italian translator, which first appeared in the *Giornale d'Italia*, Sorel took his critics to task. Small-minded democrats assume that a journal is always the work of a party; but the concern of a true "philosopher" is to study movements that seem important, and this does not necessarily mean to adhere to a party. Truly to understand a movement one must first acquire for it "an intellectual sympathy." Whatever the merits of this argument for the student of society, it was not calculated to give a great deal of comfort to Sorel's former friends, who, by implication, were led to understand that their ideas possessed little that could hold the interest of the serious thinker.

Indeed, the collapse of the *Cité française* proved only a small, and in many ways temporary, setback for Valois and his friends. Sorel, it is true, was never again to associate himself so closely with a project of the Action française. Yet it was generally known after the *Cité* episode that his sympathies were with the nationalists. Within a few months, Variot had set up the kind of review with which Sorel could feel comfortable. Entitled—not without a certain irony —*L'Indépendance*, it proved to be, on many issues, almost an echo of the Action française, although run without the royalist personnel. Here Sorel felt free enough to develop the appropriate sympathies for those movements of thought that were worthy of the philosopher's attention. Among these were an even more bellicose nationalism and a newly discovered anti-Semitism.

Berth, always more impulsive than his mentor, gave free rein to his new sympathies for the Action française. His relationship with Valois, far from being soured by the failure of the *Cité française*, was closer than ever: he would soon be involved with Valois's new project, which would lead him willy-nilly into the royalist camp.

"Le Juif, Voilà l'Ennemi"

With the launching of Janvion's *Terre libre* and the winning of Sorel and Berth to the nationalist banner, the Action française, by the summer of 1910, had some cause to feel optimistic concerning its projected entente with the revolutionary Left. Yet, at a more practical level, that of day-to-day politics, late 1909 and most of 1910 were frustrating. What the royalists sorely lacked was open confrontation between the syndicalists and the government, for, as do most organizations of its kind, the Action française thrived only in an atmosphere of crisis. Confrontation had been the habitual style under Clemenceau; but with the new prime minister, Aristide Briand, the mood of French politics mellowed considerably. For a time it seemed that there was a real possibility that the tensions of the current social crisis, tensions that had intensified under Clemenceau to the point of open warfare, might be adroitly calmed. Briand did not conceal his feeling that the syndicalists, preoccupied with disorder within their own house, would tacitly agree to live and let live if Clemenceau's penchant for blunt talk and a show of force were avoided. His ministry, without making any fundamental changes in social policy, promised to show more carrot and less stick.

All of this put the royalists in a dour mood. Clearly, the Action française was disconcerted at the prospect of relaxed social tensions. Nevertheless, the royalists persisted, despite the new mood of social calm, to doggedly pursue working-class sympathies by all means at their disposal. In the royalist daily, reports of strikes, meetings, and general syndicalist concerns were interspersed with didactic articles relating to the ultimate compatibility of syndicalism with royalism. Persistently, on the most controversial issues of the day—those affecting public order—the Action française took the side of the workers, whereas almost the entire nonsocialist press—and on occasion the socialist press—was alarmed by "the active minorities." When in late 1909 electricians threatened to darken Paris, Maurras defended them, observing that they were simply acting out the logic inherent in liberal economics: "Syndicalist concentration responds to capitalist concentration, using similar weapons."[1]

All the while, Daudet continued his forays into working-class faubourgs.[2] Many of the themes with which he dealt were inveterate royalist clichés: antirepublicanism, anti-Semitism, antiparliamentarism. But one issue especially was given new emphasis: that of the malevolent influence of Jean Jaurès and *L'Humanité*. The reformist wing of the Socialist party had, of course, never been spared by the royalists, but beginning in the second half of 1909 royalist attacks had grown more vehement. One charge in particular portended difficulties ahead for *L'Humanité*. Daudet ventured beyond vague charges that Jaurès had "sold out to the Jews." He repeatedly named prominent Jews who had given disproportionately large amounts of money to help launch the Socialist daily. The original degree of Jewish control was so embarrassingly obvious, charged Daudet, that Jaurès, at a later date, had been forced to rearrange his stockholding policy. This rearrangement, Daudet argued, did not lessen Jewish influence but only made it more difficult to trace. According to Daudet, the Jews were determined to control the socialist movement: "You workers, syndicalists, revolutionaries, who do not want to be duped any longer, do you know how it will all end up if the Republic continues? . . . In gunshots. Israel will punish you for seeing things too clearly."[3]

Daudet's long-standing insistence upon going directly to the working class was, by 1910, applied not only in Paris but in the provinces as well. Reports of provincial meetings organized by local branches of the Action française began to appear more frequently in the royalist daily. At Orléans, Bordeaux, Toulouse, and other provincial capitals the idea of the "social monarchy" was promoted.[4] Quite frequently, Georges Valois himself, who until that time had been kept out of the public eye, was sent to carry the message—one that he had done so much to develop—to provincial audiences.

Yet the results of all this expenditure of royalist time, money, and energy would come to nought, as the royalists were painfully aware, if the relations between the government and the syndicalists continued to sail a smooth course. The ideas that the royalists were cultivating could only be harvested in times of protracted social crisis. And it was this kind of crisis that Briand, with his carefully orchestrated policy of moderation, seemed determined to avoid. Yet suddenly, in October 1910, after more than a year of relative tranquillity, the Briand ministry found itself enmeshed in a dispute of major proportions with the syndicalists.

The occasion was a flare-up of one of the most recalcitrant problems in French prewar politics: whether or not workers in industries and services considered critical to national security and public order had the right to strike. The case in question was that of the railway workers. The Briand ministry had publicly stated that it would find unacceptable any strike that would paralyze national transport. No distinction was made between lines that had been nationalized and those that were still owned privately, because even in the latter case a vital public function, according to Briand, was being served. The rail workers, for their part, were growing increasingly restive in the face of long-standing indifference to their demands on the part of both companies and government.[5] Briand, early in the summer of 1910, sought to mollify them by acceding to some of their demands on the government lines and promising to put pressure on the private lines to make similar concessions. But it was a case of too little, too late. Preparations were under way for a general strike of rail workers; the date was set for 15 October. Tension once again rose as all indications pointed to another test of strength and nerve between Republic and syndicalists.

On 10 October there was premature strike action against the Compagnie du Nord, one of the private lines. The syndicalist leaders hurriedly attempted to generalize the strike in advance of the target date. Briand, undoubtedly fearing that his conciliatory attitude would be interpreted as faintheartedness, decided to bring the full power of the state to bear. The Gare du Nord was occupied militarily, and strikers on both government and private lines were notified that their failure to return to work would be grounds for dismissal. But most crushing of all for the syndicalists, rail workers subject to military service were mobilized so that they might, under military orders and threat of military discipline, be utilized to keep the railroad in operation. Meanwhile, the members of the strike committee, who had taken refuge in the offices of *L'Humanité*, were arrested. Briand, by way of justification, pointed to acts of sabotage. By ministerial declaration, noting the critical importance of national transport, the issue was raised from the level of labor-management conflict to insurrection against the state.[6]

Once again the syndicalist bluff was called, and as before the government proved itself master of the situation. The strike failed to generalize. Though the companies had made some token concessions, their victory was complete. The strike, within a few days, had been totally broken. Syndicalist planning, execution, and, most importantly, ability to rally workers in sufficient numbers were revealed in all their embarrassing inadequacy.

As complete as the government's victory was, however, it had, from the ministry's point of view, unfortunate side effects. The government had taken sides, and any chance that Briand could continue to pose with any credibility as an honest broker above parties was, to even nonsyndicalist workers, hardly tenable. However unequal the strength of the respective sides, Frenchmen were once more made aware that their society was deeply divided along class lines. The heavy atmosphere of social tension that Briand had hoped to dissipate once more hung low over the political landscape.

The new crisis was a windfall for the royalists, seemingly tailor-made to fit the cut of their propaganda efforts toward the working class. Once more, the republican state had shown itself for what it was: the executor for those interests determined to smash the organized workers. What is more, the royalists pointed out with relish, the current repression was directed by the person of Aristide Briand, the very man who scarcely a decade earlier was brought to national prominence by his defense of the general strike. Briand's career, the royalists asserted, was typical of the cycle of incitement and repression that was the lifeblood of socialist politicians. Predictably, the latter would rise to prominence on the backs of the workers by espousing the most inflammatory of programs and then, once secure in their parliamentary seats, would prove themselves ministerial by a public demonstration of resoluteness before the specter of social unrest. One could see manifest in Briand, the royalists argued, the ultimate futility as well as the ultimate danger of the strategy of a unified Left extending from syndicalists through parliamentary socialists and Radicals. Once again, the logic of the Dreyfusard alliance stood exposed for the treachery that it was.

Long before the rail strike, of course, this argument had informed the strategy of the royalists in their attempt to build a worker alliance. The men of the Action française, anxious to destroy conventional wisdom about the political spectrum, argued that the crucial line of demarcation was not between the Left and the Right but between those who supported and those who opposed the status quo. Even before the rail strike, to the great satisfaction of the royalists, rumblings of a similar argument were being heard from certain quarters on the revolutionary Left, most notably among the Hervéists and certain syndicalists. Yet, with the exception of Janvion and his cohort at *Terre libre*, the revolutionaries of the Left had not followed what to the royalists at least was the logical conclusion of this argument. In spite of the enormous strains under which it labored, even by 1910 the old Dreyfusard alliance was still a force in French politics. If no longer a positive force as in the days of the *bloc des gauches*, it was a negative one in the sense that it had prevented the definitive fragmentation of the Left.

That this was still true in 1910 was, in no small measure, the work of a single man—Jean Jaurès. Despite the fact that he was closely identified with the reformist parliamentary faction of the Socialist party, Jaurès urged, often over bitter opposition, that the unity of the Left, forged during the Dreyfus affair, be preserved. To this end he took the position that, whatever the provocation, Hervé and his followers should not be expelled from the Socialist party, and, even more importantly, he urged the Socialists not to yield to the temptation of a wholesale condemnation of the revolutionary syndicalists. Likewise, he encouraged patience toward many left-leaning Radicals, who, though often infuriatingly uncooperative, would be needed if even a modest reform program were to be written into law. *L'Humanité*, the paper that he founded and ran until his death in 1914, became a kind of institutionalized voice for tolerance, promoting a diverse but unified Left. Moreover, *L'Humanité* assumed the role of a conscience for this amorphous Left, preaching the Dreyfusard ethic that a republic and the rights of man were the sine qua non of social progress. Jealously it guarded what it considered to be a necessary minimum program for the Left: loyalty to the republican form, hostility to reaction in all guises, and— something not always avoided by pre-Dreyfusard socialists—an absolute refusal before the enticing temptations of anti-Semitism. It was in the midst of the rail strike that, quite unexpectedly, *L'Humanité*'s ability to hold together what remained of leftist unity was seriously undermined. What had been heretofore isolated attacks by certain revolutionaries almost instantly coalesced into a virtual campaign against the Socialist daily. Near the center of the controversy was an issue that the royalists, had they had a choice, would have doubtlessly chosen: anti-Semitism. Most importantly for the royalists, the controversy and its upshot would provide the long-awaited issue upon which the Action française could directly reach the working class. An important crossroad had been reached.

The controversy was ignited when a muckraking revolutionary journalist, known to the readers of the *Guerre sociale* only by his pseudonym, "Z," charged that the real villain of the rail strike was none other than the Baron Edouard de Rothschild. According to "Z," the real *patron* of the Compagnie du Nord, where the strike had begun, was Rothschild. This fact, "Z" continued, was not public knowledge because there was a great deal of genuine popular animosity toward the great financiers, of whom Rothschild was only the most illustrious. The Republic—fig leaf behind which the rich and powerful machinate affairs—took pains to conceal that the struggle was between Rothschild and syndicalist workers. Public sympathy would surely be with the workers. Instead, the struggle was masqueraded as one where *fonctionnaires* were in revolt against the public weal.[7]

The Republic's most reliable ally in this chicanery, according to "Z," was the republican press. The main function of this press, no less than that of the republican politician, was to serve and protect its financial overlords. Given this much, it was to no one's surprise that the name Rothschild did not enter public discussion through the columns of the bourgeois press. But perhaps one was surprised, "Z" wrote, that the self-appointed "journal of the working class," *L'Humanité*, would show the same reticence. "Z," however, was not surprised. *L'Humanité*'s silence concerning Rothschild, he maintained, was completely logical. "We know well," "Z" wrote, "that in the old *Humanité* big Jewish capitalists had given one million [francs] to Jaurès. It was their way of thanking him for the struggles of the Dreyfus affair." "Z," however, claimed that he was not out just to slander *L'Humanité*. He offered the Socialist daily a way out. "It could," he wrote, "start immediately a campaign against the Rothschilds. This campaign is imperative because a terrible repression is being exercised in all the branches dominated by this powerful family. Everyone will understand that this struggle has nothing to do with anti-Semitism. The railroad workers will be pleased; the socialist public of *L'Humanité*, in its entirety, will applaud."[8]

Although the staff of *L'Humanité* could claim that one does not waste time and energy engaging in polemics with the forces of reaction—whether they be represented by Daudet or the syndicalists "without mandate" at *Terre libre*—they could not ignore the charges put forward by "Z." For "Z" was not only associated with the revolutionary Hervéists but also, under another of his pseudonyms, Cratès, helped found the influential syndicalist publication, *La Vie ouvrière*. The controversy with *L'Humanité* would not only bring to light his real name, Francis Delaisi, but also give some indication of his pivotal influence on the pre-1914 French Left.

Francis Delaisi was also pivotal—although this fact has not hitherto been revealed—in the royalists' campaign to build an alliance with the revolutionary Left. Through his willingness to play the game of *politique du pire*, Delaisi became for the royalists the perfect complement to Emile Janvion. What Janvion did with relative sincerity and clumsy enthusiasm, Delaisi was to do with dissimulation, restraint, and almost consummate artistry. He was to come very close to accomplishing for the Action française the most essential prerequisite of their projected Left-Right alliance: to drive a wedge between the moderate and revolutionary Left and to undermine the code of ethics that had been promoted by *L'Humanité*.

To understand how it was that Delaisi could play such a crucial role, it will be necessary to inquire into the large, albeit discreet, influence wielded by Delaisi in syndicalist circles, the important connections that he enjoyed with certain revolutionary socialists, and, no less importantly, the shadowy relations that linked him with the Action française.

As has already been seen, during the Clemenceau ministry there had been a serious disintegration of the revolutionary leadership of the syndicalist movement. Many of those in a position of responsibility, under the heavy blows of governmental repression, were forced to moderate their actions, if not their rhetoric. This moderation led to a split in the revolutionary majority between a politique group, which favored caution, and an ultra faction, which argued increased élan as the only antidote to the government's tough line. Ultimately, the feud grew so bitter that the ultras were willing, as a tactical gambit, to conspire with the reformists, the extreme right wing of the syndicalist movement, in order to unseat the politiques.

This feud between the politiques and the ultras, however, did not extend to the philosophical level. The politiques and the ultras shared—however much they disagreed on tactics—much the same revolutionary heritage, derived largely from late-nineteenth-century anarchism. Many of the leaders of revolutionary syndicalism were ex-anarchists, who believed that society could best be transformed along libertarian lines through the ready-made vehicle of the labor movement. Syndicalist organization and practice reflected this: the basic unit was the small, independent syndicat with a minimum of centralization. Likewise, the syndicalist vision of the future society was permeated with anarchist ideals. Lines of authority—if they could be thus termed—would go up, not down. The local syndicat, not the state or some central agency, would have effective decision-making power.

By about 1910, a new force began to emerge out of the leadership crisis within the revolutionary majority, a force that was quite distinct from either the politique or the ultra factions. It broke definitively with the old anarchist underpinnings. Much of the impetus for this new direction came from the close collaboration of two men—Alphonse Merrheim and Francis Delaisi. Merrheim, a capable provincial militant who had made his way to Paris and up through the Confédération générale du travail hierarchy, refused to accept with equanimity the ineptitude that had led syndicalism from defeat to defeat. With Delaisi, a gifted journalist and something of a student of economics and modern industrial organization, Merrheim launched an on-going critique of syndicalist practice. Merrheim and Delaisi, like the politiques with whom they were for a time closely associated, distrusted violence, extreme anti-patriotism, and the notion that élan would conquer all. Their reasons, however, had less to do with making virtue out of necessity, as with the politiques, than with the firm conviction that syndicalism must be made more practical and less romantic. If workers were to have any real chance in the fight against large-scale industrial capitalism, they would have to arm themselves with something more substantial than the old revolutionary battle cries. The first task of the working class, according to Merrheim and Delaisi, would be to study seriously and come to some understanding of the intricacies of the twentieth-century plant—how it is organized and how it operates. Scholarly detachment would replace the customary syndicalist emphasis on élan. Following this would come an even more radical departure from syndicalist practice. Workers must learn to imitate industrial organization. Merrheim and Delaisi were emphatic: a technologically proficient, highly centralized capitalism could be successfully challenged only by a labor movement itself technologically proficient and highly centralized.

A recent student of syndicalism has labeled this approach to syndicalism *dirigiste* and views it as the instrument by which syndicalism was transformed from a revolutionary to a reformist movement.[9] In retrospect, one can see that the dirigiste mentality was a sharp break with prevailing anarchosyndicalism. As opposed to the decentralized, nonauthoritarian vision of Pouget and Griffuelhes, where each artisan-hero was to be his own man, the dirigiste group stressed the industrial mass man, who needed to be not so much liberated as organized. It was no longer the worker who would create a new-style economy but the economy that would create a new-style worker.

This adaptive aspect of *dirigisme* was not immediately perceived. In fact, both those associated with the Merrheim group and those opposed to it considered it part of the revolutionary majority. The identification was made largely because the dirigistes were in accord with the older anarchosyndicalist faction on one central point: the hostility to parliamentary socialism and democracy in general. The willingness to cooperate with socialists in parliament had been, and still was, the hallmark of old-style reformist syndicalism.

To be sure, the antidemocratic credentials of Francis Delaisi were in order. He had just written a long series of articles for the *Guerre sociale*, soon after published in book form as *La Démocratie et les financiers*. Delaisi's conclusion was unambiguous. "A precise fact," Delaisi wrote, "emerges from our study: the sovereignty of the people is a fiction; democracy a lie; the conquest of political power through the ballot a lure. The financiers govern France."[10]

Delaisi's study anticipated the great interwar shibboleth of the French Left, the conspiracy of the "200 families."[11] Behind the innumerable capitalist firms, according to Delaisi, and the countless stockholders, which gave the appearance of widespread ownership, there was, in reality, effective control by a relatively small number of families who, through financial manipulation rather than direct ownership, made themselves masters of the French economy. Delaisi's exposé, like almost all such conspiratorial accounts, owed its verisimilitude to the indiscriminate yet polemically satisfying mix of outright fabrication with half and three-quarter truths. It was not enough to say that deputies were often influenced and, in many cases, controlled by financial interests. Delaisi's account turned the parliamentary system into an elaborate stage production, where all politicians were in the pay of financiers orchestrating the show down to the minutest detail. It was not enough to say that the press, likewise, was influenced or controlled by outside interests. For Delaisi, journalism was another charade, manufacturing false issues to keep a gullible public from perceiving its true enemies.

The same conspiratorial imagination informed Delaisi's account of the rail strike. He offered a ready explanation for the humiliating failure of the strike. The railroad bosses, according to Delaisi, had viewed with alarm the spread of revolutionary syndicalist ideas among their workers. They realized that within the space of a few years revolutionary syndicalism would be invincible, so they had decided to provoke a premature strike, which they could easily repress. Future troubles would be nipped in the bud. This allowed Delaisi to place the entire blame for the strike failure—blame that was due, in no small measure, to inadequate syndicalist preparation and organization—upon the shoulders of the bosses.

But for Delaisi the bosses were only, of course, acting under the orders of their overlord, the Baron Edouard de Rothschild. By route of a long series of tenuous suppositions, albeit a good measure of polemical flair, Delaisi demonstrated how almost all railroads in France were "under the control" of the Rothschilds.

Anticipating criticism that his argument was racist, Delaisi, like the men of the *Revue critique* before him, admitted only cultural objections. The Rothschilds were *déracinés*:

> Are they Jewish? Of course, but through marriage they have Aryan blood in their veins. Do they attend the synagogue? That might be true, yet they eat impure meat, dine with Gentiles, and sleep with the daughters of Gentiles. Are they French? Evidently, in Paris; but they own a house in London, one in Vienna, another in Frankfurt. At the head of the family there is an English lord, a German baron, an Austrian nobleman. They have no precise race, no religion, no nation, no *patrie*; they are impersonal and international like the anonymous and sovereign force that they so well represent: MONEY.[12]

Delaisi's attack on Rothschild had important implications. The Left, since the days of the Dreyfus affair at least, had rather consistently refused to mix anticapitalism with anti-Semitism.[13] The danger of symbolizing the Jew as exploiter, given the latent anti-Semitism in French society, had been perceived and resisted. The short-term gain involved in making the enemy more concrete and in tapping anti-Semitic support would not, it was felt by revolutionary leaders, make up for the long-term damage done to the integrity of socialist doctrine.

It is not at all clear that Delaisi and his friends weighed these issues. It does seem clear, however, that Delaisi was not primarily concerned with promoting anti-Semitism among workers. His real target, it seems, was *L'Humanité* and moderate socialists, and his use of anti-Semitism was just a means to this end.

For a long time, as has been noted, relations between revolutionary syndicalists and Hervéists, on the one hand, and *L'Humanité*, on the other, were precarious. Only at the insistence of Jaurès were rather consistent provocations from the revolutionary Left passed over. This indulgence was made easier by the fact that these provocations lacked the specificity to make them truly dangerous. Most often, they were not charges that could be answered but—in the style of the revolutionary Left—vague polemical broadsides.

Delaisi, however, could bring more than polemical tools to bear. The same propensity for detailed study, for documentation, and for knowledge of organizational operation developed by Delaisi in his work on capitalism could be a formidable weapon if turned on socialists. Likewise, as he was soon to prove, he could tie the impressively documented bundle together with the long strings of conspiracy. Unwittingly, *L'Humanité* was to give him ample opportunity.

L'Humanité's response to "Z"'s original charges, as it turned out, was a serious miscalculation. As to the claim that the Socialist daily was protecting the Jew Rothschild, *L'Humanité* did not raise the level of the debate appreciably by counterclaiming that Delaisi, in his shadowy past, had himself worked for a "rich Jew."[14] But the real trouble came in response to another charge by Delaisi: that *L'Humanité* had been founded with "Jewish gold." Innocently enough, *L'Humanité* offered to allow Delaisi to visit its offices and inspect its books, the only proviso being that he would make his findings public. Delaisi was only too happy to oblige.

The revelations in the wake of Delaisi's visit were little less than a sensation. In his meticulous fashion, Delaisi listed all those who had bought original shares in *L'Humanité*. His analysis of the list reveals something of his method, a curious blend of scrupulous concern for details and figures and total abandon of logical connection.[15] Delaisi's conclusion, now buttressed with "proofs" from *L'Humanité*'s own books, supported his original contentions: *L'Humanité* had "sold out to Jewish gold." Its silence during the rail strike, according to Delaisi, followed logically.

Delaisi's charge that *L'Humanité* was launched through the good offices of the Rothschilds proved to be only the first in a series of accusations based on his examination of the newspaper's books.

The consistent theme was that, although *L'Humanité* claimed to be the "journal of the working class," it depended so heavily on sources of income outside the working class that it could not act independently.

In all Delaisi's allegations, whatever the specifics of the case, there ran a low-keyed but unmistakable anti-Semitic note. One of Delaisi's favorite adjectives was the word "Jewish." If there existed Christian bankers or financiers, it did not seem, to Delaisi, worthwhile to point them out.

The importance of Delaisi's campaign against *L'Humanité* cannot be underrated. It grew daily more acrimonious and threatened to open a no-holds-barred fight among French leftists. The Hervéists, who had always attacked *L'Humanité* for its lack of revolutionary fervor, joined in the chorus of condemnation. But even more important was the promise of support from another quarter: the syndicalist leaders published an open letter proclaiming their sympathy with Delaisi's campaign. The letter was signed by Griffuelhes, Merrheim, Monatte, and the new secretary of the Confédération générale du travail, Léon Jouhaux. Despite the scurrility of Delaisi's attack, its unmistakable anti-Semitic tone, and its blatant exploitation of themes currently being promoted at the Action française, official syndicalism joined the Hervéists and stood foursquare behind the offensive against *L'Humanité*.

The significance of Delaisi's crusade against *L'Humanité* did not long await its interpreters. Marius Riquier, in *Terre libre*, noted how much the times had changed. In the good old days, he recalled, everyone rushed to defend the "persecuted race." The myth of a persecuted race, Riquier wrote, is giving way to the brutal truth: "One may no longer remain ignorant of the fact that France is a conquered country, that its resources are regularly exploited by a gang of intruders, who benefit from the solidarity of race and who, in the most natural way in the world, come to an agreement every time it is a question of exploiting, plundering, and bullying the native."[16]

Another recent convert to this "brutal truth" was Gustave Téry. The ex-Dreyfusard had gathered a staff of some of the ablest, if most idiosyncratic, young Parisian journalists for his fortnightly,

L'Oeuvre.[17] The controversy and interest sparked by Téry's brand of journalism would make *L'Oeuvre* into a leading Paris daily within a few years. For now Téry busied himself, like Valois and Janvion before him, with a public act of contrition for his Dreyfusard sins. According to Téry, the eager young men of the Left who had joined the Dreyfusard crusade, seeing it as a chance to realize their hopes for a new society, had been cruelly deceived by those "crafty *you-pins.*" "I still do not know," Téry wrote, "if he was innocent, their captain, but good God of Israel *we* certainly were."[18]

For the royalists, who had been courting Téry, his growing anti-Semitism seemed a vindication of their own propaganda efforts. His expressed difficulty in coming to anti-Semitism made it seem all the more meaningful. "I know everything that can be said about anti-Semitism," Téry wrote, "I said it myself. And I am mad for not believing it anymore. Basically, do you know what I will never forgive the Jews for? It is for having made me an anti-Semite."[19]

As to the monarchy, Téry was skeptical but willing to open a dialogue with the royalists. One hardly knows how to answer Maurras these days, Téry admitted, for the existing Republic is a source of embarrassment for all those who call themselves republicans. As one might have expected, when Delaisi opened his campaign against *L'Humanité* Téry was in the front rank of those joining the attack.[20]

Thus, by the end of 1910 it seemed that the royalists' long and patient cultivation of leftist fields was about to yield its first harvest. The revulsion against democrats in any guise, including social democrats, had reached its culmination in the explosion against *L'Humanité.* Royalists had long argued that democracy and true socialism were incompatible: the thrust of Delaisi's polemics was to convince syndicalists and revolutionary socialists. Even more ominous from the point of view of republicans was the complementary theme: at important points along the old revolutionary Left, as has been seen, anti-Semitism was once again coming into vogue.

All this, from a royalist perspective, was healthy liberation from the shackles of Dreyfusard morality. Once the revolutionary Left had learned to savor delicacies such as antirepublicanism and anti-Semitism, they would be ready, the monarchists reasoned, for even more exotic forbidden fruit—active collaboration with reaction to bring down the encrusted Republic.

The circumstances surrounding Delaisi's campaign against *L'Humanité* leave one intriguing question as yet unanswered. Was there any collusion between Delaisi and the Action française, considering the fact that Delaisi's and Daudet's campaigns against *L'Humanité* were not only concurrent but emphasized nearly identical themes? Given the available evidence, it is difficult to answer this question definitively, but it is clear that certain of Delaisi's later involvements do not leave him above suspicion.

By 1912 the police had gathered enough evidence to implicate Delaisi directly with the royalists. Early that year, Delaisi had been seen at both a meeting of the Action française and a royalist social gathering.[21] Upon further investigation, it was reported that a noted playwright and intimate in royalist circles, Robert de Flers, was an intermediary between Delaisi and the cashbox of the duc d'Orléans. Later in the same year, this information was confirmed by a second report, which stated that a police agent had received an assurance from a staff member of the *Guerre sociale* that Delaisi "had his hand in the royal cashbox."[22]

One is tempted to react with skepticism toward such reports, as Delaisi's public statements, unlike those of Janvion, indicated no fondness for royalism. But testimony from sources other than police reports lessens one's resistance to seeing Delaisi in the role claimed for him by the police. Christian Gras, a recent historian of syndicalism, who has had access to the Merrheim archives in Moscow, has uncovered a revealing incident, one that portrays Delaisi as a man of little scruple, a man who would find few moral qualms in playing a ruthless game of *politique du pire*.[23]

Sometime in late 1912 or early 1913, according to Gras, Delaisi suggested to Merrheim that covert government subsidies might be available for the *Bataille syndicaliste*, a newly launched syndicalist daily in serious financial straits. The government subsidies were being distributed as part of a stratagem, engineered by certain officials, to weaken *L'Humanité* by strengthening certain of its rivals. Merrheim, indignant that Delaisi would even hint at such a scheme, refused. Doubtless feeling that Merrheim's scruples were a commodity that the sinking newspaper could ill afford, Delaisi, in early 1913, began sending contributions in small amounts under fictitious names. When Merrheim discovered Delaisi behind the badly forged contributions, he demanded that they be stopped. Significantly, wishing to avoid scandal, Merrheim did not bring the matter up with the editorial staff of the *Bataille syndicaliste* but dealt with Delaisi privately. The result, according to Gras, was that Delaisi withdrew from active collaboration at the *Bataille syndicaliste*.

Though the police reports—given a measure of credibility by Merrheim's testimony—establish that Delaisi acted in collusion with the royalists by 1912, they do not indicate how far back his covert relations with the royalists extended. It therefore cannot be contended with any certainty that Delaisi and the royalists were party to a direct conspiracy during the 1910 campaign against *L'Humanité*.

But if the charge of collusion cannot be substantiated at this early point, there can be little question of Delaisi's connivance. At a minimum, Delaisi could not but have been aware that he was exploiting emotions aroused by Daudet's charges—promoted from the front page of the *Action française*—that *L'Humanité* had been founded and run by "Jewish gold." Nor could he have been oblivious to the fact that anti-Semitism and attacks on parliamentary socialists were the route by which the royalists hoped to reach the working class. It seems an unavoidable conclusion that Delaisi attempted to play the perilous game of profiting from the suspicions and passions excited by the royalists for the furtherance of his own ends.

With the Dreyfusard alliance threatening definitive collapse and the rekindling of anti-Semitism on the revolutionary Left, time seemed ripe for the royalists. Yet, despite these propitious circumstances, all was clearly not well at the Action française. For several months before the rail strike the royalists' antirepublicanism and prosyndicalism seemed somehow muted; the familiar themes were still present, but the old stridency was gone. What was more, the Camelots, who had done so much to keep the Action française in the public mind, now seemed to have collapsed into lethargy. In reality, the Action française—just as the circumstances looked most favorable for its campaign toward the working class—was in the midst of the most serious internal crisis in its ten-year history.

The crisis had been sparked by the growing resentment building among the older monarchist clientele toward the neoroyalists, who, in a few short years, had succeeded in making the monarchist cause identical with the fortunes of the Action française. Though tension between old- and new-style royalists had existed since the founding of the Action française, real trouble began about 1908. This coincided with the neoroyalist shift from what was essentially an intellectual study group to a serious political movement. This change disturbed not only republicans, who thought that they had finally laid the reactionary threat to rest, but also avowed monarchists, whose royalism had become more a badge of social distinction than a true political program. In this latter group respect for the law and commitment to order, even republican law and order, was not taken lightly.

It is not surprising that older royalists would be shocked by the most flagrant neoroyalist violations of the spirit of law and order— the antics of the Camelots du roi and the initiatives toward the workers. Both inside and outside the Action française, the two issues were seen as interconnected, different facets of a policy of provocative action. Certainly they were mutually reinforcing. Perhaps the greatest asset of the Action française in the attempt to attract worker support was the Camelots. The humiliation they served up republican officials could not but have been savored by workers frustrated by the same officials in their strike efforts. On the other hand, the most enthusiastic supporters of a prosyndicalist policy in the Action française were Camelots. If Daudet's success with workers in the faubourgs was modest, he at least convinced the squads of Camelots accompanying him that the monarchy would be a social monarchy or would not be at all. Likewise, Valois and his coterie at the *Revue critique* found their most enthusiastic support among the young Camelots.

To the older royalists, both workers in revolt and young toughs breaking up statues and into meetings became a source of growing irritation. As early as August 1908 the police reported a certain number of cancellations of the *Action française* and even more numerous letters of complaints from outraged royalists over the Action française support of the Confédération générale du travail. The issue was discussed "at length" by the staff of the *Action française*, where at least one member of the inner circle had grave doubts about the wisdom of continuing the prosyndicalist policy.[24] With increasing Camelot activities in 1909, pressures for moderation grew, and, although they were resisted within the Action française, they began making themselves felt at the political bureau of the pretender, the duc d'Orléans.[25]

Under these pressures the pretender wavered, and matters came to a head in June 1909 when Roger Lambelin, a neoroyalist sympathizer, was forced to resign as director of the duke's political bureau. His replacement, the comte Henry de Larègle, was known not only to oppose the Action française but to be prepared to take the necessary steps to bring the neoroyalists to heel.[26]

The Action française braced itself for the worst. Even before de Larègle's appointment, they had felt the stiffening of resistance at the political bureau. In March 1909 the duke himself, in an interview in *Le Gaulois*, repudiated the exploits of the Camelots and suggested in the strongest possible terms that their adventurism had better cease. The very next month the political bureau ordered the Action française to stop meddling in working-class affairs.[27]

How to best respond to the traditionalist offensive became a debated issue within the Action française and reveals, by the problems that it raised, something of the inner dynamics of a movement of the radical Right. As has been noted, from the very beginning there were certain voices arguing that the Action française could ill afford to cut itself off from its potentially large conservative clientele. By mid-summer 1909, with de Larègle installed at the political bureau, those counseling prudence had grown not only more insistent but also more numerous. Léon de Montesquiou, Frédéric Delebecque, and, most significantly, Charles Maurras, although not admitting capitulation, seemed at least ready for strategic retreat. Maurras was convinced, according to the police, that the best policy would be to allow the pretender at least the illusion that his advice was being heeded: the Action française must be more discreet in its effort with workers, and the Camelots, for the time being, must lay low. All the while, as Maurras's scheme would have it, neoroyalist friends near the pretender would work to win him over.[28] Apparently Maurras felt that he could be as effective in intrigue as his traditionalist opponents.

Not everyone at the Action française agreed. Opposition to any change in policy that might smack of surrender was running strong. It was led by Daudet and Pujo—not surprisingly, as the latter was the head of the Camelots and the former had made the worker campaign his personal project.[29]

For a time at least, it seemed that Maurras's arguments had won the day. The summer and early fall of 1910 were, by earlier neoroyalist standards, tranquil. It did not take long, however, for the Camelots to grow restive. Rumors began to circulate about Maurras. He was a man of talk, not of action. His highly touted connections within the Confédération générale du travail were becoming an excuse rather than a stimulus for action. Camelots were no longer satisfied with theoretical statements in support of syndicalism; they were eager to join their forces to those of the syndicalists where they believed they counted most—in the streets.

The Action française was on the horns of the classic dilemma of the radical political group: either risk allowing enemies to use its defiance of the law to dismantle it or become more lawful and run the danger of consigning itself to obscurity. Daudet and Pujo were unequivocal as concerned the Camelots: they had to have action or they would disintegrate.[30] The other side, of course, could raise its specter: excommunication by the pretender. It appeared that the Action française was doomed to be a cause without followers or followers without a cause.

Whatever Maurras might have argued within the inner sanctum of the Action française, the issues confronting the movement were larger than strategy. Would the Action française move from radicalism to respectability? Would neoroyalists carry on with their project of organizing a threat to the existing regime, or would they, as had so many radical groups in the past, find a comfortable niche for themselves in the ranks of the domesticated opposition? Despite the hesitancy of Maurras, already the dominant figure, the Action française suddenly regathered its lost momentum and surged forward to meet the challenge head on. This refusal to surrender was not, however, a conscious decision; the force of events over-whelmed a hesitant leadership.

One incident in particular—almost surely unplanned—forced matters to a head; for the older royalists it symbolized all that was wrong with the Action française. In November 1910 a young Camelot du roi, after listening to a speech by Prime Minister Bri-and, ran up to him and slapped him in the face. The neoroyalists did not fail to connect the incident with their worker campaign: Lucien Lacour, the Camelot in question, was avenging the honest worker, victim of Briand in the rail strike. In fact, the neoroyalists went out of their way to play up the incident. Lacour, through his symbolic act, was not only settling scores for workers but redress-ing the honor of the nation, besmudged by the hypocrisy of its prime minister.[31] One suspects at this point that the dog was being wagged by the tail; a hesitant leadership was making the best of the ill-timed impulsiveness of the Camelots.

This latest outrage by a Camelot made any further attempt at a neoroyalist reconciliation with the political bureau seem im-possible. De Larègle began working on a formal disavowal of the Action française, a disavowal that, according to the police, would be signed without hesitation by the duc d'Orléans. Sensing that nothing could now save them, the neoroyalists, recovering some of their nerve, decided on a daring ploy. They would beat de Larègle at his own game, take the offensive, and disavow him before he had a chance to disavow them. Accordingly, on 30 November 1910 the *Action française* announced that evil machinators around the king, led by the comte de Larègle, were out to destroy them with calum-nies. Henceforth they would refuse to obey orders sent out by a political bureau under his control. The duke himself sharply repri-manded them and demanded that they recant. When they refused, their excommunication became official.[32]

The Action française was now fighting for its life. To call for a royal restoration was difficult enough; to call for the restoration of a king who, in advance of his coronation, was already a prisoner of evil counselors was beyond the ingenuity of even Maurras's po-lemics. Its only hope was to prove itself the stronger party—to convince the pretender that he needed the Action française more than it needed him. Astonishingly, within a few short months the Action française had won a complete victory. The political bureau was purged of all anti-Action française personnel, and, from mid-1911 on, royalism in France became synonymous with the Action française. In order to win a victory of such magnitude, the neoroyalists spared no energy or available resource; nor did they let themselves be hampered by the strictures of commonplace decency. It was an all-out war that they waged, one that took on aspects of a fanatical crusade against the forces of Satan.

The battle plan that was to be followed by the Action française had been hinted at by Maurras some months before. That syndicalism and royalism—the only movements with enough vigor to challenge the corrupt but all-powerful Republic—were both undergoing severe internal crises was not, according to Maurras, coincidental. Behind both stood Briand the intriguer; he worked covertly to crush all who refused to be incorporated.[33] And behind Briand stood those grand manipulators for whom the entire political game was staged in the first place, the Jewish financiers. They, as the Action française had long preached, were the new masters of France and feared no force save the one with the power to undo them, anti-Semitism. Thus, Maurras argued, as he would time and again, that the only true radicalism was anti-Semitism; it was the brave refusal of the Action française to protect the Jew that made it a target of attack.

This overarching explanation of the dynamics of French society formed the backdrop for the neoroyalists' assault upon the political bureau. Traditional royalism, like all other movements in France, had suffered *enjuivement*. If the Action française was now under attack from all sides, the neoroyalists reasoned, it was only because it stood against the corruption of the monarchist principle.[34]

What is more, the Action française pledged to wage more than a defensive battle. It would take the offensive and carry its fight directly to the people. It would undertake a public subscription for funds to fight the treason in the king's council, "the Jewish treason." We will fight, the neoroyalists vowed, until the Jewish conspiracy that has temporarily gained the ear of the king is vanquished.[35]

Thus, as 1911 began, the neoroyalist fight against de Larègle had turned into a frenetic anti-Semitic campaign. The police noted, not without a certain apprehension, that the official condemnation by the pretender, when it finally came, was like a burden being lifted. Months of pent-up energy could now be released in a program of action. Those friends of the Action française who feared, toward the end of 1910, that neoroyalism would follow the older nationalist leagues into a premature middle age could take heart. The Action française was its old self.

The bitterest enemy of the Action française, Marc Sangnier's *Démocratie*, was not unaware of the danger. Sangnier, like the police, saw the real import of the pretender's condemnation: the neoroyalists, if they could survive the initial shock, would be cut loose from all conservative constraint. The neoroyalists could now, Sangnier predicted with foreboding, move more freely and "realize the junction with the most turbulent and the least republican elements of revolutionary syndicalism."[36]

What was even more ominous, from the republican perspective, was that there was a new basis for such a juncture. The neoroyalists' struggle against "Jewish influence" at the pretender's political bureau was contemporaneous with Delaisi's campaign against the "Jewish gold" that had founded and continued to manipulate *L'Humanité*. The parallel was too poignant to be overlooked.

[9]

The Year of Decision: 1911

Marc Sangnier's fear of a revitalized royalism joining forces with the revolutionary Left was only one side of a coin. The other was the state of the Republic. A robust Republic, commanding the confidence of its people, Sangnier reasoned, could easily resist the likes of the Action française. But the truth, as Sangnier saw it, was that the Republic was in serious trouble: the French were sick of politicians, sick of scandals, and what was still worse, no one could even manage much enthusiasm for the very concept of republicanism: "The fashion is no longer with the principles of 1789 but with the acts of violence of the C.G.T. or the Camelots du roi." One might argue, Sangnier continued, that these new currents agitate the masses only superficially; yet it is apparent that they are coming into vogue with the nation's intellectual elite. Sangnier observed "that the 'intellectuals' today pretend to look down with contempt on democracy and that it is good form with the older *lycéens* to swear by Maurras and Georges Sorel."[1]

This very problem was the subject of a long series of articles, appearing through 1910 in the *Revue de métaphysique et de morale* and published in 1911 under the title *Le Procès de la démocratie*. The author, Georges Guy-Grand, was an apologist for democracy, but, as the defensive tone of his argument hinted, some of the terrain in question was already in the hands of the enemy. What worried Guy-Grand was the disaffection from the democratic ranks, which, as recently as 1900, had been victorious over the reaction and swollen with idealistic recruits. At that time, the Republic was a great symbol to the working class; today, according to Guy-Grand, one can find among workers only hostility and scorn for the Third Republic. Among the population at large, the notion of parliamentarism and those connected with it are in general disrepute. But most important for Guy-Grand, as for Sangnier, was the alienation of the nation's young intelligentsia. They would be, Guy-Grand realized, the arbiters of future intellectual fashions, and at the present time they were much impressed with Maurras and Sorel and their implacable critiques of democracy. Though they started from very different intellectual positions, the thoughts of these two men came together on the issue of their opposition to democracy: "Whether disciples of Proudhon or of Comte, of M. Sorel or of M. Maurras," Guy-Grand wrote, "they see in the isolated 'man' presented by the democratic or anarchistic apologists for individualism only an abstract and therefore unreal being."[2] Not that Guy-Grand was won over by either Maurras or Sorel. He remained a democrat; yet he hoped that democracy would be capable of growth through the selective incorporation of the critiques of its avowed enemies.

Others echoed these doubts. Léon Vannoz in the *Annales de la jeunesse laïque* posed the problem with an almost embarrassing candor: "Is it not a sign of the times that, [even] in this review where the democratic faith is very much alive, we are led to discuss such problems [the problems of democracy]?"[3] But discuss such problems they did. And they were not alone. This genre of democratic soul-searching was very much the dernier cri in the years just before the war. It was widely accepted that parliamentarism, democracy, and the Republic were undergoing a crisis of confidence.[4]

Scarcely a decade before, the victory of the Dreyfusards had boosted the prestige of the Republic to unprecedented heights. But times had changed, and so had intellectual fashions. If it was avant-garde in the late 1890s to be an idealistic democrat, a free thinker, and a foe of militarism, by 1911 all this had become passé; the men of the new generation stood against democratic *nuées*, were Catholic, and set great store in military men and traditions. In Roger Martin du Gard's only slightly fictionized *Jean Barois*, the hero, a veteran of the Dreyfusard campaign, is confronted by two men of the new generation. They are self-assured to the point of truculence, as if their nationalism was a self-evident principle; Barois, by contrast, is a defeated man. Painfully, he is made aware that his ideas—as well as the heroic struggles that had given his life meaning—offer little inspiration to the men of the new generation.[5]

The Action française had made no mean contribution to the change of mood. Yet this new mood certainly went beyond the bounds of neoroyalism. Extravagant expressions of patriotism, by 1911, were no longer the exclusive preserve of reactionaries. Good republicans—or so the electorate was told—were just as patriotic as the men of the Right. The Church and the military were losing the stigma attached to them in the days of the Dreyfusard Republic. For some on the Right, this was good enough. Maurice Barrès, speaking when this mood had somewhat matured, expressed his satisfaction: "What does it matter to us that the nationalist party is fading away if, at the same time, we see the opposing parties being nationalized!"[6] Maurras and the Action française, of course, were not satisfied with this half-a-loaf victory. They felt themselves on the crest of the wave and fully intended to ride it in. They had, working on their side, not only their own recently fired enthusiasm but a good deal of self-doubt haunting their adversaries.

The rising fortunes of the royalists and the disarray in the republican camp manifested themselves for all to see by the beginning of 1911. The anti-Semitic campaign, which had been directed for some months by the royalists at the pretender's political bureau, abruptly shifted gears. Losing none of its momentum, it focused on a new target, a Jewish playwright, Henri Bernstein, whose play *Après moi* was being staged by the Comédie-Française. The "Jewish invasion" of French theater had long been a preoccupation of the Action française.[7] The royalists maintained that not only was the theater becoming disproportionately Jewish, depriving French talent of its place in the sun, but it presented a threat to French moral values by promoting degenerate Jewish themes rather than heroic French ones. For the Action française, Bernstein was more than they had the right to expect in a symbolic target: not only was he a Jew and his play sufficiently antiheroic, but he had as a young man deserted from the French army. Bernstein was a most concrete manifestation of a consistent royalist theme: the Jew as an agent of subversion.

These same themes had been echoed by Gustave Téry's *Oeuvre*, and there too the prospect of a campaign against Bernstein was eagerly seized. Téry accused Bernstein not only of having deserted but, by virtue of the kind of chicanery that one might expect of a Jew, of having managed to scheme an amnesty for himself. What is more, Téry revealed, he had tried to arrange things discreetly so that *L'Oeuvre* would drop its opposition to *Après moi*. Of course, Téry's journal had stood firm. The result, as Téry portrayed it, was that the full fury of Jewish finance was about to turn upon *L'Oeuvre*. Jaurès is only a theoretical radical, he attacks nameless capitalists; we are real radicals, we attack the Jew by name. "[Bernstein] can have me convicted," Téry wrote, "he even can, by dint of trials and fines, kill *L'Oeuvre*; but do the Jews think that they can frighten us when, after having robbed us of France, they threaten to rob us also of the miserable few *sous* left in our cashbox?"[8]

But the Bernstein campaign was not to be simply another affair of the pen. The Action française took it to the streets. After attempting to disrupt the performance of Bernstein's play from inside the Théâtre-Français—and not without a modicum of success—the Camelots decided to mass large numbers outside the building in order to prevent the play from being staged. At first police took a tough line. Leading royalist personalities were arrested, including Daudet, while demonstrating Camelots were treated to charges by mounted troops. But authorities soon became convinced that they had taken the wrong tack. Clearly the royalists intended to see the issue through, and the police show of force only served to steel their resolve. Moreover, they were beginning to rally other nationalist groups to their side; the crowds, which had gathered before the Théâtre-Français, were becoming unmanageable. A police report of 3 March 1911 noted that the earlier firmness had had the effect of rallying protest from "all sides" and that the army and police were suspected of being "used in the service of a rich Jewish deserter." Things, the report concluded, could be expected to grow worse.[9] On 4 March, under pressure from the ministry, Bernstein withdrew his play.

This was the most important victory won by the Action française since its formation. Clearly the royalists had pushed the situation to the point where republican officials feared that they could no longer maintain public order—and the harder they tried, the more they seemed to lose control of events. A police report of 8 March reveals a new respect for the royalists. At first, according to the police, the violent language of the royalists was taken as bluster; nowadays one takes it seriously, as one knows how often the royalists pass from verbal menaces to action.[10] Even more worrisome than the royalist agitation was the inaction of all those groups that had for so long stood against the reaction, especially in its most dangerous form, anti-Semitism. Public opinion in Paris, when it was not openly sympathetic to the royalists, was indifferent. Republican officials could not have forgotten that without an out-pouring of public concern during the Dreyfus affair the nationalist mobs could have made themselves masters of Paris.

In case they had forgotten, Marcel Sembat reminded them in a lead editorial in *L'Humanité*. His motivation was largely political: the new ministry, under Ernest Monis, showed signs of snubbing the Socialists, and Sembat was using the nationalist and anti-Semitic resurgence as a point of leverage. Yet his description of the situation, as he addressed those in power, was not inaccurate:

Look around you. You will see another proof that, in order to maintain the republican preponderance in the streets, the police are not enough. What is needed is the will of the people. Last week, around the Théâtre-Français, the fearless fellows of the Action française forced your police to withdraw with the cries of "Death to the Jews!" and "Long live the king!"

You then capitulated. . . .

Encouraged by their success, the anti-Jews and the Camelots du roi will do it again at the first opportunity. They will again force you to withdraw and thus will gain new forces. Then what?

Then, gentlemen of the . . . [government], your hour will come, won't it? Then will be the time to show yourselves! You don't need the *peuple*, you who all alone have tamed Boulangism and nationalism! Go ahead gentlemen! Take heart! Go down into the streets![11]

Sembat's editorial, more charitable than most references to the Action française in *L'Humanité*, was received with scorn by a puffed-up Daudet. It was not, Daudet charged, as if *L'Humanité* had deliberately stood on the sidelines during the Bernstein affair, as Sembat intimated. *L'Humanité* had not acted because it could not act. "It [*L'Humanité*] understood very well," Daudet charged, "that a call in favor of the deserter Bernstein would not be heard, and would risk, on the contrary, unleashing the latent anti-Semitism of the working-class world."[12]

The issue of anti-Semitism in the working class had not been forgotten by the Action française. Indeed, they saw the continuing anti-Rothschild tenor of some of the leftist press as a logical extension of their campaign against Bernstein. Since the end of the railroad strike, pressures had been building to reinstate the workers who had lost their jobs during the strike. The *Guerre sociale*, where Jaurès and his allies had been castigated because of their fear of offending Rothschild, had taken the lead in calling for the reinstatement of the railworkers. By early February, Gustave Hervé— showing visible alarm at the turn of events since his diatribes against Rothschild—was forced to declare: "There are no *anti-Semites* here!" This affirmation was, however, weakened by further qualification:

But all the same, when you see a family of foreigners, who have been established in France for less than a century, thanks to a popular revolution of which they had been the main beneficiary, a race until then held in disgrace and persecuted, . . . when you see this family dominating the Parliament, mastering the press of the whole country, publicly treating ministers like lackeys, driving to poverty and hunger three thousand working-class families that have committed no crime—and this out of pride—you catch yourself detesting Drumont a little less.[13]

However provocative this statement might have sounded to republicans, to Emile Janvion it was sheer pusillanimity. To the editor of *Terre libre*, Hervé's attack on Rothschild was too nuanced; it was interpreted as a manifestation of that old proclivity of the Dreyfusard Left—favoritism toward Jewish capitalism. As for Janvion himself, however, he remained above nuance. By February, *Terre libre* began to rival the *Action française* in sheer vituperativeness with its attacks on Jews, now more often *youpins*. "They came from their ghettos," Janvion wrote, "full of vermin and wearing clogs, one hundred years ago; they now have everything at their discretion: power, magistracy, industry, banking, commerce, railways, mines, and food supplies."[14] Janvion took Hervé's affirmation— "There are no *anti-Semites* here!"—as an accusation and attempted to turn it back on Hervé. Referring to *Terre libre*, he challenged: "There are no *philo-Semites* here!"[15]

The view that Hervé was suffering a failure of nerve was not restricted to the staff of *Terre libre*. At the height of the Bernstein campaign, Victor Méric, a mainstay of the *Guerre sociale* staff and one of Hervé's personal friends, had further qualified Hervé's already highly qualified statement that there were no anti-Semites at the *Guerre sociale*. Without going over to a "systematic anti-Semitism," one must, Méric wrote, rethink the whole issue. Certainly, one cannot but be concerned over harsh police treatment of journalists unfavorable to Bernstein. Moreover, the number of Jews in high places—a number that is swelling out of all reasonable proportion—is disturbing. Not only in the theater but among authors, critics, and journalists, the increase is becoming a veritable "wave." Despite all this, Méric reassures his reader, it is difficult to take the last step: "Well, my word, no, one does not become an anti-Semite, because . . . well, because! . . . but one eagerly grabs the writings of the anti-Semites in order to cure oneself of the irresistible desire to become one."[16]

After the Action française victory at the Théâtre-Français, even Hervé was favorably impressed. "The Camelots du roi," according to Hervé, "have just shown us what one does to bring the *radicaille* to heel. You can see that it did not take long for the authorities to capitulate!"[17] The methods of the Action française could also be applied to the solution of other problems, Hervé reasoned— for example, the problem of railroad workers, whom Rothschild had refused to reinstate. Perhaps, Hervé offered, a demonstration "under Rothschild's windows" would make the latter more amenable.[18]

The idea of using the rising anti-Semitic tide fed by the Bernstein riots to further the campaign against Rothschild not only was current at the *Guerre sociale* but had also been in the air for at least several days in certain syndicalist circles. This became manifest in an open letter to Rothschild written by an important syndicalist militant—a letter that was to cause quite a stir. The controversy surrounding the letter focused on two key paragraphs:

We are not anti-Semites yet, but confronted with these observations [that is, the fact that Rothschild had not reinstated the rail workers], we would almost be tempted to become so, to the point that, very recently, we had to dissuade our comrades from demonstrating under your windows. For agitation is growing among us. . . . Can't you see that you will not be able to act this way very much longer with the working class?

Now that the new minister is getting ready to put off social reforms till doomsday by brandishing again the specter of anticlericalism, beware lest the workers, . . . parodying the phrase of a staunch anticlerical, answer with these words: "LE JUIF, VOILA L'ENNEMI."[19]

Had this statement come from an ordinary militant it would have been a cause of consternation; coming from Emile Pataud, head of the powerful Syndicat des industries électriques, it was positively alarming. Partly because of the strategic importance of his office—he liked to brag of the role of electricity in the future revolution—and partly because of the force of his personality, Pataud had established himself as a leading figure on the Parisian Left.[20] When he spoke, regardless of official sanction, his words were taken as more than his personal opinion.

Pataud's letter seemed a vindication of Daudet's long-held conviction that anti-Semitism would someday seal a worker-royalist alliance. Now, on the heels of the government's retreat at the Théâtre-Français, worker hostility to Rothschild could be joined to the royalists' anti-Semitic drive. The exact role played by the royalists in the inspiration and timing of Pataud's letter is uncertain. What is certain is that Pataud had for some time been in contact with the royalists—one of those shadowy "connections" between syndicalists and royalists that the police were sure existed but about which they lacked much specific information.[21]

Pataud wasted little time in making good on the threat contained in his letter. He was soon busy with Emile Janvion planning a huge worker rally. The official theme of the rally would be the Masonic infiltration of syndicalism; but as was now well established—at least as far as Janvion was concerned—anti-Masonism was only a stalking-horse for anti-Semitism.

By late March, as preparations for the rally neared completion, the police expressed apprehension about two not unrelated developments. First, the hall where the rally was to be staged was chosen so that it might be convenient for the nationalist and anti-Semitic student groups of the Latin Quarter.[22] Second, the offices of the Action française were buzzing with talk of the rally, an event, the police observed, to which the royalists were attaching "great importance."[23]

Meanwhile, Téry's *Oeuvre* was hoping to form some kind of front organization that could coordinate the efforts of all the various anti-Semitic groups. Its goals, for the time being, would have to be modest. "There is no doubt," Téry wrote, "that in the Bernstein affair public opinion was in our favor. Our main concern must be that it remains favorable to us; if our program is just, clear, practical, it will remain so."[24] Téry, who prided himself on his "realism" in regards to "the Jewish question," could write without a hint of irony: "*'Death to the Jews!'* a demonstrator was shouting on the place du Théâtre-Français. 'No,' said I, 'let us be content to cry *Down with the Jews!*'"[25] Following Téry's suggestion of a league, there ensued a discussion in the anti-Semitic press as to what should be the maximum and the minimum programs. Téry's main worry was that the Action française, with its disdain for moderation, would undercut the wide public support that could be rallied by a "moderate program." He pleaded with Maurras not to act impulsively, for to do so would kill the "wide and profound movement" already afoot.[26] Maurras, although he had little taste for Téry's schemes involving electoral politics, let himself be cajoled. With Maurras's resistance broken, Téry launched the Oeuvre de défense française on 30 March. Its first goal would be the modification of naturalization laws regarding Jews.[27] The real focus of attention, however, was to be centered on 3 April—the date set for the Janvion-Pataud rally.

Earlier police apprehensions over the rally were justified. The crowd was large and tumultuous and the speakers provocative.[28] With Pataud presiding, Janvion began with a long tirade against the Freemasons. The fine energies of the working class, Janvion inveighed, are being diverted by the Masons, who have successfully infiltrated the syndicalist movement. Since the Dreyfus affair, the goal of Masonry has been to turn workers from the task of revolution and to channel their force "to the benefit of Judeo-Masonic politics." The newly initiated syndicalist, Janvion argued, is surprised to find his ferocious union leader, who lectures only of direct action and class struggle, practicing the most demeaning form of class collaboration. With his "dear brothers" of the lodge—often *patrons*, army officers, and local police officials—he engages in degrading rituals and pledges fraternal solidarity. The ultimate beneficiaries of this treason to his class are, on the one hand, the Republic, and on the other, "cosmopolitan and capitalist Jewry," for which Masons are only "a shield."[29]

With mention of the anti-Semitic theme, the tenor of the meeting reached a fever pitch. Amid cries of "Down with the Jews!" Janvion took to task the "rapacious *youpins*," who have fed upon the working class.[30] When Pataud tried to make the distinction between the "capitalist Jew," who was the enemy, and the "little Jew," who was not, he was drowned out by the crowd, who protested his nit-picking: "Down with the Jews! Down with all the Jews! The small as well as the big!"[31]

The only real attempt to challenge the prevailing mood came from Eugène Merle, member of the staff of the *Guerre sociale*. He protested the anti-Semitic slurs and attacked Janvion for collaboration with the Action française. A tumult of catcalls and countercharges—among them, ironically, that the *Guerre sociale* was controlled by Jewish finance—greeted his efforts.[32]

The rally closed with a resolution condemning the Freemasonry and demanding that the working class be given "more substantial nourishment than that of anticlericalism." Anticipating what that "nourishment" might be, the resolution went on to denounce, "without giving in to anti-Semitism, the directing complicity [in the Freemasonry] of the main Jewish capitalists and particularly Rothschild."[33] The auditors filed out to the familiar strains of the Internationale interspersed with shouts of "Les youpins, hou, hou!"[34]

The composition of the audience, so enthusiastically anti-Semitic, became immediately controversial. *Libre Parole* affirmed that two-thirds in attendance were workers; *L'Humanité* saw only royalists and nationalists, among them "several priests in cassock."[35] The police, although admitting that the royalists were there in number, gave no figures.[36] Whereas *Libre Parole*'s estimate seems obviously exaggerated, no one seemed very convinced by *L'Humanité*'s assurance that there were no workers there. Hervé, who was now thoroughly alarmed by recent events and would have no reason to see workers where there were none, was not so complacent. He noted that there were workers there, and, what was more, they were vigorously applauding Janvion.[37]

However many workers actually attended the rally, it was apparent by early April that a great deal of apprehension was building up in republican quarters over the prospect of an anti-Semitic outburst in the working class. Even before the rally, in late March, one of the elder statesmen of the French Left, Alfred Naquet, attempted to sound the alarm. "The Bernstein incident," he wrote, "and the events accompanying the rail workers' strike have renewed anti-Semitic activity, and it is not only among M. Drumont's faithful, it is also in the socialist and revolutionary ranks that the racist ferment has manifested itself."[38] Naquet singled out the recent statements of Méric and Pataud for criticism. Because they were in positions of leadership, they had special responsibilities. But it was not individual indiscretion, Naquet made clear, that alarmed him the most. "What worries me," Naquet explained, "is that such attitudes are symptomatic. They demonstrate that the old hatreds among races persist in our France, and that they are not restricted solely to the reactionaries and the clericals; that even among the most devoted socialists and syndicalists the fire is smoldering under the ash, and that the slightest puff of wind is enough to rekindle the blaze."[39]

The day after the rally another of the Left's most respected sages, Sébastien Faure, expressed an even more pressing concern over the recent turn of events. He addressed a public, although very personal, letter to Pataud, expressing both surprise and anguish that Pataud had taken part in the rally. Janvion alone, Faure argued, was no threat, but with "you, a serious syndicalist, you, a respected militant, you, a revolutionary, loved, listened to, and influential," one has cause to worry.[40] Faure expressed confidence that, once Pataud understood the fragility of the "house of cards" presented by Janvion as "an indestructible fortress," he would mend his ways. To further that end, Faure concluded, he was going to search for a hall large enough to hold all "our interested friends" so that the issue could be resolved.[41]

Even at *L'Humanité* there was a noticeable sense of urgency about the situation. In the past *L'Humanité* had pointedly ignored the *réunions contradictoires* of the Action française designed to lure workers into open debate. A few days after the Janvion-Pataud rally, *L'Humanité* gave full coverage to just such a debate in the eighteenth arrondissement: it reported with pride how socialists in attendance had distinguished themselves in defense of the Republic. The enemy must be met head on, *L'Humanité* now argued, and socialists must play their part and "[manifest themselves] in the most manly way and [oppose] resolutely, squarely, any attempt that goes against the socialist, syndicalist, and revolutionary effort."[42]

The undercurrents of the anti-Semitic issue were also clearly felt at the Socialist party congress, which met in mid-April at Saint-Quentin. As the congress opened, the Socialists felt it necessary to reassure officially their Jewish brothers that the party "will never compromise itself with the anti-Semitic reactionary slime."[43] As it soon became apparent, however, not all the party faithful were above suspicion. Pierre Myrens, deputy from Boulogne, who had long been a vehement opponent of Freemasonry, was charged with seasoning his attack on the lodges with anti-Semitism.[44] From the floor of the congress Myrens was explicitly warned "not to mix or to risk being mixed with men like Gustave Téry, Janvion, or Pataud."[45]

The controversy surrounding Myrens was just a prelude to a more serious explosion of the anti-Semitic issue at the congress. Charles Rappoport, writing in the Guesdist review, *Le Socialisme*, on the eve of the congress, had referred to "the vices and the miseries" that had attended the founding of *L'Humanité*. Rappoport, although a Jew himself, apparently felt Delaisi's charges suitable grist for the anti-Jaurès mill—a mill then being ground with abandon by the Guesdists hoping to wrest control of *L'Humanité* from Jaurès and his allies.[46] When part of the text of Rappoport's article was read before the congress, Jaurès, jumping to his feet, vented a rage that had been smoldering since Delaisi's first article. "I am used," he charged, "to seeing our common adversaries slander me, calumniate me, cover me with insults. I am used to that, but I cannot accept it from a comrade."[47]

Rappoport, taking the floor in his own defense, did not help his cause by repeating a charge made by Delaisi, one particularly offensive to Jaurès. Everybody knows, Rappoport said, that Lévy-Bruhl, who reportedly has contributed 100,000 francs to help found *L'Humanité*, is not a rich man.[48] Jaurès exploded and accused Rappoport of "the worst anti-Semitic calumnies." Pushing the now visibly shaken Guesdist even further into the tangles of his own innuendo, Jaurès asked if the implication was that Rothschild money had actually founded *L'Humanité*. Rappoport brought the house down on himself with his hapless reply: "Materially, I cannot prove it."[49] Despite the overwhelmingly hostile reaction of the delegates to Rappoport's tactics, the Hervéists could have taken heart from the fact that even the highest councils of the Socialist party were not immune from the contagion of suspicion unleashed by Delaisi.

The Hervéists, however, did not take heart. In fact, Gustave Hervé was among those most apprehensive over the events following in the wake of the Bernstein affair. As early as 15 March, his editorial—entitled significantly "Le Réveil de l'antisémitisme"—revealed a new Hervé emerging, a frightened Hervé in search of allies to join in the fight against what he now saw as a dangerous movement. As he looked across the battlefield into the camp of the bourgeois enemy, the editor of the *Guerre sociale* could now discern two distinct forces, where before there had been only undifferentiated evil. There were, after all, Hervé maintained, two bourgeoisies: a liberal, Dreyfusard faction and a clerical, reactionary faction. About the former, he waxed lyrical. "Since the Revolution," he wrote, "no, since the beginning, since Voltaire, since Rabelais, there has been this freethinking bourgeoisie, in good part Jewish, Protestant, Freemason, whose elite, for centuries rebelling against all traditions [and] all dogmas, has been the glorious educator of the proletariat."[50]

This was an odd profession of allegiance by Hervé, who, at least since 1908, had worked to break up what was left of the Dreyfusard alliance. The *Guerre sociale*, in fact, had been the first to announce that revolutionaries would no longer run to the aid of the endangered Republic. It had further suggested that revolutionaries would feel free to make alliances of convenience with whomever it pleased, including the royalists. Finally, the *Guerre sociale* had launched both Janvion's anti-Masonic campaign and Delaisi's attacks on *L'Humanité*. But now its editor was running scared. On the day following the Janvion-Pataud rally, Hervé wrote: "Le flot monte [the flood tide is rising]. Blind are those who do not see it!"[51]

The extent of Hervé's commitment to a new *défense républicaine* was revealed in an interchange with Pataud shortly after the rally. Pataud, furious over Hervé's sudden change of heart, pointed out that the *Guerre sociale* not only had itself counseled anti-Rothschild demonstrations but had attacked *L'Humanité* for remaining silent. Further, Pataud charged, Hervé's new concern for the fate of Rothschild smacked of philo-Semitism. Hervé refused to be intimidated. I am a philo-Semite, Hervé retorted, because in France there are too many people who hate Jews, not because they are capitalists but because they are part of "the Jewish race"; my "philo-Semitism" is only in reaction to this "'racist' nationalism." Hervé went on to point out that Pataud himself was responsible for the fact that the anti-Rothschild campaign had to be stopped. It could have continued only if it had been clearly differentiated from the Bernstein affair and the Action française, a differentiation certainly not respected by Pataud.[52]

Hervé's reaction to this revival of anti-Semitism was not limited to his newspaper. Almost simultaneously with the Bernstein affair, the Hervéists began organizing the Jeunes Gardes révolutionnaires, a socialist version of the Camelots du roi.[53] It was not long before the Jeunes Gardes were challenging Camelot preponderance in the streets, a preponderance that had made possible in the first place their victory in the Bernstein affair.

The new mood at the *Guerre sociale*, as later events were to prove, was an important victory for the moderate Left. Led by *L'Humanité*, the moderates had always argued for a preservation of the Dreyfusard alliance and warned against any compromise with reactionary elements. In contrast, the men of the *Guerre sociale* had long maintained that come a crisis the treason of the Dreyfusards in power would be avenged. Serious revolutionaries had more to gain, the Hervéists had consistently maintained, by working with forces undermining the Republic than by running to its defense. One such force was, of course, royalism.

But the real question was how much stock the Hervéists had placed in this strategy. How much of it was simply blackmail against republicans? Only a crisis would reveal the answer. With the decline of confidence in the Republic and the reawakening of nationalism—apparent to all by the beginning of 1911—that crisis was approaching. The staff of the *Guerre sociale*, according to a police report of January 1911, had been deeply divided as to how to proceed. One tendency, represented by Almereyda,[54] was to hold firm and resolutely oppose the Republic, even a Republic "in great danger." This group had "natural affinities" with the Action française; should the day come when the Palais-Bourbon is stormed, they would not hesitate to "chime in" with the royalists. Another faction, led by Hervé himself, was increasingly faint-hearted before the threat to the Republic; their republican idealism proved stronger than their thirst for revenge.[55] For a time, policy seemed confused and the Hervéists wavered, but Hervé, from his prison cell, won out. "Paris révolutionnaire," as Hervé liked to refer to the staff and readers of the *Guerre sociale*, would rally to the Republic.

The reaction of Hervé proved pivotal. The *Guerre sociale* began to serve not only as an inspiration but as a clearinghouse for an antiroyalist coalition. Very soon it became apparent that Janvion and Pataud were embarrassingly isolated. Janvion, habituated to isolation, fought back from *Terre libre* with all the more vehemence.[56] Pataud attempted a partial, strategic retreat. Marshaling his reserves of courage, he tried to defend himself before a large, hostile meeting called by several Jewish working-class organizations to protest the rekindling of anti-Semitism. Pataud claimed that he was a victim of the socialist press: they made out that he had attacked Rothschild as a Jew when he had attacked him only as a capitalist. He also attempted to dissociate himself from Janvion and the Action française. Sangnier's *Démocratie* reported that, given the circumstances, he defended himself with "a great deal of cleverness"; yet a resolution was passed condemning him for his letter to Rothschild.[57] At a second meeting—this one arranged by Sébastien Faure, as promised—notables of the Left cheered enthusiastically as Faure lectured to Pataud on the dangers of anti-Semitism. Once again, Pataud claimed he had been misunderstood. Once again, he took pains to separate himself from Janvion and the Action française.[58]

It soon became abundantly clear that the Action française had overplayed its hand. The Janvion-Pataud rally had been too bla-

tantly anti-Semitic, and royalist connections with its organizers too
patently obvious. Maurras—always more cautious than Daudet and
Pujo—had expressed doubts on the very eve of the rally.[59] Yet
even Maurras had not anticipated Hervé's reaction. His turnabout
left the royalists stunned and discouraged.[60] The Action française
could no longer expect sympathy from the *Guerre sociale*; further,
they could anticipate an organized revolutionary challenge in the
streets from the Jeunes Gardes.[61]

Thus an important corner had been turned. Just as the men of
the Action française were expecting the solidification of Hervéists,
revolutionary syndicalists, and radical republicans of Téry's stripe
around the complementary themes of antiparliamentarism, anti-
Semitism, and antirepublicanism, the linchpin of this ad hoc alliance, Gustave Hervé, executed an abrupt volte-face. This, despite
the fact that times had never seemed so auspicious: parliamentarism
and the Republic had never been in such low repute; Jaurès and his
efforts to preserve a united Left had run aground; and, finally, anti-
Semitism—the cement by which the neoroyalists had hoped to seal
their cause to that of the Left revolutionaries—had shown itself to
be in the midst of a popular renaissance.

The Action française had obviously suffered a setback of major proportions—but not one that was necessarily foreordained. It
might be tempting to see the events of the spring of 1911 as "logical," meaning that royalist designs for a working alliance with the
revolutionaries were an inherently impossible undertaking. Yet to
do so would ignore the facts of the matter. Clearly, for certain
revolutionaries the game of politique du pire was not only feasible
but necessary; Hervé himself had argued its logic for several years
and succeeded in convincing not a few of his disciples. As police
reports make abundantly clear, the decision to calm the waters
that the *Guerre sociale* had done so much to stir up was bitterly
contested. It took all of Hervé's reputed tenacity to prevent the
Hervéists from doing what they had long promised: to take revenge
on the Dreyfusard Republic at the first opportunity and with all
means at their disposal.

The Hervéists, though important, were not as crucial to the royalists as another element of the revolutionary Left—the syndicalists.

Hervé the royalists could pretend to dismiss lightly, because "he [remained], in spite of everything, [just] a well-bred bourgeois"; his followers could likewise be passed off as an intellectual coterie somehow peripheral to the working class.[62] The sole legitimate source of revolutionary energy, the royalists now argued, was to be found in the organized working classes. The real measure of their efforts toward the revolutionary Left, the royalists themselves would no doubt have insisted, could be calculated only on the basis of their success in influencing and infiltrating the syndicalist movement.

On the surface at least, however, the royalist initiatives toward the syndicalists had fared scarcely better than the initiatives they had directed at the *Guerre sociale*. Once again, the Janvion-Pataud rally seems to have been an important juncture. All of the momentum of Delaisi's offensive against *L'Humanité* came to what the royalists considered a healthy fruition in the explosion of hostility against Rothschild; but all too soon, from the royalist perspective, this hostility was dissipated in the backlash following the rally. As a result, Janvion was again isolated. And Pataud, whose influence, the royalists had hoped, would bring together a formidable anti-Semitic coalition, was now publicly, and somewhat inelegantly, trying to extricate himself from his former involvements. Meanwhile, to add to their problems, the royalists were being openly repudiated by the syndicalist leadership from the pages of the newly founded and officious syndicalist daily, the *Bataille syndicaliste*. "If the program of monarchical restoration of the A.F.," the editors of the *Bataille syndicaliste* explained, "does not seem to us overly sacrilegious, if its criticisms of the democratic regime sometimes meet our own criticisms, nothing authorizes the organ of integral nationalism to think that there may exist between them and us the least conformity in tendency and action." The *Bataille syndicaliste* concluded with a list of the profound differences separating the two movements.[63]

This public denial of any coincidence between syndicalism and royalism was not merely part of the general repudiation of the Action française by the Left in the wake of the Janvion-Pataud rally. It was sparked by a revealing incident. Sometime in the spring of 1911, a notice had been sent by the *Bataille syndicaliste* to various

Paris newspapers, including the *Action française*. The notice, which the syndicalists wanted published, protested a decision by the rail companies to ban the selling of the *Bataille syndicaliste* in their train stations. The royalists graciously published the notice, adding, however, the following impertinent preface: "At the *Bataille syndicaliste*, where one finds new elements of sympathy for the A.F., they strongly expect *a word or an insert* . . . [concerning] the prohibition of the *Bataille* in railroad stations. Complete silence would be a veritable disillusion for them, because feelings of esteem and admiration for the independence and the courage of the A.F. play a great part in their sympathy."[64]

The only conceivable explanation for this bit of presumption seems to have been the one admitted publicly by the Action française a few days later. The above was an interoffice memorandum attached to the notice from the *Bataille syndicaliste*, which, not meant for external consumption, had been printed by mistake.[65] The subsequent *mise au point* by the *Bataille syndicaliste* denying "sympathy" for the Action française, had it not come voluntarily, would certainly have been demanded.

Given this formal and public disavowal, however, could one assume that these "new elements of sympathy," of which the Action française boasted, were simply figments of overripe royalist imaginations? The police, at least, were not convinced. Despite the fiasco of the Janvion-Pataud rally, covert relations between royalists and certain syndicalist leaders, according to the police, continued. The police, for example, reported conversations having taken place just before May Day 1911 in the offices of the Action française concerning strategy in worker demonstrations—conversations attended by Janvion, Pataud, and a third syndicalist leader, a founder and administrator of the *Bataille syndicaliste*, François Marie. The latter, the police reported, had also been part of the anti-Semitic "combination." Obviously, royalists and certain syndicalists still felt that they could be of use to each other. The police were not clear as to syndicalist expectations at this point, but they were unequivocal about the royalists: they wanted May Day to be the first act in the "insurrectionary and revolutionary drama, which, in MAURRAS's mind, must facilitate, voluntarily or not, the famous 'coup.'" The police saw in these expectations a sign that the royalists were still maintaining a pervasive optimism about the revolutionary potential of the syndicalists. The royalists anticipated "very seriously" the beginning of the "revolutionary *reprisals*," which the Confédération générale du travail had long promised the government and the bourgeoisie.[66]

By 1911, police suspicions of royalist-syndicalist relations went beyond the more or less open connections with Janvion and Pataud and the anti-Semitic campaign. Unspecified reports persistently suggested royalist relations with men closer to the center of syndicalist power; royalist-syndicalist cooperation at this level, the police reasoned, was both more subtle and more dangerous. It was only late in the game, however—the spring of 1913—that police suspicions were confirmed. Their investigations had uncovered evidence implicating one important figure in the syndicalist movement and further implicating a second. The two figures were, respectively, Charles Gogumus, director of the *Bataille syndicaliste*, and Francis Delaisi.

As has been already recounted, Delaisi and Merrheim had broken relations, sometime early in 1913, over the issue of covert government funds offered to the *Bataille syndicaliste*.[67] It had apparently been assumed by Merrheim that Delaisi, disgraced by his willingness to use government subsidies in order to attack Jaurès, had severed all connection with the *Bataille syndicaliste*. It seems clear, however, that not everyone on the staff of the *Bataille syndicaliste* was as incorruptible as Merrheim. A short time after Delaisi had purportedly withdrawn from the *Bataille syndicaliste*, the police reported that he returned, bearing a gift of 3,000 francs. Not only did the director of the paper, Charles Gogumus, accept the money from Delaisi, he was, in fact, reported as having expected 2,000 francs more.[68] The intermediary was once again de Flers, and the police had good grounds for believing that this time the money came directly from the offices of the Action française.[69]

The kind of agreement made by Delaisi in exchange for royalist money cannot be known for certain. Obviously, Delaisi or anyone else at the *Bataille syndicaliste* would have had difficulty promoting royalism openly. It seems, at a minimum, that there was cooperation in the form of information exchanges and willingness to participate in joint newspaper campaigns.[70] Freemasonry, antire-publicanism, attacks on Socialists were all areas where royalists and syndicalists could find common ground.

If police information concerning Delaisi was incriminating, although sketchy as to details, the police had more solid information concerning Gogumus. The commissaire de police was able to reproduce three letters written by an important Camelot du roi, Henri Lagrange, and addressed to the director of the *Bataille syndicaliste*. The letters, written in early April 1913, establish that Gogumus had asked Lagrange for further information about a dossier previously discussed. A meeting was arranged at Lagrange's home, which Gogumus attended. Lagrange wrote Gogumus afterward, assuring him of the authenticity of the information exchanged. The letters are fully reproduced in the report of the commissaire de police.[71]

The police attributed special importance to this exchange of information when they learned, shortly afterward, of the contents of the dossier. It concerned the Moulins de Corbeil, a center of flour production for the Paris area, and gave information as to how Paris would be supplied with food in case of war. The Action française had received the information contained in the dossier, the police had learned, from two well-placed sources: an employee at the Moulins and one at the Ministry of Interior.[72]

That the royalists would collect and pay for the information contained in the dossier revealed the seriousness of their conspiratorial intent, if nothing about their ability to act upon it. Further, that they would transmit such delicate information to the director of the *Bataille syndicaliste* suggested not only a confidence in the revolutionary potential of syndicalism but some prior agreement between royalists and syndicalists about a joint exploitation of a revolutionary situation. It is abundantly clear that certain well-placed syndicalist leaders—their public denials notwithstanding—were quite prepared to play a serious game of politique du pire. As will be demonstrated, the fact that in the end this game had rather limited repercussions was due more to the circumstances that overtook these syndicalist leaders in the years just before the war than to their own intentions.

[10]

Le Cercle Proudhon

> [These are] men who find their sole pleasure in run-
> ning the most violent risks, in involving themselves
> in the most hazardous adventures. They need action
> and defeat, for a calm and monotonous life, gray
> days, [and] quiet pleasures are deadly to them and
> offer only boredom.   Henri Lagrange

For the young generation at the *Revue critique*, where the alliance of
worker and royalist was first conceived, conspiratorial activities
with syndicalists were only one facet of their program. Their interest in syndicalism did not originate in simple calculation, in *politique du pire*. It was their sincere conviction that nationalism, if it
was to be the truly renovative force they envisioned, must incorporate the energies of the working class. The "social monarchy"
—however opportunistic a gambit it might have appeared to the
outside observer—was for the men around Georges Valois the
vision of a new society, a society that would be at once national
and social.

Henri Lagrange, the Camelot in secret communication with the
staff of the *Bataille syndicaliste*, was representative of these young
national socialist idealists of the Right. He had come to the Action
française at the ripe age of sixteen. His taste for action had put him
in the forefront of royalist demonstrations and led him to an early
acquaintance with La Santé.[1] But he was more than an impulsive
young tough; his leadership capabilities soon earned him the position of secretary-general of the Etudiants d'Action française, one of
the most important royalist organizations in the prewar years.

Maxime Brienne, a young poet and friend of Lagrange, recalled the frenzied pace of Lagrange's life after he had joined the Action française. Though Lagrange was a participant in many of the *réunions contradictoires* organized by the royalists, Brienne remembered that he was never too busy to join the Camelots for action in the streets. He argued half his nights away in the brasseries of the student quarter, and after they had closed he carried a reservoir of energy home where he studied and wrote through what remained of the night. "Thus," wrote Brienne, "were the short years of his youth consumed, without rest, without joy, without sorrow." Lagrange was to die, an early victim of the war, at the age of twenty-one.[2]

While still in his midteens, Lagrange was writing literary pieces for the *Revue critique*, pieces possessing an acuity that earned him praise from outside the confines of the Action française.[3] It was at the *Revue critique* that Lagrange met Georges Valois; the two immediately became intimates, sharing the same *tempérament frondeur*. Lagrange, from the start, took the ideas of the second-generation royalists to heart: to destroy the *nuées* of the democrats and to build a bridge toward the working class.

This was the same spirit that had first animated the *Revue critique*. Since its founding in 1908, the publication had gone from one success to another. By 1911 it had established itself as one of the most influential of the avant-garde reviews, mixing, in enticing proportions, scholarly seriousness with verve and audacity. According to Eugen Weber, the *Revue critique* was becoming for the chic Right what André Gide's *Nouvelle Revue française* was for the Left.[4]

Many of the contributors to the review never ceased to be concerned with the social question first introduced by Georges Valois. Pierre Gilbert, the editor, had joined with Valois on the ill-fated *Cité française*. The literary critic Henri Clouard, who became editorial secretary at the *Revue critique*, was likewise a proponent of a vigorous social policy. Gilbert Maire, the most philosophically inclined of the review's staff, had developed into a serious student of Georges Sorel.

Yet there were problems. Not all of the second-generation royalists, as Maurras was fond of calling his followers at the *Revue critique*, were of one mind. Valois's impulsiveness and the personal following that he had developed among the students and Camelots did not sit well with some of his colleagues. The *Cité* project was seen by a few as too daring. One could borrow from Sorel, but only with the proviso that one was clear about what one was leaving behind. Jean Rivain, who had done much to stimulate the original interest in syndicalism at the Action française, was convinced that Valois and his friends paid altogether too much attention to Georges Sorel and not enough to La Tour du Pin.[5] By 1911 it was clear to Valois that the *Revue critique* was no longer the open forum it had been in 1908 when he had first launched his enquête on the working class.

This was frustrating to men like Henri Lagrange, for whom the alliance with the syndicalists was now a veritable passion. The problems surrounding the "social monarchy" were far from resolved, Lagrange reasoned; most of them had barely been touched upon. With the conviction that the work of construction must be carried forward, Lagrange approached Valois in the spring of 1911 and inquired about the possibility of a study circle. Lagrange conceived of a laboratory where those fired by the idea of the social monarchy might begin to tackle problems heretofore sketched out in only the most general terms.[6] Characteristically, the idea, once in the hands of Georges Valois, became something more than the original conception. Ever since the collapse of the *Cité française* in the fall of 1910, Valois had entertained hopes of rekindling interest in a joint nationalist-syndicalist enterprise. The spring of 1911 seemed an auspicious moment.

The spring of 1911 upset the conventional wisdom of many republicans. One article of faith among republicans—that anti-Semitism was dead in working-class circles—was shaken by Pataud's letter to Rothschild and the Janvion-Pataud rally.

A second item of conventional wisdom among republicans was the conviction that, however much royalists and syndicalists might unite in negative opposition to the Republic, they could never unite on a positive program. Maurras's *entente naturelle* was, at best, an entente of common animosities. This view was reinforced by an influential critic of both movements, Georges Guy-Grand. He argued that the critiques leveled against democracy by Sorel and Maurras were indeed serious and needed to be taken seriously, but that Sorelians and Maurrassians could ever formulate a joint program was unthinkable. Whatever they shared as antidemocrats and practitioners of direct action was insignificant compared to the profound differences that separated them on the question of the shape of the future society. The ideas of a Sorel or a Berth could never be squared with those of a Maurras or a Valois, Guy-Grand assured his readers.[7]

Doubtless Guy-Grand expected that the young royalists would attempt to rebut his arguments. He and the royalists had already been party to a long polemical interchange.[8] Guy-Grand, however, probably did not expect an argument from Edouard Berth— one of the very authors he had used to prove his case. Berth, in a long and spirited article in the *Revue critique*, not only challenged Guy-Grand's presumption but added new reasons why the two movements—syndicalism and royalism—were tending toward a convergence.

Like his teacher Sorel, Berth had for some time been brooding over the bankruptcy of revolutionary syndicalism. Berth saw syndicalism, like socialism before it, as sinking into the democratic morass. Sorel had already analyzed the reasons why a revolutionary movement could not succeed in a democracy; the very mechanism of democratic politics, he had concluded, ensured the cooptation of revolutionary ideals. Berth took a slightly different tack. He asked why a collectivist movement could not succeed in a democracy; his answer was no less pessimistic than Sorel's. But rather than undertaking the analysis of democratic institutions as Sorel had done, Berth looked for his answers in the philosophical underpinnings of the democratic mind. He hoped to complement Sorel's sociological critique of democracy with his own philosophical one.[9]

Berth started from the premise that in its very essentials—its philosophic base—democracy was profoundly anticollectivist. In philosophic terms, democracy was incurably nominalist, that is, it denied the reality of collective categories—whether in the realm of ideas or social forms.

With regard to ideas, Berth argued that democrats prided themselves on being pragmatists. They detested metaphysics—but only because they no longer had ideas that could stand up to rigorous philosophical criticism. They had traded ideas and thinking for ideals and believing; a democrat would dismiss metaphysics as the last vestige of theology but would subscribe to the most banal and sentimental of ideals—those of the ballot box, of the sovereignty of the people, of universal progress.

But it is in the realm of social forms, Berth argued, that democratic nominalism is most pernicious. Because he is a nominalist, the democrat denies the existence of what to him are "abstract" categories; social groups have reality to the democrat only as associations of individuals. The groups themselves can have no reality; they are only convenient fictions. However, according to Berth's realism, what is abstract is not the social group but the individual. The isolated individual exists nowhere save in the mind of the democrat. Yet somehow this fiction of the individual became the democratic reality, the building block of democratic society.

This preoccupation with the individual, according to Berth, has become a democratic passion. Democrats seem to talk about little else but the "development of their personalities, the blooming of all their faculties." For Berth there is a supreme irony behind all this; despite the pious talk of the democrats, never more than in contemporary democracy has the personality been "more colorless, more insignificant, more flattened, more impalpable." A true individualism, Berth argued, has thrived only when it has had roots in the collective reality; here Berth pointed to the "magnificent specimens of strong and powerful individuality offered by the ancien régime."[10]

The revolt against democratic nominalism, against abstract individualism, had led Berth to that most concrete reality, the reality of the historically sanctioned group. Here the analyses of Sorel and Berth—the one sociological, the other philosophical—came together: the fight against democracy can be buttressed by traditionalism. The genuine traditionalist—as opposed to the conservative, who works only to protect his interest—is the archenemy of the democrat. The genuine traditionalist is necessarily both revolutionary and collectivist: revolutionary because he can never compromise himself by accepting the existing order, collectivist because the very notion of the individual is anarchistic. The stumbling block, however, is that no one in contemporary society is capable of thinking outside the democratic framework, a framework that, since the Enlightenment, has been the sustaining myth of all right-thinking men. No one, that is, except Charles Maurras.

As has been indicated, Georges Sorel discovered Maurras early.[11] It took Edouard Berth longer to come to similar conclusions, but when he did so he threw himself in with an abandon foreign to Sorel. To Guy-Grand, who denied that there could be any grounds, save expediency, for an alliance between Sorelians and Maurrassians, Berth answered that there existed the most profound philosophical reasons for such an alliance. Democratic pragmatist that he was, Guy-Grand was blind to the larger philosophical forces operating above the superficial play of parties. Berth argued that, above their seeming diversity, liberal Protestants, modernist Catholics, Freemasons, Jews, and Jacobins, on the one hand, were all united by a "spirit of democratic abstraction." The Action française and the revolutionary syndicalists, on the other hand, Berth continued, can "make an alliance against this unity, . . . because a similar spirit of realism moves them, and they depend on the very realities that democracy destroys or dissolves: national realities or professional realities, the reality of the *patrie* conceived—and it cannot be conceived otherwise—as a territorial reality."[12]

Berth's philosophic excursion seemed to justify Maurras's long-standing optimism about the entente naturelle. A true syndicalist, by the logic inherent in his position, would come to see the Action française as a natural ally. Stripped of the remaining trappings of democracy—trappings such as electoralism and notions of natural progress—syndicalism would find royalism complementary. Berth had been working to purge syndicalism of one of the most persistent of the remaining democratic nuées, internationalism. There was no longer an inherent contradiction, Berth could now argue, between the syndicat and the patrie. Democratic ideology, forever vacillating between an egoistic individualism and a sentimental idealism, missed the intermediate level, a concrete level, where the reality of groups could be understood. Royalists had come to see the importance of the strong, independent syndicat: syndicalists, for their part had to see the necessity of the strong, independent patrie.

The first lines of the declaration of purpose of the Cercle Proudhon, appearing in the first number of the main project of the group, the *Cahiers du Cercle Proudhon*, read as follows: "The Frenchmen who came together to found the Cercle P.-J. Proudhon are all nationalists. The mentor whom they chose for their group introduced them to other Frenchmen, who are not nationalists, who are not royalists, and who joined them in order to participate in the life of the Cercle and the writing of the *Cahiers*."[13] It is curiously straightforward. There is little effort to conceal the fact that the royalists saw Proudhon as their passport into nonroyalist territory. The idea of using Proudhon was not new. In January of 1909, a committee of royalists had tramped out to the Montparnasse cemetery to place a wreath on the grave of Proudhon. The inscription on the wreath read: "To P.-J. Proudhon, to the French patriot, . . . to the socialist man of justice, who denounced the social crimes of the Revolution and the economic lies of Jewish collectivism, to the immortal author of *Du principe fédératif*."[14] From the beginning, the Action française had served notice: its interest in Proudhon was to be highly selective. Even those closely connected with Valois could not be considered students of Proudhon. They read Proudhon—a few even labored over him—but they knew what they were looking for and passed over anything else. At best, they pointed out things in Proudhon that democrats and socialists chose to ignore: his nationalism, his distaste for revolutionary romanticism, his attachment to certain traditional values, and even a pronounced strain of anti-Semitism.[15] But Proudhon, as the declaration of purpose of the Cercle frankly admitted, was seen primarily as a bridge to the Left, especially to those two men whom the royalists had long courted, Edouard Berth and Georges Sorel.

Both Sorel and Berth considered themselves serious scholars of Proudhon and were in a perpetual state of irritation over the Proudhon emerging from the contemporary democratic and socialist literature. Would they not be interested, Valois asked, in joining with men earnest about exploding the myth of the social-democratic Proudhon? Sorel did not take the bait. The royalists, he wrote to Berth in late 1911, understood Proudhon as badly as the democrats. According to Sorel, the royalists of the Action française, because of their monarchist preoccupations, were incapable of placing Proudhon in the perspective necessary to understand his thought.[16] Sorel had been soured by the *Cité française* experience and was not ready for more of the same.

Sorel's young disciple, however, would not let his enthusiasm for the Cercle Proudhon be dampened. He knew full well that the Cercle was not intended as a place where a scholarly exhumation of the real Proudhon was to be undertaken.[17] The men of the Cercle saw as their real goal the study of how nationalist and syndicalist energies might be fruitfully combined. For this task, Proudhon might, on occasion, be a source of inspiration; he might, more often, be a convenient stick with which to beat nonnational socialists; but he must always—following the established royalist precedent —be read selectively.

If the Cercle Proudhon was not intended as a center of Proudhonian scholarship, neither was it intended as a political movement. It was organized strictly as an intellectual study group with two primary functions. First, there was to be an open discussion of issues. To this end, the Cercle sponsored monthly lectures, usually given by members of the group; in addition, there were to be weekly workshops to discuss the theme of the lecture. Second, the Cercle would publish the fruits of its work in its own publication, the *Cahiers du Cercle Proudhon*. Later, there were to be a few works published by the Nouvelle Librairie nationale gathered in a "Collection du Cercle Proudhon."

Another aim of the founders of the Cercle Proudhon was that it would not be a mere auxiliary of the Action française. Valois liked to emphasize the heterogeneity of the group: there were nationalists, to be sure, but also syndicalists and *républicains fédéralistes*. Yet few were deceived. The majority of those actively participating were royalists. Of the eight men who signed the original declaration of purpose and who also formed the core staff of the *Cahiers*, five were members of the Action française.[18] The three nonroyalists were Jean Darville, Berth's pseudonym, Albert Vincent, an *instituteur* calling himself a federalist republican, and Marius Riquier from *Terre libre*, who could pass for a nonroyalist only with considerable difficulty.

This failure of the Cercle Proudhon to move out from under the shadow of the Action française was a serious limiting factor. The members knew it and tried desperately to enlist Sorel, who, they reasoned, would make it much easier for disaffected syndicalists to adhere. They even sponsored a special soirée where they hoped to honor the celebrated author of *Reflections on Violence* in person. But Sorel kept his distance: their acknowledged mentor had to be feted in absentia. Undaunted, the men of the Cercle Proudhon devoted an issue of their *Cahiers* to Sorel, reproducing the panegyrics of the soirée and more.[19] The best that Sorel could manage in return was to allow the anonymous publication of a letter written earlier. The letter mocked Lagardelle who had criticized the Cercle and urged socialists to recapture Proudhon; according to Sorel, there were as yet no socialists capable of writing on Proudhon with any authority.[20]

As a result of the failure to rally Sorel, the Cercle Proudhon remained a modest affair. Its *Cahiers* attracted only some two hundred regular subscribers.[21] Its meetings were attended by no more than two dozen or so faithful.[22] Almost all of them were young— many still students—and comfortable with royalism. The large input from the Left eagerly sought by Valois never materialized.

Yet despite these limitations the work of the Cercle Proudhon was significant. The two leading figures in the Cercle, Berth and Valois, though not first-rate original thinkers, had a talent for seizing upon novel ideas and combining them with other novel ideas in an audacious and polemically effective way. They were able not only to entice their readers with lively renderings of Sorel and Maurras—removing the discursiveness of the former and the logical dryness of the latter—but they felt free to experiment and take liberties with which neither Sorel nor Maurras would feel comfortable.

It is in this experimentation that the work of the Cercle Proudhon takes on significance. In the short time between its founding and the outbreak of the war, Valois and Berth—and to a lesser degree the other members of the Cercle—fashioned together an amalgam of ideas that were at once national socialist and fascist. Their ideas were national socialist in a specific sense: they tried to find a common ground not only where national and social concerns could reach some mutual accommodation but where these concerns might reinforce and energize each other. Their ideas were fascist in a necessarily less precise way. As has already been proposed,[23] fascism is not to be found in a concrete program but in a mood, a temper. It is predicated on a deep-seated pessimism and a gnawing dissatisfaction with both contemporary social reality and the proposed Marxian alternative; the Gordian knot can only be cut with a thrust of heroic action, the regenerative power of the violent deed. This atmosphere of heroic pessimism hung heavy above the activities of the Cercle Proudhon.

Despite the persistent individual differences dividing its members at times, there was enough intellectual coherence to allow one to speak of an ideological construction emerging from the Cercle Proudhon. This construction was most apparently a negative one. The members of the Cercle knew and were most anxious to specify what they were against. The declaration of purpose of the Cercle Proudhon, much like that of the *Cité française*, was, in the first instance, militantly antidemocratic. "Democracy is the greatest error of the past century," the declaration read. "If one wants to live, if one wants to work, if one wants to possess in social life the highest human guarantees for Production and Culture, if one wants to conserve and to increase the moral, intellectual, and material capital of civilization, it is absolutely necessary to destroy democratic institutions."[24]

This antidemocratic stance, as might be expected, was not the mere rejection of a political form. The outward political form was simply, for the men of the Cercle Proudhon, the superficial manifestation of a deep malaise that had overtaken not only France but the West in general. These self-proclaimed neo-Proudhonians argued that this malaise had such catastrophic implications for civilization that it was crucial to investigate and articulate its precise nature as well as all of its ramifications.

Almost all members of the Cercle, at one time or another, attempted to come to grips with this central problem. All had a similar instinctual reaction; the differences in the way that each treated the problem stemmed largely from differences in sophistication and degree of facility with abstract thought. Albert Vincent, the federalist republican, was as usual the most rustic and the most concrete.

The apologists for democracy, Vincent observed, have made it synonymous with the growth of liberty. But the problem with democratic liberty is that it matured under the tutelage of the bourgeoisie: democratic idealism reached its apogee at the same time as bourgeois materialism. For this insight, Vincent credited Marx. Vincent continued to invoke the authority of Marx, whom he quotes on the nature of democratic liberty: " 'The liberty of the egoistic man . . . [is only] the right to an unbridled flight of all the spiritual and material elements that form the content of his life.' " Leaving Marx aside, Vincent gives his own interpretation of the sorry results of this "unbridled flight": "It is, very truly, the excuse for all turpitude, the incitement to total license." The concrete results, according to Vincent, have been destructive for society: they constitute the "balance sheet of democracy": "First of all, alcoholism! The consumption of alcohol in France is rapidly increasing. . . . Morphine and opium are secretly consumed. . . . Must one mention lust and pornography?"[25] This, for Vincent, is but part of the problem. The list of the evils caused by the infiltration of the democratic ideal was extensive. The increase in the suicide rate, the declining birth rate, the mounting incidence of mental illness, the destruction of the family, and the depopulation of rural France are no less a part of the balance sheet of democracy.[26] "This balance sheet," according to Vincent, "is clear. Democracy destroys everything it touches."[27]

Whereas Edouard Berth was no less than Vincent convinced of the categorical evil represented by the democratic ideal, his argument took somewhat higher ground. Where Vincent contented himself mainly with condemning the destructive effects of this ideal, Berth was determined to search out and destroy its roots. It has already been indicated how Berth attacked "nominalist" democracy and contrasted it to the "realism" of historically sanctioned institutions. Berth did not simply conceive of this dichotomy as a clever device to sustain an article; by 1911 it had become a virtual obsession.

Like Sorel, Berth's original interest in the syndicalist movement had little to do with that of the many anarchists who had come to syndicalism at about the same time. The anarchist goal of the total liberation of the human personality was viewed by Berth—nurtured as he was in Sorelian pessimism—with suspicion. To preach that man could be liberated from morality was for him a dangerous heresy. He fully agreed with Sorel that syndicalism, if it was to be a truly constructive force, must be a vehicle capable of promoting morality—not one involved in a cheap demagogy promising a release from morality. Berth's disavowal of anarchy was one of the major thrusts of his most important work to that date, *Les Nouveaux Aspects du socialisme*, published in 1908.

The worst aspect of the anarchist doctrine of total liberation, Berth wrote in *Les Nouveaux Aspects*, was that it refused to realize that civilization was built through constraint, a constraint that was, in no small measure, the legacy of capitalism. Capitalism was historically important not so much because of the material wealth that it created but because of the moral habits that it instilled in the masses—the habits of work and discipline. The masses, through the mechanism of capitalism, had been raised up from "their primitive laziness and their individualistic anarchism, in order to be made capable of a collective work, more and more perfected." Syndicalists should realize that their hope of "a regime of freedom, without patronal tutelage and without the tutelage of the state," could never have been even a hope without this "regime of constraint," which rendered man "little by little capable of elevating himself to free and voluntary work."[28]

Anarchists, however, according to Berth, rejected such a notion: they not only denied the necessity of historical constraint but detested its contemporary legacies, work and discipline. They, in fact, reject everything connected with civilization, for civilization demands that man leave that anarchist Garden of Eden, the state of nature, and build institutions calling upon him to subdue "his instincts, his passions, his thorough laziness." Their deity is the first anarchist, Jean-Jacques Rousseau: "Consider Rousseau: one knows his vagabond inclination, his love of independence . . . , his misanthropy, his hatred of society. Man is good, he exclaims, when he comes out of the hands of his Creator; civilization depraves him: there lies all of anarchist thought; a candid, idyllic optimism, a naive faith in the good instincts of man, the idea that human nature can be abandoned to its instincts and can only be corrupted by social institutions."[29]

This utopian view of man, left to his instincts and without institutional support, Berth considered as the most naive and dangerous of chimeras. But as of 1908, at least, Berth still placed great hopes in syndicalism. Rather than attempt to resuscitate institutions long dead, new working-class institutions were being constructed that would incorporate all the best of the past and eliminate all that was merely anachronism. He was soon to be disenchanted. Everything he saw as constructive in syndicalism was losing ground; through a series of cowardly compromises, syndicalism was giving up the vision of a new society and was becoming just the most advanced of the democratic parties. Sorel, for his part, had seen this early. His influence—especially the influence of *Les Illusions du progrès*, published at about that time—was considerable. Democracy was the source of all evil. Berth now came to believe that the flaws he had detected in anarchism—its naive view of man, its glorification of passions, its aversion to work and discipline—were inextricably bound with democratic institutions and ideals.

It was no longer, for Berth, a maverick sect, the anarchists, that threatened the advance of civilization. The situation was far more serious: an entire civilization had wedded itself to a metaphysical framework that was anticivilization. From the perspective of 1914, Berth explains the predicament: "If one wonders why the syndicalist idea has been carried so quickly into the same degeneracy as the socialist idea, one will find only one answer, [namely, that] the working class has not yet managed to effect a *moral separation* from the bourgeois philosophy, that is to say, from the philosophy of the eighteenth century."[30]

Likewise, Valois had by 1914 come to the conclusion that the problem was, above all, metaphysical. The Enlightenment had produced a philosophy, a false philosophy, but one that had become a veritable countertheology. It taught that man is "indefinitely perfectible" and that the real measure of his progress toward perfection was the removal of "constraining institutions."[31]

As a necessary first step against this "prodigious metaphysical error," Valois proposed "the cleansing of minds." A more "realistic" picture of man must be resurrected, one "both scientific and religious, which [would] present man as subjected to the consequences of original sin or as limited by the imperfection of his nature; one on which [would] stand the political and social institutions maintaining human societies in an order where man [would] find his salvation and his greatest terrestrial good."[32]

For the men of the Cercle Proudhon, the malaise afflicting contemporary society was here: namely, in the refusal to see man for what he was, a finite creature. The eighteenth-century vision of man as a creature of infinite possibilities had become the new religion, replacing the less flattering but more earnest vision of the great Christian pessimists. By 1911, Berth had come to see the dichotomy with terrifying simplicity: "Democracy, in its essence, wants to be independent of all bond of time and place: it dreams of the absolute independence of pure spirits, it pretends to be all spiritual, it aspires to be angelic, [but] it only partakes of the bestial."[33] The other side of the equation Berth had been perceiving more and more clearly since the *Cité française* project and his association with Valois: "Family, class, nation, Church—all this is founded on blood, on tradition, on extraindividualist and supranational influences; nothing in all this has anything to do with a simple individual adhesion; these are *mystical realities*, which are denied any valid existence by the abstract rationalism of democracy."[34]

There can be little question that the men of the Cercle Proudhon worked toward an early and highly self-conscious version of what Ernst Nolte has called "resistance to transcendence." As was manifest in many later fascists, this resistance was only discernible by implication or expressed in sloganeering. In Valois and Berth it was not only fully articulated but articulated as a metaphysical proposition—a clear, considered, and unequivocal rejection of transcendence. Yet, to say this much is only to uncover one component, though an important one, of the fascist mentality. This "resistance to transcendence" was also part of the mental makeup of reactionaries. As Nolte has demonstrated, it was certainly central to the thinking of Charles Maurras; Berth and Valois, as they admitted publicly, were in Maurras's debt. Yet they also went beyond Maurras. What made the Cercle Proudhon venture characteristically fascist was not this "resistance to transcendence" alone but its combination with a more elusive although no less important element, the idolatry of heroic activism and the cult of violence.

Henri Lagrange had been won over to the Action française by the seduction of Maurras's logic. He had found in Maurrassian doctrine, as Pierre Andreu recalls, "a complete and coherent system of man, society, and the world."[35] Lagrange found this intellectually satisfying, no doubt; yet the real import of integral nationalism, for Lagrange as for many young *ligueurs*, was not its logical consistency but its emotional appeal. An astute observer of prewar royalism likened the process of becoming a Maurrassian to that of a conversion experience: "everything is saved, everything is clear again, luminous, golden! *Evohé! Evohé!* Joy, joy, and tears of joy!"[36] Once Lagrange had imbibed Maurras's teachings, he adhered to them —again, according to Andreu—"with a rigor and a violence that 'terrified' Maurras."[37]

This was, in one sense, a vindication of Sorel's earlier judgment concerning the power of the nationalist myth and his confidence in Maurras as its effective propagator. Sorel had reasoned that a myth must be able to rally men capable of heroic action and inspire them with a sense of mission. In Lagrange, and others like him, both functions were served. Speaking of his generation, "vingt ans en 1914," Lagrange could say that "at the age of twenty they did not dream of love but of the satisfaction of some great and noble action. The idea of a vast world, of a role to play, of revolutions to make, inspired their judgment and dominated their resolutions. . . . [It was a] generation happy only in the exaltation of violence and combat."[38]

Henri Lagrange was the prototype of the new man that the Cercle Proudhon had hoped to help create—he was the incarnation of "martial virtues." The Action française also talked of combat and of the superiority of military virtues. History was made, Maurras liked to say, not by impersonal historical forces but by men of will. However, the men of the Cercle Proudhon had overtaken Maurras. Their attitude toward violence revealed itself more Sorelian than Maurrassian. For Maurras, violence was always a means to an end. His much-discussed coup was illustrative: it would require force, but surgical force, just enough to accomplish the task. For the Cercle Proudhon, violence had its own rewards: it was sought for its purifying effect, for its capability to energize men, to move them to heroic deeds.

From its founding, the Cercle Proudhon interested itself in the "martial spirit." At the dedication of the Cercle Proudhon, Valois had selected a passage from Proudhon's work, *La Guerre ou la paix*, which would set the tone of all the later pronouncements of the Cercle on the subject of violence: "Hail to war! It is through war that man, hardly emerged from the slime that served him as a womb, assumes majesty and valor; it is on the body of his first slain enemy that he dreams his first dream of glory and immortality. Our philanthropy abhors these streams of spilled blood and these fratricidal slaughters. I fear that this flabbiness forebodes the cooling of our virtue. . . . Death is the crowning of life: how could man, an intelligent, moral, and free being meet a nobler end?"[39]

Berth was also fond of quoting Proudhon on the virtues of war. But his interest in the martial spirit went beyond that of the other members of the Cercle. Berth was convinced that this spirit, as with everything else he studied, could be understood properly only if one searched out its philosophic foundations, became aware of the historical context in which it grew up, and, of course, identified all that tended to corrupt or diminish it.

As a student of Georges Sorel, Berth was familiar with the value of military virtues. The modern worker, in Sorelian terms, was simply the warrior of yesterday transformed; the good worker was filled with the same discipline and passion that had fired the soldiers in the armies of the French revolutionary wars.[40] Of course, as a syndicalist Berth had believed that this discipline and this passion were no longer properly put at the service of the state, a state acting as a committee for the defense of bourgeois interests. And modern wars, losing all semblance of heroism, had degenerated into disputes among the various national bourgeois committees. This was Berth's position circa 1908.

The change came gradually, it seems, but by 1912 it was complete. In late 1912 Berth was excited by two events: first, the outbreak of the Tripolitan war; second, the offensive of the small Balkan states against the Ottoman Empire. He congratulated the Italians on their audacity and the Balkan states on their "heroic will." For the rest of Europe, unnerved by the fear of a general war, he could feel nothing but disdain: "What a spectacle of high comedy," he wrote, "this attitude of plutocratized Europe in the face of these two martial initiatives—it is seeped in pacifism as an old slut in retirement is seeped in devotion; in front of the irruption of the fact of war it shrieks as a person whose modesty has become, a trifle too late, overly sensitive and pinched."[41] Thus Berth wrote in the *Cahiers du Cercle Proudhon*; the article, entitled "Satellites de la ploutocratie," was an extended gloss of an epigram by Nietzsche: "A society that refuses, definitively and *by instinct*, war and the spirit of conquest is in decadence: it is ripe for democracy and a government of small shopkeepers."

The older nations of Europe, as Berth now saw it, were hopelessly decadent, dominated by the international capitalist plutocracy, pacifist "by instinct and out of interest." Materialism and heroic values were always in opposition: it is the eternal struggle between the moneychanger and the warrior, between "gold" and "iron." If the former had won the day, how could the latter contest the victory? Berth, borrowing from Vilfredo Pareto, finds only one recourse left to the men of iron: "brutal force." "Against gold," according to Berth, "only iron can prevail, and that is why in this modern world, plutocratized to the marrow, there is universal prejudice against violence and why in all classes the spirit of conciliation is so strong. Transaction is, naturally, the essential law of a merchant world: on the marketplace everything can and must be bargained for."[42] But this spirit of the merchant is not limited to the world of finance: "It will corrode Catholicism through modernism, which is essentially a transaction between the Christian faith and the modern world; it will corrode philosophy through pragmatism, which is a philosophical modernism; it will corrode socialism and nationalism through parliamentarism: wherever it senses a spirit of martial intransigence capable of raising and maintaining *against it* [something] Absolute and Supernatural, . . . it immediately tries to break into it, to surround it, to 'pacify' it."[43]

In tracing back the victory of the merchant over the warrior, Berth found himself, once more, in the century that was the source of all modern ills, the century of the Enlightenment. The philosophes were men of peace par excellence, because they had revolted against the heroic vision of life perpetuated by Christianity —a vision of man born to sin, surrounded by corruption, and capable of attaining salvation only through incessant struggle. Behind the reveries of the philosophes, Berth argued, stands the idyllic dream, the alternative theology, of a natural and eternal harmony.

The democratic ideal, reduced to simplest terms, is the victory of Rousseau over Pascal.[44]

This democratic ideal of universal peace insinuates itself into the modern world at two levels. At the internal level, under the guise of *solidarisme*, it preaches the conciliation of class antagonisms, the resolution of social conflicts. At the international level, it promotes *humanitarisme*, the concept of a brotherhood of men above nations.[45] At both levels, the interests of the moneychanger and the philosophe come together in the bleating for peace. But it must be resisted, Berth urges: "We are forever disgusted—I repeat—with this optimistic philosophy, and far from believing that the attenuation of antagonisms in the world is possible—even far from thinking that this attenuation, should it be possible, would be good—we proclaim the sovereign virtue of war, whose intervention in human affairs is always comparable to that of a strong, bitter, and salubrious wind renewing the putrid waters of the human swamp."[46]

But the virtues of war must not only be proclaimed, Berth argued; they must be practiced. As with everything else, force that remains dormant tends to dissipate. "All force needs to be tested," Berth concluded, "so that its degree of resistance, the purity of its temper, the necessity of its eternal mission be known. All force is mollified and lulled to sleep by peace; war exists to draw it out of its sleep and its torpor."[47]

The fascist temper of the Cercle Proudhon is thus unambiguous: the men of the Cercle not only developed a classic formulation of "resistance to transcendence" but also proposed what has been called the fascist alternative to transcendence—the escape through the mystique of heroic action, violence, and war.[48] But they were also interested, at a lower level of abstraction, in formulating a practical program by which their monarchist and syndicalist concerns might be joined. By the end of their first year, after much discussion, the men of the Cercle Proudhon could speak of a coherent position. Their "national socialism,"[49] as the few that preceded it and the many more that would follow, was a unique combination, borrowing as it did from varied intellectual and national traditions.

It shared with other national socialisms, however, a common inspiration: the conviction that the democratic Center had lost the capacity as well as the will to govern and that the impasse could only be broken by the combined energies of the nationalist Right and the collectivist Left.

As with later national socialisms, the monarchist-syndicalist construction was first and foremost antiplutocratic. One of the Cercle's favorite themes was the domination of the modern world by the power of "gold." Unlike most of the older members of the Action française, who confined themselves largely to anti-Semitism, the men of the Cercle Proudhon dared to speak out, loudly and frequently, against the "capitalist regime." This caused no small amount of consternation in conservative circles. Rumors circulated that the Cercle Proudhon, supported by funds from capitalists (through the Action française), was openly promoting anticapitalism.[50] Valois was forced to publish a *mise au point* in the *Cahiers*, where he explained the "anticapitalism" of the Cercle. The document is revealing in its anticipation of much of the later national socialist rhetoric on the very same topic; it manages to display a genuine hostility to what it considers the excesses of capitalism, while steering clear of an attack on the capitalist mechanism per se.

Valois makes a distinction between "capitalism in production," which it would be foolish to contest, and the "capitalist regime." The latter is an aberration of the capitalist principle, born from its unnatural extension outside of the realm of production. A society that allows itself to be overwhelmed by laissez-faire principles invites disaster. "Thus religious life is diminished," according to Valois, "the working life degraded, the family destroyed, the foreign worker brought in, the natural resources exploited without restraint, the political institutions transformed into organs of coercion in order to increase the excessive output of capital. In everything the national interest is gravely compromised."[51]

The problem, as Valois conceived it, is thus more than economic: it is more properly political, for the political structure of the society is unable to contain capitalism within its "natural" bounds. This brings Valois back to that favorite theme of the Cercle Proudhon: antidemocracy. Democracy, as has been seen, encourages all license and breaks down all sense of responsibility. It is no accident, according to Valois, that rampant materialism and unbridled acquisitiveness have grown up side by side with the rise of democracy. The bourgeoisie, the acquisitive class par excellence, once served valuable historical functions; that it has suffered a degeneration cannot be laid, as some have attempted, at its door: "Is this degradation the product of a vice inherent in the bourgeoisie? This passion for gold and the passion for pleasure . . . , are they the normal passions of the bourgeoisie?" Valois asked. His answer was a categorical no. "It would be greatly unjust to charge the French bourgeois with these vices. The truth is that the evil is of an entirely political nature. It is engendered by democratic life, which gives the will to power antisocial aims. Historic democracy, which has destroyed the professional and regional bodies of the nations, has made the bourgeois—organizer of production, exchange, and economy—a merchant of gold and a denationalized pleasure-seeker."[52] Thus, in the end, the problem of plutocracy is a problem of political mismanagement: the proper political regime would be one that would destroy the "capitalist regime" and return capitalism to the confines of production.

What that proper political regime would be was never seriously in question. At the outset of the Cercle Proudhon, Valois liked to advertise the variety of opinions represented. Yet those who came regularly to meetings were for the most part royalists; those who were not were already on their way. No one was very surprised when Albert Vincent and Edouard Berth announced their conversion to monarchy. But this is not to argue that there was no serious interchange about the *kind* of monarchy that would be promoted by the Cercle Proudhon. The "social monarchy" that emerged from the Cercle Proudhon bore unmistakable Maurrassian traits, yet it was also fundamentally different: the men of the Cercle could legitimately honor Maurras as an inspiration and also argue that their "social monarchy" was a product of discussion, debate, and compromise.

The obvious Maurrassian input was the monarch with limited functions. He would be the protector of the national interest but would still allow a great deal of "real liberty" to those intermediate bodies that would make for the health of the nation. Maurras's concept of monarchy was decidedly nontotalitarian, and for the men of the Cercle this was its greatest attraction. Berth claimed that he yielded none of his syndicalist principles to come to the monarchy: Maurras's vision of monarchy was perfectly compatible with syndicalism. "It would be," Berth explained, "an antiparliamentary Monarchy, decentralized, hereditary, and traditional; namely, it would be a State that, instead of being abstract, would be incarnated in a family, that is, in what is most concrete, most lively, most realistic: it would be the State made Man, no longer this monstrous bureaucratic abstraction, the modern democratic State."[53]

This clear Maurrassian contribution sat rather uneasily with another aspect of the "social monarchy" as conceived of by the Cercle Proudhon, an aspect clearly Sorelian in inspiration—albeit Sorelianism filtered through Valois and Berth. As has been noted, Valois, from his very first meeting with Maurras, had insisted on antagonism, a system of mutual constraint, as a necessary first principle of the new society. Although Valois had been converted to Maurras's notion of limited but responsible monarchy, he had been unimpressed by what he considered Maurras's lack of imagination as it concerned social dynamics. Maurras could only repeat the hackneyed conservative call for social peace. To Valois, each class in society could contribute its fullest share only if it was spurred on by pressure from other classes: capitalists would benefit from the stimulus of organized syndicats demanding full remuneration for workers, whereas workers, for their part, could test their mettle only if the capitalists they opposed were worthy adversaries. The king, whose function it would be to oversee, would trouble to make sure that the game was fairly played. Rather than impose the stagnation of social peace, he would benefit by this orderly antagonism of a society in tension.

This propensity to raise antagonism to a first principle was reflected in a short position paper published in the *Cahiers*. After much discussion, the members of the Cercle had drawn up a sketch of the kind of monarchy they envisioned. The king was to have three functions: responsibility for the police and national defense; protection of the state from the plutocracy; defense of the independence of the intermediate bodies. The "republics," or local provincial authorities, not only would jealously guard their liberties in an abstract sense but would be "fully armed" so, if need be, they could defend their liberties with force. The syndicalist organizations under the new monarchy would likewise be proudly independent. Although the state would always have responsibility for public order, the "worker republics" would know their interests and be able to defend them: "If some forms of violence are necessary to them," Valois wrote, "the worker republics will go . . . beyond the will of the royal State and oppose it with all their force: equilibrium, it must be repeated, is born of antagonism."[54]

In these respects—the limited central authority and the antagonistic pluralism—the national socialism of the Cercle Proudhon revealed itself different from the many later varieties of national socialism tending toward totalitarianism. Yet there is no imperative that a national socialism be necessarily totalitarian. The national socialism of the Cercle Proudhon reflected its Maurrassian and Sorelian legacies: it was decentralized and pluralistic.

Clearly, the vision of the future monarchist society emerging from the Cercle Proudhon was something quite different from the version being promoted in the columns of the *Action française*. In earlier days, Valois had gone out of his way to square his social theories with La Tour du Pin's. From the beginning this was an impossible task; but that he had made the effort revealed the desire not to alienate the more traditional elements. However, the excitement of the discussions at the Cercle Proudhon left these eager "neo-Proudhonians" little disposed to be so accommodating. It is significant, as Pierre Andreu has observed, that the name La Tour du Pin was never mentioned in the *Cahiers du Cercle Proudhon*.

It has already been noted that at the *Revue critique* there had been growing opposition to Valois, his enthusiasms, and his camp followers. This opposition, although it resented Valois's activities at the *Revue critique*, was not any happier with the Cercle Proudhon. Jean Rivain, who knew La Tour du Pin personally and was a devout Catholic, was especially enraged. By early 1912 the police were reporting a serious split between the young royalists siding with Valois and those siding with Rivain.[55] The split was important because each man was influential in a different way. Rivain was a member of the executive committee of the Action française and, through marriage, connected with a most prestigious family.

Valois's influence came largely through the amount of support he was rallying to the cause. He represented the kind of dynamism that had allowed the Action française to prevail over the old royalists in the controversy with the pretender's political bureau.

Maurras, who from the beginning had distrusted Valois, was apparently realistic enough to sense that a disavowal of Valois, although it might be ideologically satisfying, would be inopportune. It would certainly go a long way toward wrecking whatever capital the royalists had succeeded in building up on the Left. For a time, at least, Maurras was tolerant of the Cercle Proudhon. Despite increasing criticism, the Cercle Proudhon continued its meetings and its controversial *Cahiers* through 1912 and 1913.

But pressures mounted. In January 1914 it became public knowledge that on the advice of La Tour du Pin himself Rivain had left the Action française. The Catholic press was in an uproar over everything connected with the Cercle Proudhon: Valois, Berth, and their "paganism"—especially their public appreciations of Nietzsche and Proudhon, neither of whom were great favorites in clerical circles. The January–February 1914 issue of the *Cahiers du Cercle Proudhon* (it was to be the last) was one long answer to the Catholic critics.

The leadership of the Action française did not act directly against Valois. Instead, they turned against Henri Lagrange. Lagrange, with his sizable student entourage, was an important point of support for Valois and the Cercle Proudhon within the Action française. The immediate issue was a feud between Lagrange and Pujo. To settle the matter, Maurras arranged a mock trial where Lagrange would be judged. According to Dimier, the trial was both "cruel and ridiculous." Maurras portrayed himself as a government official distracted from the national interest, whereas he cast Lagrange in the role of Dreyfus—guilty of sowing the seeds of dissension. The "trial," according to Dimier, turned into a bitter and emotional scene, one that left deep scars.[56] Valois, from the perspective of 1928, remembers it as "a rather deep schism"; it meant the expulsion from the Action française of Lagrange and his radical student followers, the natural clientele of the Cercle Proudhon. Valois speculated that, had not the war intervened, there would have been another schism by 1915, this time with the rest of the Cercle Proudhon.[57]

The difficulties encountered by the Cercle Proudhon were not limited to the Action française. By the end of 1912, scarcely a year after its founding, there was a rather abrupt change in the political atmosphere. Between 1908 and 1911 this atmosphere had been favorable to propaganda for a Left-Right alliance: government-syndicalist clashes had been frequent and bloody. After 1911, however, new issues emerged, deepening the gulf between nationalists and syndicalists. The most obvious was the debate over military preparedness. The effort to extend military service from two to three years became the focal point of French politics. Royalists supported the three-year bill; syndicalists stood against it.

Of course, this was not a problem for the Cercle Proudhon alone. All aspects of the Action française initiative toward the revolutionary Left were rather suddenly in jeopardy. The Action française was slow to give up the ground that it felt it had gained in its worker campaign. But it found its options severely limited. During the year 1912, royalist pretensions of a community of interest with syndicalism became steadily less credible, and the Cercle Proudhon, tied to the Action française by the bond of their common nationalism, was carried along helplessly by events. The collapse of the Action française efforts toward an alliance with the Left, detailed in the next chapter, was no less the final blow to the hopes of the Cercle Proudhon.

A first important indication that a breakdown in royalist-syndicalist relations was imminent came with the unraveling of a highly exotic intrigue seemingly unconnected with the great issues of war and peace. This intrigue came to be known in the leftist press as the Bintz affair. The startling end product of this affair—which began in the pettiest of circumstances—was the formal exclusion from the syndicalist movement of two men upon whom the royalists had placed such large hopes—Messieurs Janvion and Pataud.

Decline and Collapse

Victor Bintz, a young plumber by trade and a revolutionary syndicalist by avocation, found himself in jail after trying to put some of his ideas into practice during a strike. While still in jail, he was drafted into the army, which had little success in dampening his revolutionary ardor. Bintz was in and out of the stockade, always protesting with a great deal of vehemence that he had been victimized on account of his beliefs. Sometime in late 1911, while Bintz was on a hunger strike, his commanding officer decided to send the troublesome soldier to a disciplinary unit.

Bintz's cause was taken up by both the *Bataille syndicaliste* and the *Guerre sociale*, where the general conviction prevailed that young militants professing revolutionary idealism were not always treated evenhandedly by the French officer corps. Bintz's case, however, seemed well on its way to being settled when a staff member of the *Guerre sociale* was promised by the military that any disciplinary action against Bintz would be dropped if the *Bataille syndicaliste* and the *Guerre sociale* would agree to silence the press campaign against the officer in question. At this point, Bintz—who, even his defenders admitted, was less than an engaging personality —sabotaged the efforts being made on his behalf. He refused to obey an order, and his commanding officer used the incident to take his revenge; Bintz was reordered to the disciplinary unit. Thus, matters stood at an uncomfortable impasse: the campaign supporting Bintz had been stopped on the prompting of a staff member of the *Guerre sociale*, yet the young syndicalist-soldier was being sent away with little prospect of release in the near future.[1]

All of this had not passed unnoticed at *Terre libre* where Emile Janvion kept one ear to the ground attuned to just such distant rumblings.[2] Despite the generally unfavorable reaction to the anti-Semitic rally of April 1911, Janvion continued with his characteristic stridency to press the argument that only treachery and conspiracy could properly explain the precipitous decline of revolutionary élan in the syndicalist movement. Now, with the Bintz case, Janvion once again could raise the oft-repeated charge that Jewish and Masonic influences had infiltrated and subverted syndicalism. As early as March 1912, Janvion published a letter from Bintz to *L'Humanité*, in which Bintz criticized the Socialist paper for its reticence in his hour of need. Contemplating the polemical potential of the case, Janvion announced magnanimously that *Terre libre* would make no accusations but would wait for answers as to why the *Guerre sociale* and the *Bataille syndicaliste* had "mysteriously" stopped their campaign in favor of Bintz. We at *Terre libre*, Janvion wrote, do not want to think that the fact that Bintz's commanding officer was a Freemason "would alone have deflected from him the legitimate anger of the syndicalists."[3]

Janvion spent the next several months propagandizing and organizing, raising the Bintz case to the status of an affair. By the end of 1912 he had formed with other syndicalists, including Emile Pataud, a Bintz committee, which promised not only to work for Bintz's release but to expose the Masonic intrigue lurking behind it.

The issue was not inconsequential. Even before the Bintz affair, Janvion's anti-Masonic campaign, promoted from the pages of *Terre libre*, could not easily be dismissed as the rantings of an isolated figure without real influence. Hostility to Freemasonry, which was viewed as contrary to the spirit of class struggle, ran deep on the French Left, and it was clearly becoming more pronounced. Many of the charges raised by Janvion were being widely echoed, albeit in more nuanced tones, and by 1912 the whole issue of Masonic influence in both socialist and syndicalist circles had taken on serious proportions. At the Socialist congress held at Lyon in February 1912, for example, there was a long and impassioned debate over whether or not a Socialist could be a Freemason. The final vote was a defeat for the anti-Masonic forces, but the margin of victory was uncomfortably close.[4] There were strong pressures for a kind of revolutionary purism: Freemasonry was class collaboration and fraternization with Radicals, and, as such, should be condemned. The Socialists, at least since the Dreyfus affair, had not carried their anti-Masonism to the anti-Semitic conclusions reached by Janvion, but the two issues had become so connected that, to many, anti-Masonism seemed only a stalking-horse. Janvion's position, as one party member argued before the congress, was only a logical extension of the anti-Masonic campaign. He warned that if Socialists were willing to purge Masons now they had better be ready to purge Jews a few years hence.[5]

Within the syndicalist movement, the Masonic issue was an even greater source of friction. By 1912 certain syndicats were bitterly divided between Masonic and anti-Masonic forces, virtually paralyzing effective action.[6] At the Paris bourse du travail, renamed the Union des syndicats de la Seine, the leaders were constantly harassed because of their association with the Freemasonry.[7] Janvion's propaganda took special aim at Jules Bled, a secretary of the Union des syndicats and long an influential syndicalist leader.

By late 1912 Janvion's Bintz committee claimed to have evidence that Bled was actually behind the failure to have Bintz released. According to the committee, a high-ranking officer and Freemason had been irritated by the commotion made in the syndicalist press over Bintz and had sent word to his Masonic brother Bled that the campaign in the *Bataille syndicaliste* would have to stop. Bled, according to the committee, passed the word on to Edouard Sené, the journalist who had launched the original campaign for Bintz at the *Bataille syndicaliste*, and as a result Bintz was sacrificed to higher Masonic interests.[8]

To expose this "Masonic crime in syndicalism," the Bintz committee sponsored a series of rallies where Janvion and Pataud were the featured speakers.[9] By early December 1912 the furor raised by the charges from the committee was sufficient to force the *Bataille syndicaliste* to print a mise au point by Edouard Sené. Bled had indeed come to see him, Sené admitted, but it was at the beginning of the affair and had nothing to do with the decision to stop the campaign in favor of Bintz; the decision to stop the campaign had come only after Bintz had requested it. But then Sené, who claimed to be anti-Masonic himself, agreed with Janvion that there had been a "Masonic crime." According to Sené, the Masonic crime had been committed not in Paris by Bled but by a Freemason union president in the town where Bintz was stationed. This union president, because of his fraternal bonds with Bintz's commanding officer, had refused to stage a demonstration for Bintz. Despite Sené's criticism of the Bintz committee for inventing "somber conspiracies," his mise au point hardly laid the issue to rest.[10]

The scope of the affair, however, had been extended even before Sené's mise au point. Almost by accident, it seems, Janvion had picked up a juicy scrap of information while on one of his frequent visits to the offices of the *Action française*: Sené had been exchanging information with the royalists on the Bintz case. In fact, Maurice Pujo, for a time, had had in his possession parts of the *Bataille syndicaliste*'s dossier on Bintz.[11] Janvion and Pataud, who themselves had been castigated by the *Bataille syndicaliste* for playing "the game of reaction," were ecstatic over this new revelation. Publicly, they used it to discredit Sené and the *Bataille syndicaliste*, while privately various members of the Bintz committee demanded explanations from the *Bataille syndicaliste*.[12] Finally members of the *Bataille syndicaliste*, including Jouhaux himself, were forced to meet with Pujo in order to clear up Sené's involvement. Meanwhile, Janvion was sending letters to the *Bataille syndicaliste*—letters he demanded to be published—further incriminating Bled.[13]

The situation, from the perspective of the syndicalist leadership, was now clearly alarming. Faced with increasingly factious disputes on the issue of Freemasonry and compromised by charges of collusion with the royalists, the syndicalist leaders found it impossible to maintain their long-standing pose of impervious silence vis-à-vis Janvion and his allies. But just as the full disruptive possibilities of the Bintz affair seemed about to unfold, Janvion and Pataud made what proved to be a fatal miscalculation. On 2 January 1913, with some of the members of the Bintz committee, they forced their way into a staff meeting held in the offices of the *Bataille syndicaliste*. Janvion demanded to be told why a certain article sent by him had not been published; as the answer was not to his satisfaction, he physically attacked the director of the *Bataille syndicaliste*, Charles Gogumus. Janvion, Pataud, and their followers then began to sack the offices in search of the Bintz dossier, which they found and took with them.[14]

The next day the *Bataille syndicaliste* announced a general assembly of all shareholders in order to clear up the Bintz affair definitively. Both Pataud and Janvion refused to attend, but other members of the Bintz committee were there ready to defend their work. Although there was almost unanimous castigation of Janvion and Pataud for their methods in obtaining the Bintz dossier, there was also a good deal of serious questioning of the role played by the *Bataille syndicaliste* in the Bintz matter. The issue was soon narrowed to Janvion's motivation: the partisans of the Bintz committee argued that he only wanted to get to the bottom of the "Masonic intrigue," whereas the staff of the *Bataille syndicaliste* claimed that he was out to deliberately discredit the syndicalist daily. At a crucial point in the debate, Merrheim read a letter from a militant, whom all factions trusted, testifying that Janvion had in the past attempted to convince the editors of the anarchist *Libertaire* to attack the *Bataille syndicaliste*. Given the reaction to the letter, there was little for the committee to do but to disavow Janvion and Pataud and demand that Sené be sanctioned for his collusion with the Action française. Merrheim assured the assembled shareholders that Sené had been reprimanded as soon as his act had been known to the editorial staff of the paper. As for Janvion and Pataud, a motion was passed declaring that both had *"placed themselves, definitively, outside of the organized working class."*[15]

The staff of the *Bataille syndicaliste*, obviously embarrassed by the affair, seemed little inclined to discuss the matter further. It was left to Gustave Hervé, in an article in the *Guerre sociale*, to spell out the lessons to be learned from the affair by the revolutionary Left. The article, seen in retrospect, is a revealing commentary on the degree to which involvement with royalist themes and personalities had contributed to the *crise du syndicalisme*. There was, of course, no small amount of irony in the fact that Hervé—whose *Guerre sociale* had so consistently urged a policy of *politique du pire*— should be the one to draw up the somber balance sheet.

First and most obvious, Hervé wrote, was the damage done by the anti-Masonic campaign to the morale of the Left. Comrades of good faith had been lured into the tempting thesis that the working class had been caught in the tentacles of "an octopus," while *Libre Parole* and the *Action française* stood cheering from the sidelines: "The gang of those who invaded the offices of the B.S. [*Bataille syndicaliste*] and, who, in reality, are better than their wild gesture would indicate, were convinced—Lord, protect us from idées fixes! —that the B.S. . . . had abandoned Bintz to the furor of the military bullies in order to please the Freemasonry. Oh! the disease of suspicion, verging with some people on a persecution complex, one will never know the evil it has operated in France at all times among people with advanced ideas!"[16]

A second lesson, according to Hervé, could be drawn from Sené's behavior. Sené was a "very respectable" comrade, but his association with the royalists was inexcusable. His actions revealed more than individual indiscretion; they were part of a general pathology of the syndicalist movement, which propagates "the reactionary sophism according to which the Republic is often worse than monarchy." This attitude, wrote Hervé, whatever it might mean elsewhere, was a dangerous game in France, where "monarchy is only, and can only be, the most reactionary and the most ferocious form of capitalist conservation."[17]

The exclusion of Janvion and Pataud was, of course, a serious defeat for the Action française. With the help of their intermediaries they had twice tried to spark campaigns that might have opened the working class to royalist propaganda, and twice they had failed. In 1911, with the opportunity open for them to hitch their anti-Semitism to the mounting anti-Rothschild campaign, they had been sabotaged by the unexpected defection of Hervé and his *Guerre sociale*. Now, with a promising anti-Masonic drive reaching high gear, Janvion and Pataud, through their ill-considered raid of the offices of the *Bataille syndicaliste*, had given their enemies the ammunition to destroy them. Clearly, the men of the revolutionary Left upon whom the royalists had depended had disappointed them: Hervé and the men of the *Guerre sociale* were less desperately revolutionary than the royalists had calculated, Janvion and Pataud simply less capable.

But royalist initiatives toward the Left did not run aground primarily because of personalities. Other forces, more important than personalities and specific events, were working to ensure that an alliance of the radical Right and the radical Left would fail to coalesce.

The worker initiative had always been a three-cornered affair: royalists in one corner flirting with the revolutionary socialists at the *Guerre sociale* in another and with the revolutionary syndicalists in a third. Viewed from the perspective of the Action française, this triad was a revolutionary one, each part exerting its force upon a moribund Republic, each drawing upon the energies of an increasingly adamant clientele. The testimony of the police and the republican press from 1908 to 1911 can be called upon to show that there was at least some truth in this royalist boast. Not since the Dreyfus affair had the Republic been surrounded by so many enemies who were so vocal, so organized, and seemed, to many of the best minds, to be so much the wave of the future. Yet 1912 and 1913 brought with them a rather surprising reversal of this situation. By 1913 all three of these movements had modified their attitude toward the Republic. Hervéism, royalism, and revolutionary syndicalism had, each in its own way, reached an accommodation with the Third Republic—an accommodation that in the end eliminated the possibility of a serious conspiracy to overthrow it.

The most dramatic reversal was that of Gustave Hervé. His accommodation with the Republic came piecemeal, but when completed it was so total as to leave his closest associates incredulous. The first stages of his turnabout were already discernible in his frightened reaction to the Bernstein riots and the Janvion-Pataud rally.

Those of his friends who waited for him to turn his polemical fire back toward the Republic once the dust had settled in the wake of these events were disappointed. Hervé, now convinced that the nationalist revival was a serious threat to the Republic, continued to work from his prison cell to organize the Left into a new coalition. By midsummer 1911, he was worried not only by the Action française but also by the new lease on life given to other rightist groups by the nationalist upsurge—most notably to the Bonapartists.[18] Hervé observed that in the large-circulation Paris press one now spoke openly of the need to end the parliamentary quagmire and to find "a master" to put the French house in order. All the while, Hervé lamented, the one force that could head off such a take-over remained in a state of torpor. "An eminent person" in "the working-class world," Hervé confided, was recently saying to one of our friends: "Whether Prince Victor Napoléon or the Republic, who gives a damn?"[19]

In order to dispell this lethargy, the *Guerre sociale* sponsored another rally featuring Sébastien Faure in late June.[20] But the cutting edge of the counteroffensive led by the *Guerre sociale* was to be the Jeunes Gardes. By early summer the *Action française* and the *Guerre sociale* were threatening each other with their respective shock troops. Following an article by Maurice Pujo in the *Action française*, insinuating that the Jeunes Gardes were being subsidized by the police, the *Guerre sociale* announced that Pujo would no longer be able to speak in Paris.[21] Though the *Guerre sociale* did not make good on its threat, it did succeed in challenging the royalists' freedom of action.[22] What was more, it introduced a new tension between reactionaries and revolutionaries, a tension conspicuously absent in the preceding several years.

By mid-1912, with the nationalist clamor reaching its peak, Hervé was publicly criticizing the Confédération générale du travail for its overtly hostile attitude toward electoral politics. Hervé justified the *Guerre sociale*'s long-standing use of the very same arguments on tactical grounds: we were simply reacting against the overemphasis on electoralism then prevalent in the Socialist party. But now, with the parliamentary institutions of the Republic in such low esteem, Hervé concluded, the pendulum had swung the other way.[23]

Hervé took the Rousseau bicentennial, held in the summer of 1912, as a sign of the times. The Camelots had rudely upset the republican-sponsored festivities, and, Hervé lamented, no counter-demonstration had even been attempted. But, as a report on the Latin Quarter by a student leader made all too clear, counterdemonstrations were becoming difficult for the Left. With nationalism the fashion of the day, the ranks of the nationalist leagues were swelled with recruits.[24] What was urgently needed, Hervé argued, was a reconciliation between republicans and the working class. He made an impassioned plea calling for republicans to make their peace with workers, who, although abused, had not lost touch with their roots. "The socialist and revolutionary people," he wrote, "despite the disgust they feel for the *radicaille*, will not let the Republic drown, for they are the Republic; the Republic is the flesh of their flesh; they founded it with their blood, and it remains the necessary condition to the accomplishment of their dream of equality and social justice."[25]

On 14 July 1912 Hervé, who had been in prison for over two years, was released under the terms of a general amnesty. Responding with a clenched fist to this gesture of reconciliation, Hervé saluted his erstwhile republican jailers with a banner head in the *Guerre sociale*: "Et je vous dis: Merde!" Beneath this defiant posture, however, was a different Hervé. Within a week the onetime enfant terrible of the Left and archenemy of militarism had announced two "tactical" shifts in the *Guerre sociale*'s revolutionary strategy. First, admitting the damage done to the socialist ranks by his past vehemence, he promised to cease attacking all fellow socialists. Second, he revised his antimilitary strategy. Rather than attack militarism from the sidelines, revolutionaries must join the army and learn from it. Hervé's rationale for this was that a revolution could only be carried out by the force of arms and the best laboratory for this was the military itself.[26] Hervé's claim that all this was consistent with his original revolutionary position rang somewhat hollow—both to contemporaries and to later scholars. Maurice Rotstein, a sympathetic student of Hervé's career, has concluded that by the summer of 1912 "there was, in truth, no longer anything revolutionary in his politics."[27]

After 1912 Hervé's evolution continued apace. First, he came into the camp of those willing to fight a defensive war. By the summer of 1914 he had become a vocal advocate of preparedness. And, as the last hopes of peace flickered out, Hervé voted against a motion for a general strike.[28] The final ironic touch came only in January 1916 when the *Guerre sociale* was rechristened the *Victoire*, and Hervéists and royalists, who as late as 1909 had toasted the demise of the Republic, were once again united—this time as its staunchest defenders.

With the opening of the second Moroccan crisis in July of 1911, an important turning point had been reached in French preoccupations. The period from about 1906 to mid-1911 was one of unremitting civil strife. Confrontations between government and worker mark the epoch: Villeneuve–Saint–Georges in 1908; the postal strike in 1909; the rail workers' revolt in 1910. Starting with the second Moroccan crisis, French attentions turned toward the increasing threat of war. This put the Action française in an uncomfortable position. Royalists could easily join internal opposition to the Republic, but could they maintain their opposition when the threat was external? The facile distinction between a hated Republic and a beloved France—such a favorite of Maurras before 1911—was put to the test.

At first the Action française seemed determined to hold its ground. At the outset of 1912, the police were convinced that the Camelots were building strength for a coup d'état.[29] Further, the Action française was hostile to the avowedly patriotic ministry of Poincaré, which took office in January 1912.[30] For some on the Right, the fact that many republicans—some with shaky past associations on the issue of patriotism—were now spouting nationalistic slogans was a victory. For the royalists, it was still only a source of irritation.

By mid-1912, however, there were signs that the Action française was sagging under the pressure of events. Daudet's meetings in working-class areas, although they continued to be numerous, subtly shifted their theme. Daudet had embarked upon a series of articles in the *Action française* alerting his countrymen to the unhealthy number of Germans in French industry. This new theme began to be the central motif of his speeches. From the Republic as enemy of all workers Daudet had subtly gravitated to the German as enemy of all Frenchmen.

The specter of Germany would, from 1912 on, begin to color all issues taken up by the royalists. A maritime strike in mid-1912 found the royalists less prosyndicalist than was their wont. Though they tried to separate themselves from their "conservative colleagues," who could only castigate workers, they nevertheless had to view the strike from a "national" point of view. Where before they had seen this kind of conflict as antirepublican kindling, they now showed a new concern with its deleterious effects upon the nation. Germany, the royalists concluded, had been the sole beneficiary of the strike.[31]

The issue that most revealed the royalists' increasing accommodation with patriotic republicans was military preparedness. They shrank before the inescapable conclusions of their own logic: a military defeat would bring about the most propitious time for the fall of the Republic and the institution of new political forms. The members of the Action française, by declaring themselves in favor of raising the period of military service to three years, broke in several respects with their long-standing policies. First, they brought themselves into the parliamentary arena—a place they had vowed never to enter—by actively supporting the three-year bill. Second, once the bill was passed, they came to the side of the Republic by defending the new law against those who wished to revise it. Finally, and most importantly for this study, their support of the Three-Year Law led, first, to strains and, ultimately, to a break with their policy of accord with the working class.

As early as September 1912, police spies reported that royalist policy was being pulled in divergent directions. The vigorous stirrings of other nationalist groups, most notably the Bonapartists, made the royalists fear that attention might be drawn away from them. When the Bonapartists organized a demonstration celebrating the departure of a new class for military service, the royalists felt pressured to outdo them. Pujo suggested sending the Camelots to disrupt an antimilitary rally of the Left rather than organizing a counterdemonstration; at the rally the young royalists could heckle those who would dare to dishonor France. Such a plan, the police reasoned, would put the Action française one up on the Bonapartists. Royalist leadership, however, was wary of the idea because it would interfere with the "good relations" that had been maintained with the revolutionary Left. Because the royalists still valued these "good relations," the police ventured, the Camelots, at least for the time being, would not be sent to antimilitary rallies.[32]

Meanwhile, throughout the fall and winter, the issue of preparedness increasingly took over the center stage of French politics, first with the presidential election campaign and then with ministerial activity in favor of the Three-Year Law. The Action française proved itself on both counts to be less immune to the lure of republican politics than its theories would admit. Although there seems to have been no formal alliance between royalists and Poincaré, the propreparedness candidate, there was, as Maurras later delicately put the matter, a "reciprocal circumspection based on national interest."[33] The immediacy of a patriotic president of the Republic seemed suddenly more alluring than the more distant dream of a king of France.

Once Poincaré had been installed at the Elysée, events moved swiftly. Within weeks, a three-year bill was before the Chamber of Deputies, and France was in the midst of a debate that would end only with the outbreak of war. Once again, royalists allowed themselves to be seduced onto a territory that, had they followed the dictates of their earlier pronouncements, would have been out of bounds. Without doubt, as the royalists had preached, all parliamentary debate was a sham and must be exposed as such. Yet the royalists took uncommon interest in the debate over the three-year bill.

However unconsciously, the Action française was in the process of reordering its priorities. By early 1913 it was apparent to all that national security was taking first place—before the worker alliance, even before a royal restoration.

The syndicalists were also forced to take sides. They had long argued that parliamentary debate was no substitute for direct action and that syndicalists must energetically resist the temptation of being drawn into alliances with socialists. Syndicalist leaders had not hesitated to line up behind Delaisi's vicious campaign against Jaurès and *L'Humanité*. Yet, now, circumstances began to limit options. The first press reaction to the ministry's three-year bill was ominous: not only the Right but also the Center and important segments of the Radical party were showing signs of rallying behind the government. It was abundantly clear that a rapprochement between the various sections of the Left was a precondition for any effective opposition to the bill's passage.

In late February and early March, the *Bataille syndicaliste* made it plain that syndicalist leaders were moving toward a working agreement with Socialists. Symptomatic of both the strength of the sentiment in favor of the three-year bill and the willingness of syndicalists to forget old animosities was an incident occurring in early March. Jaurès, already a symbol of resistance to the three-year bill, was greeted by an unfriendly crowd in Nice. The *Bataille syndi-*

caliste observed that *L'Humanité* had tried to whitewash the incident by claiming that Jaurès had been welcomed in Nice. It was no good, the *Bataille syndicaliste* claimed, to pretend: Jaurès was actually hooted and scorned by the "nationalist hordes." We have had our differences with Jaurès, the syndicalist daily admitted, but we respect him as a courageous and honorable man; if those who proclaim themselves nationalists had any sense they would realize "that he [Jaurès], whom they insult, is one of the best representatives of the classical culture of our country, whose purest traditions he protects and perpetuates."[34]

The real turning point came with the announcement of an important rally at the Panthéon against the "military panic." The meeting was of the kind long avoided by the syndicalists. It would include, besides syndicalists, leftist reformers of all stripes. No one, not even the royalists, could be deceived. The struggle against the three-year bill was reconstituting the old Dreyfusard alliance. All its components would be accounted for at the Panthéon: the academic and literary intelligentsia, the socialists (parliamentary and otherwise), and the organized working class. The *Bataille syndicaliste* let it be known that it would brook no nationalist opposition. It pointedly invited all its comrades to be on hand and not to hesitate, if need be, to "bring to their senses the fanatics" who would be tempted to disrupt the meeting.[35]

The royalists' hand was forced. They would be able to avoid a clash with syndicalists only by withdrawing from the field. Instead, they took up the syndicalist challenge directly: they sent Camelots to infiltrate the Panthéon meeting. When the Socialist Francis Pressensé rose to speak, the Camelots tried to spark an antisocialist reaction. The move failed, and a pitched battle between Jeunes Gardes and Camelots ensued. The numerically inferior Camelots were subdued and led unceremoniously from the hall.[36]

The next day, the *Bataille syndicaliste* emphasized the significance of the evening: "The socialist students and the people have recovered the Latin Quarter." The syndicalist daily went on to warn the royalists: "The young brawling bourgeois will henceforth know that they cannot, with impunity, provoke the people." To add insult to injury, the *Bataille syndicaliste* suggested that a Camelot procession down the boulevard St. Michel, after their ouster from the Panthéon, had been protected by the police.[37]

The royalists took the role of the offended party. Pujo, in a letter that the *Bataille syndicaliste* refused to publish, was especially dismayed over the fact that the *Bataille syndicaliste* had invited workers to help defend Dreyfusard "intellectuals." The *Bataille syndicaliste* was in no mood to open a dialogue. It summarily dismissed Pujo's objections, reaffirmed that royalists and syndicalists could have nothing in common, and, in parting, charged Maurras with bad faith for underestimating attendance at a recent antimilitarist rally.[38]

The final break came on 30 March 1913 in a lead editorial by Maurice Pujo on the front page of the *Action française*. The current excitation against the three-year bill, Pujo contended, must be put into historical perspective. For the last few years, the working class had succeeded in freeing themselves from the tutelage of the politicians. After Clemenceau, Briand, and the part they had played in the repression of the working class, Dreyfusard politicians had little credit with workers, who proclaimed their independence from all politicians. With the debate aroused by the three-year bill, the politicians were seeing their chance to exploit the issue and thereby regain favor with the workers. Pujo noted that, when he had asked the *Bataille syndicaliste* for an explanation of the flagrant violation of the syndicalist policy of independence represented by the Panthéon meeting, the syndicalist daily had only replied that syndicalists did not heed counsel from outside the working class.

Given this blindness on the part of the syndicalist leadership, Pujo continued, royalists could only conclude that the syndicalist movement, so promising in its origins, had spent its force. Pujo went a step further. "Let us confess it frankly," he wrote, "syndicalism has no longer anything in common with working-class organization. What goes by this name is a political party, the internationalist party, in the tow of the Socialist party, itself tied, through the parliament, to the game of all the parties of the bourgeois Republic."[39]

With this repudiation, the Action française turned its full attention to the issue of preparing France for the war, a war that it now saw as inevitable. Syndicalism, so long an object of special consideration, began to melt indiscriminately into the negative side of the royalist equation, a side that Charles Maurras liked to call *l'anti-France*. The public campaign for worker support was drowned out by the issues of war and peace. Though conspiratorial activities continued, according to the police, at least throughout May of 1913,[40] the conspirators were working more from past momentum rather than on energy derived from the realities of the contemporary situation.

If patriotism proved to be an issue upon which the Action française found it difficult to compromise, the syndicalists seemed no less resolute in their commitment to avoid a European war. It was especially among the ultras, in whom the royalists had placed their highest hopes, that antimilitarism ran the deepest. One could plausibly argue that nowhere was the incompatibility of royalism and revolutionary syndicalism more manifest than here; and yet it was precisely this issue, in the light of developments after 1911, that was destined to take the center stage of French politics. In fact, the debate sparked by the three-year bill so dominated French politics from late 1912 down to the outbreak of the war that old alliances and old divisions faded before a single question: *troisannéiste ou antitroisannéiste?*

Yet behind this all-too-apparent issue of the three-year bill existed another, more subtle, reason why royalist-syndicalist alliance had become a moot question. Syndicalists, in a quite different way but with similar results, were making their own accommodation with the Republic. This accommodation did not, of course, involve an acceptance of the preparedness policy. On this issue syndicalists remained officially antimilitarist, and so vocally antimilitarist that a more profound accommodation was obscured—one that involved the abandonment of much of what was left of the revolutionary heritage of syndicalism. The years just before the war witnessed the continued evolution of syndicalism from a revolutionary movement committed to the overthrow of the republican state to a corporative one agreeing—whatever its continued allegiance to revolutionary rhetoric—to work within the existing political structure.[41]

The first public admission of any change came in the aftermath of Hervé's much discussed "conversion" in the summer of 1912. Hervéists, syndicalists themselves confessed, had been very influential in syndicalist circles; certain Hervéists hoped now to use this influence to convince syndicalists to take a more prorepublican stand. Syndicalists publicly refused, declaring their independence. But what must be noted is that they rejected not only Hervé's new position but, explicitly, his old position as well. They took pains to point out that Hervéism had been a mistake; it substituted the "theatrical gesture" for the organized action of the working class; it overemphasized violence, making it into an end in itself; finally, it overdid antimilitarism, turning it into antipatriotism. Hervéism, the syndicalists concluded, "is excess without a counterweight, without equilibrium. It is propaganda without a base. . . . It could not go on. . . . A change was inevitable."[42] One could well interpret this as a definitive rejection of the ultra position, which had so long been at odds with the politique leadership of the Confédération générale du travail. After all, adventurism and commitment to revolution could be separated. But, as was soon apparent, the men now in control of France's largest labor confederation were in the process of rejecting more than old-style Hervéism.

It has been noted above that by 1910 an entirely new concept of syndicalism was beginning to emerge and challenge the existing leadership at the Confédération générale du travail. Led by Merrheim and Delaisi, it proposed that workers imitate their capitalist counterparts and organize. The old syndicalist notion of "acting minorities" was giving way before the logic of a new principle, "organized majorities." This conception of syndicalism was more than a challenge to Hervé and Janvion; it was also a challenge to Griffuelhes and Pouget. For some time the politiques, who were running the Confédération générale du travail, talked of revolution, yet acted, for the most part, with prudence. They invariably explained this prudence by the necessities of the hour; the group forming around Merrheim and Delaisi claimed that this prudence followed naturally from weakness. The only remedy for this weakness, they claimed, would be a new kind of syndicalism built upon the realities of the new industrial world, not on the vagaries of nineteenth-century anarchy.

This new conception of syndicalism, this "new reformism," developed slowly. For a long time the new men were indistinguishable from the politiques with whom they worked. The launching of the *Vie ouvrière* in 1909, undertaken by Merrheim and his good friend Pierre Monatte, marked an important stage: Merrheim now had a platform for his studies that, although technical rather than polemical in style, became an indictment of existing syndicalist practice. Around the *Vie ouvrière* gathered a group of younger men, impressed by Merrheim's approach and desiring to carry it into practice.[43]

Open debate came only at the beginning of 1913 when Griffuelhes, representing old-style syndicalism, challenged the growing influence of Merrheim and his ideas. Griffuelhes claimed that the *crise du syndicalisme* was the result not of too little organization but of too much. He pointed to the huge Fédération des métaux where Merrheim was a secretary and where many of his ideas had been put into practice. The federation was a conglomerate of several federations brought together by Merrheim. Griffuelhes argued that, as it grew larger, it also grew more unwieldy: the factionalization that was a concomitant of growth ensured that decisive action would not be taken. In short, the federation had lost any revolutionary potential. Organization Merrheim-style would lead, at best, to social amelioration, never to social revolution.[44]

Debate intensified in the summer and fall of 1913. At an important syndicalist conference in midsummer, Merrheim argued for a "rectification of the aim." Just what this "rectification" involved, Monatte, writing in the *Vie ouvrière*, explained:

For years, the syndicalists have remained silent before the insurrectionary uproar of the *Guerre sociale*, old-style. This silence has cost the working-class movement dearly. For it has allowed an unfortunate confusion to settle not only in public opinion but also in the minds of many comrades. For several years, syndicalism and insurrectionism have appeared as one and the same conception.

Which sentiments have dictated this silence? With some, the fear to appear less revolutionary. With others, more numerous, the hope that, in spite of its vices, the insurrectionary publicity would stimulate, in the end, a spirit of revolt.

Were we not deceived enough? Here are the results in front of our eyes: tired people, disgusted with the movement, have thrown themselves aside;

others have cynically become turncoats. Yes, the whole Hervéist dema-
goguery could not lead to anything else. But we had to live that experience
till the end in order to be convinced of it. Will we heed this lesson?[45]

Whether consciously or not, Hervéism had become in the hands
of the new reformists a whipping boy for more than the insurrectionism of the *Guerre sociale*: it had become synonymous with much
of what was integral to old-style revolutionary syndicalism. All talk
of general strike, the syndicat as a combat unit, and the revolutionary mission of syndicalism was now suspect and associated with
Hervéist adventurism.

Despite all this, Merrheim and his friends did not admit that they
were changing revolutionary syndicalism in any fundamental way;
they vociferously defended themselves as guardians of the revolutionary tradition. Merrheim's "rectification," according to Monatte,
did not repudiate "one inch of the revolutionary ideal of syndicalism or of its methods."[46] Yet the distance traveled by the new
syndicalists from the old conception of revolutionary syndicalism
was inadvertently revealed by Monatte himself. "There will be a
true revolutionary situation," Monatte could write, "only when we
have set up strong economic organizations at home and reerected
in Europe the old International."[47]

The most important convert to this new-style syndicalism was
Léon Jouhaux, secretary-general of the Confédération générale du
travail. At both the syndicalist summer conference, where the "rectification" was announced, and later at the congress of the Fédération des métaux, where Merrheim was under fire, Jouhaux rose to
defend him. Two of Léon Jouhaux's more recent biographers, Bernard Georges and Denise Tintant—although hesitating to suggest
that Jouhaux had forsaken his revolutionary heritage—admit, by
indirection, how wide the gap had become between Merrheim's
syndicalism and old-style revolutionary syndicalism: "But it seems
fair to us to mention that, from now on, in Jouhaux's mind Merrheim's strategy outweighs Griffuelhes's; [he now subscribes to a]
conception of an organizing syndicalism, guiding great masses toward a positive action, of a documented syndicalism, more concerned with statistics than with meetings, *in short, a completely new*

conception, which takes the place of the old French tradition of revolutionary syndicalism where a handful of militants leads small numbers to the final assault against the bourgeoisie."[48]

Thus the long crise du syndicalisme was resolving itself on the eve of the war in favor of a new reformism, one that would concern itself more with organization and less with the maintenance of revolutionary élan: syndicalism, abandoning its claim to be the cell of the new society, was taking up the more modest position of a pressure group within the old. Despite its noisy opposition to the three-year bill, syndicalism, not unlike Hervéism and neoroyalism, found itself less and less disposed to plot the downfall of the Third Republic.

[12]

Conclusion

At the outset of this study, the reader was both warned and promised. The warning had to do with the extensive snooping that would be carried out in obscure corners. The project of a worker alliance was, after all, a failure. No one is fond of failures, especially those that with the passage of time seem to grow more incriminating. So a historian must go at a failure with patience; they seldom leap out as successes do. The reader can only be forewarned.

But failures—and here is the promise—can be revealing. To study them can add another perspective to the understanding of men and movements, whose complexities often demand more than one dimension. It is hoped that the assurances of larger historical concerns, made in the introduction, have become apparent to the reader through the narrative. It is fitting that some attempt be made to fill out and summarize the outlines of these concerns.

The period between 1906, when the issue of separation between the Church and the State began to exhaust itself, and 1912, when the debate over the three-year bill took center stage, French political life was dominated by persistent social conflicts. These conflicts first took serious proportions when the Clemenceau ministry decided to take a resolute stand against the growing influence and pretensions of revolutionary syndicalism. A series of dramatic confrontations between the government and the Confédération générale du travail followed. The government proved itself much the stronger party, handing the syndicalists a succession of crushing defeats. These ill-conceived confrontations led to a crisis of confidence within the syndicalist movement, a crisis that manifested itself in a decline of morale and a prolonged, serious examination of the revolutionary conscience. Partaking in this examination were not only syndicalists but also the greater revolutionary Left community, which had placed such large hopes in the revolutionary potential of the syndicalist movement.

It was in the midst of this disarray that the initiatives of the Action française were launched. Not a few revolutionaries, syndicalist and nonsyndicalist alike, were impressed with the audacity displayed by the Action française in its attacks against the Republic. Could revolutionaries pass over the royalist overtures, especially the royalist minimum program of an alliance against a common enemy? This study suggests that at several important points along the Left, desperate revolutionaries, with varying degrees of abandon, had come to feel that the royalists could be of service. It remains to summarize the degree of complicity from case to case and to assess the total impact of this complicity on the French Left on the eve of the First World War.

Outside of the syndicalist movement per se stood Gustave Hervé's *Guerre sociale*. The influence of this paper, and of Hervé in particular, in the prewar years has been admitted, however grudgingly, by both contemporaries and later historians. The *Guerre sociale*, more than any single syndicalist publication, and more than many combined, was a favorite source of information for those syndicalists who bothered to read more than the large-circulation dailies. As has been shown, it was in the pages of the *Guerre sociale* that flirtation with the royalists was first publicly contemplated. It was a first forum for Janvion's anti-Semitic drive; it played a pivotal role in Delaisi's anti-Rothschild campaign; and more importantly, it worked by every means available to break up what remained of the Dreyfusard alliance. This included propagating the notion—a notion later called by Hervé a "reactionary sophism"—that the Republic is often a worse enemy of the worker than the monarchy.

One measure of Hervé's success in this venture was his own frightened reaction in the wake of the Bernstein riots and the rising tide of anti-Semitism. His dramatic reversal in the spring of 1911 and his impassioned defense of "philo-Semitism" marked an important turning point in the royalist opening toward the Left. Had the *Guerre sociale* not reversed itself, Janvion, Pataud, and their allies would have had the most popular newspaper of the revolutionary Left as a platform. The forces of a resurgent nationalism and an embittered revolutionary Left would have been combined and sealed with the bonding agent of popular resentment against the Jew. This possibility—if police reports concerning the state of opinion at the *Guerre sociale* are correct—was certainly a real one. The staff of the *Guerre sociale* was deeply divided on whether to take an ethical stand against Janvion or, forgoing what some considered excessive concern for scruple, to proceed full throttle against the Republic. That scruple won the day can hardly be attributed to the logic of events; indeed, Hervé's logic, promoted from the pages of his newspaper until the spring of 1911, was consistently a logic predicated on politique du pire.

The most blatant case of collaboration with the royalists within the syndicalist movement was, of course, that of Emile Janvion. His *Terre libre* became an echo on the Left of royalist themes, including the most virulent form of anti-Semitism. He and many of his collaborators on the staff of *Terre libre* propagated what the Action française most wanted workers to hear: that the working class would be better off under a monarchy than under the Republic.

One might argue that Janvion was an isolated figure without influence in the syndicalist movement and that his *Terre libre* was a failure. There is certainly some truth in this. Although in 1908 Janvion was clearly an important figure in the Confédération générale du travail, his influence in the inner leadership cadres waned considerably in the next few years. With the ultra bid for control of the confederation defeated in 1909, the most outspoken ultra, Janvion, was relegated to a permanent opposition. *Terre libre* was at best a forum where the disgruntled could vent their spleen without restraint.

Yet, despite this isolation, Janvion's invectives were not without their effect. Had times been good and had the syndicalist leadership enjoyed the general confidence of the membership, Janvion might have presented no threat. But given the crisis of confidence shaking the very foundations of the syndicalist movement, the number of the discontented was at its peak and the vulnerability of the leadership high. It was significant that influential militants like

Benoît Broutchoux, former leader of the revolutionary faction of the miners' union, and Marius Blanchard, a secretary of the powerful metalworkers' federation, wrote for *Terre libre*. Even more important was the fact that the highly influential Parisian militant, Emile Pataud, joined in the anti-Rothschild activity and threatened to become the center of a serious anti-Semitic coalition.

One measure of Janvion's influence was the disrupting effect of his various campaigns on the syndicalist movement. It was openly admitted by syndicalist officials that Janvion's long-standing opposition to Freemasonry had a divisive influence. At the Union des syndicats de la Seine, for example, the issue of Freemasonry virtually paralyzed the leadership. Jules Bled, one of Janvion's favorite targets, ran into formidable opposition in January 1913 when he sought reelection as a secretary, a post that he had long held. The police report an "indescribable tumult" when his candidacy was posed. One of Janvion's allies there threatened to "rough up" all Masons; he, in turn, was asked to conserve his "ardor for the Camelots du roi."[1] Bled was finally elected but by a margin so small that he quit, returning only at the insistence of his friends. The issue was resolved only when he promised to leave the Freemasonry.[2] The incident was not an isolated one. Victor Griffuelhes, in a series of articles analyzing the crise du syndicalisme, lay no small part of the blame on the rancorous dispute over the Masonry, exemplified by Bled's problems. "Let us not hide it," he wrote; "the case of Bled marks a weakening of working-class consciousness, and the prestige of the C.G.T., already injured, would soon vanish if new manners were not introduced in syndicalist life."[3]

Even more important was Janvion's anti-Semitic campaign. There can be little doubt that the anti-Rothschild propaganda, first launched in the pages of the *Guerre sociale*, then given impetus by the Bernstein affair, threatened to explode into a full-scale outburst of anti-Semitism. The anxious warnings expressed by Hervé, Faure, and Naquet are testimony that the threat was perceived as real.

As for Janvion's motivation, it is problematic. One could make a case of him as someone who had lost his job and then his influence in the syndicalist movement and was therefore selling out to the highest bidder, which just happened to be the Action française. His own story appears more believable. He was a genuine revolutionary, embittered by the failure of revolution: first had come the treason of the Dreyfusards, then of the syndicalists. He was not the first, or the last, to perceive behind these failures the outlines of a dark conspiracy. Freemasons and Jews conspired to defeat the revolution; socialists and syndicalists were too timid to attack them directly. Only the Action française displayed the requisite courage.

The case of Francis Delaisi is of a different order. Unlike Janvion, he did not seem to take the royalists any more seriously than he took anti-Semitism; but both had their uses. When funds were desperately needed, the royalists did not drive a hard bargain. If in the popular imagination the Jew and Rothschild had unsavory connotations, they were fair game in the fight against one's enemies. Delaisi gives every indication of being a master at the art of *politique du pire*. Further, there cannot even be the pretense that Delaisi was an isolated figure. His vicious attacks against *L'Humanité*, complete with their anti-Semitic overtones, were not only celebrated at the *Guerre sociale* but underwritten by the highest officials of the syndicalist movement—Griffuelhes, Merrheim, Monatte, and Jouhaux.[4] Moreover, if police reports are correct, certain officials at the *Bataille syndicaliste* not only accepted badly needed royalist funds but even expected Delaisi to deliver them.[5]

Finally, beyond the open complicity of Janvion and Pataud, and the conspiratorial activities of Delaisi, there were the more commonplace examples of collaboration. The Bintz affair, for example, revealed that at least one member of the *Bataille syndicaliste* staff had exchanged documents with the royalists; he could have few illusions about how they would be used by the Action française. Further, the letter of Henri Lagrange shows beyond doubt that the Action française had contacts with the director of the *Bataille syndicaliste*, Charles Gogumus. The sensitive nature of the information exchanged suggests more than a casual relationship between royalists and syndicalist leaders.

Needless to say, many questions remain unanswered about royalist-syndicalist relations. What the police were able to piece together was far from the complete story. Very probably, however, a full reconstruction will not be possible. Syndicalist leaders themselves, as indicated earlier, were not of one mind about relations with the Action française; those who considered certain relations useful were not disposed to be candid even with other militants. Time has certainly not made them more ready to discuss such matters.

But this much is certain. The royalist initiative toward syndicalism was tied rather intimately with the crise du syndicalisme. The crisis, as this study has demonstrated, revealed syndicalism in a state of agonized transformation: old-style revolutionary methods had failed in practice, and concrete alternatives were emerging only slowly. This left many with a sense of desperation—a desperation that manifested itself in many ways: the willingness to collaborate openly in the case of a few, covertly in the case of a number of others. The persistent anti-Masonic issue and the low-grade anti-Semitism, both of which found support in the most responsible circles, were other manifestations of this desperation. Eruptions such as the Bintz affair and Delaisi's campaign against *L'Humanité* were but symptoms of a serious malaise, a malaise that the historians of heroic syndicalism have chosen largely to ignore.

This leads to a more general but related consideration. Even the casual reader of French historiography cannot help but be impressed by the still considerable power of the stereotypes surrounding the militant working-class leader and the professional socialist politician in prewar France. Tainted by careerism and corrupted by his proximity to the world of the bourgeoisie, the socialist politician typically suffers by contrast with the worker-militant, whose disdain for the political arena is akin to a badge of moral incorruptibility. An important corollary of this stereotype is the proverbial penchant of the worker-militant to preserve his independence, and the corresponding penchant of the socialist politician to deflect working-class energies into political channels—a deflection, it is usually implied, ultimately beneficial to the career of the politician in question. There are, to be sure, enough examples to give some substance to this stereotype; yet the picture remains unbalanced by the fact that the coin has seldom been turned. The seamier underside of heroic syndicalism has received little attention. Yet, as this study makes plain, socialist politicians were not always the perpetrators and syndicalists not always the victims; clearly there were cases where the lines of aggression were reversed. As has been demonstrated, certain revolutionary socialists outside of parliament and certain syndicalists adopted rather unabashed neo-Machiavellian tactics in dealing with parliamentary socialists.

This neo-Machiavellianism was, of course, inspired by devotion to the revolutionary cause. Some prominent revolutionary socialists and syndicalists alike had come to the conclusion that the revolutionary potential of the proletariat had been seriously endangered not so much by the reactionary Right or the status quo as by the moderate Left. The practical consequences of this position were best manifested in Francis Delaisi's activities: his attacks on reform socialists, however vicious, had their own justification, and politique du pire was a suitable weapon in the arsenal of the serious revolutionary conspirator. Revolutionary purism demanded that one rise above petit bourgeois moral considerations and such an attitude, judging by the support received by Delaisi, was widely shared.

This mentality would come to maturity only during the interwar period, when the full fire of the revolutionary Left was loosed upon reform socialism, and reform socialists became, in the charming idiom of that epoch, "social fascists." From this perspective, the years before 1914 contain important anticipations. Jean Jaurès became a first sacrificial "social fascist" before the letter; the campaign against *L'Humanité*, supported by official syndicalism, was a pale, nonetheless real, foretaste of the scurrility and ultimate destructiveness of a revolutionary purism that viewed ethical decency as a form of decadence.

To all appearances, the Action française represented everything dynamic in the new nationalism of the immediate prewar years. Singlehandedly, the men of the Action française took the concept of royalism, which by 1900 was becoming something of an anachronism, and pumped new life into it. Their publications, especially their newspaper, fashioned royalism into a respectable intellectual doctrine capable of rallying the elements of inchoate anti-Dreyfusard nationalism into a fighting creed. Further, they showed a willingness not only to write and talk about their creed but to take their case to the streets. Men of reason, they said of themselves, but men unafraid to put violence at the service of reason.

Their forward momentum seemed—at least to many contemporary observers—irresistible. They quickly overshadowed the existing nationalist organizations and made themselves arbiters of opinion on the Right. Even their king, to whom they had sworn loyalty, seemed incapable of harnessing their energies.

Yet, despite all this, the Action française was entering upon a crisis of its own. Maurras's promises of uncompromising activism had attracted a young following that took him at his word. A few of these young recruits had come from the Dreyfusard Left, disappointed by the stagnation they had found there; others, even younger, could have scarcely remembered the affair. Their relation to Maurras was, at first, complementary: he provided a sure doctrine, the unshakable belief in first principles; they provided a source of energy, the necessary muscle to make the Action française something more than a newspaper. Very soon, however, relations between Maurras and the younger men became strained.

Part of this strain came from Maurras's increasing hesitancy to risk the organization in questionable adventures. In his writing he was an advocate of the deliberate, even the provocative, act; but as has been seen, in critical situations Maurras inevitably leaned toward prudence. By 1910 he and others around him favoring caution were having difficulty controlling the Camelots du roi. As police reports made clear, if Maurras had had his way relations with the political bureau of the pretender might never have reached the breaking point.

Another, though related, difficulty was Maurras's tendency to rely on the abstraction of monarchy to solve all problems. His royalism became intransigent, a deus ex machina that would avoid either struggle or compromise. This tendency revealed itself especially in the spring of 1911 when many of the younger royalists were excited by the prospect of a Left-Right coalition based on the anti-Semitic issue. Gustave Téry, eager to find common ground, virtually pleaded with Maurras to come halfway so that a joint program might be formulated. Maurras, however, seemed more interested in a logical demonstration of how monarchical principles could not be compromised. Téry, after the venture had collapsed, analyzed the failure in these words: "The most beautiful reasoning that I know is the demonstration of the existence of God by Saint Anselm. He proves very well that, by essence, God must have all perfections. 'It is true,' Kant remarks, '[although] there is only one that he lacks: existence. You can prove to me that God, if he exists, is a perfect being; but as beautiful and as strong as your reasoning is, it is not enough to give him existence. . . . ' Don't you think that Charles Maurras's king has some resemblance with Saint Anselm's God?"[6]

Both these issues—Maurras's hesitancy to act and his retreat into logical abstraction—separated him from the younger men who founded the Cercle Proudhon. They shared with Maurras the reactionary trait of resistance to any form of transcendence. Yet they went beyond him. The decadence of contemporary democracy, they insisted, could be overcome not through logical demonstration alone but through the catharsis of the destructive act.

Maurras was no more enthusiastic over their "social monarchy" based on an *esprit guerrier*—armed republics and armed workers. For Maurras, as has been seen, workers were interesting only as they might be of service in restoring the king: their place in the newly established monarchy would be resolved not by antagonism but by the natural propensity for all problems to resolve themselves under the proper political order. Armed force in this new and harmonious order would be as inconceivable as it would be unnecessary.

For a time the growing tensions within the Action française were successfully contained, but by 1914 these tensions reached the breaking point. The exclusion of Lagrange and his young student following came at about the same time as another important schism: the staff of the *Revue critique* declared itself independent of the Action française.[7] We have Valois's testimony that the break with the Cercle Proudhon, had the war not intervened, would have been but a matter of time. Maurras was in the process of making himself indisputable master of his own house, a process that, once completed, would make the Action française unambiguously reactionary and no longer interested in the winning of the working class.

Meanwhile, Valois and the group at the Cercle Proudhon were moving in an altogether different direction. Many parallels—striking in their anticipations—between later European fascisms and the prewar doctrines of the Cercle Proudhon have been suggested. Demonstrably, the men of the Cercle Proudhon, far more than their erstwhile mentor Charles Maurras, had gone beyond conservatism and arrived at a highly articulate version of "early fascism." From this perspective, this study contributes yet another episode to the growing literature that, refuting the traditional argument that fascism has no "native roots" in France, sees the prewar period as an important harbinger of later developments.[8]

In this connection, one final consideration seems to beg comment. The cases of Valois, Berth, and Janvion suggest what was to become an almost archetypical pattern. Their individual biographies illustrate the facility with which the transmigration might be made from the extreme Left to the extreme Right. The issue is not inconsequential. The proportion of European fascist leaders who had begun their careers on the Left is impressive—and in the specific case of France is doubly impressive.[9] The common denominator, both before and after the war, was the attempt to revivify what were perceived to be decaying forms of collectivism—be they anarchism, syndicalism, socialism, or communism—with an energetic and popular nationalism. Here Georges Sorel's early interest in the Action française was symptomatic: he was one of the first to perceive the enormous potential of the nationalist "myth" in galvanizing men and preparing them for heroic action. Although his experimentation along these lines was both modest and hesitant, his disciples, Georges Valois and Edouard Berth, were to feel none of his inhibitions. Disappointed with what they considered to be the vagaries of the "abstract" and international conception of revolution promoted on the Left, they found inspiration in the "realistic" and national conception of revolution developing on the Right. Their prewar enthusiasms at the Cercle Proudhon had their eccentricities; yet they cannot easily be dismissed as marginalia in the light of later developments. Their writings stand as highly articulate statements of "resistance to transcendence," a phenomenon presented explicitly by Ernst Nolte—implicitly by many others —as the most essential quality of the fascist mentality. Further, in their eager, if naive, desire to combine the social and the national, in their conviction that patriotism was the moving force of contemporary politics, and, especially, in their promotion of the cathartic potentialities of violence, they stand as important as well as ominous twentieth-century prototypes.

Notes

Chapter 1

1. Georges Guy-Grand, *La Philosophie nationaliste*, p. 1.
2. Published in book form in 1908; originally appeared in installments in the *Mouvement socialiste*, January–June 1906.
3. For the last significant bibliography of syndicalism, see Robert Brécy, *Le Mouvement syndical en France*.
4. F. F. Ridley, *Revolutionary Syndicalism in France*, pp. 77–78. According to Ridley, out of more than 4 million potential union members, the Confédération générale du travail, which espoused revolutionary syndicalist doctrines, could rally only about 600,000 members at its apogee in 1912. This latter figure is the one given by the Confédération générale du travail itself and includes many members who never paid dues.
5. There is a paradox here, for, as Carl Landauer has pointed out, French unions, before 1908 at least, were actually more successful in day-to-day strike activity than their English or German counterparts. This practical success vis-à-vis foreign competition, however, was obscured by the emphasis placed on the general strike by the leaders of the Confédération générale du travail and their subsequent humiliation when even the most elementary attempts at "generalization" fell flat (Carl Landauer, *European Socialism*, 1:340–55).
6. Henri Dubief, *Le Syndicalisme révolutionnaire*, pp. 42–44. Dubief is one of the French historians who questions Dolléans's framework; his work on syndicalism is, however, all too brief. The above is a collection of readings, with a fine introduction.
7. In addition to Dubief, French critics of heroic syndicalism include Robert Goetz-Girey, *La Pensée syndicale française*, Michel Collinet, *Esprit du syndicalisme*; and, more recently, Christian Gras, especially "La Fédération des métaux en 1913–1914 et l'évolution du syndicalisme révolution-

naire français," pp. 85–111, and "Merrheim et le capitalisme." Outside of France, in contrast, the reaction against heroic syndicalism has been much more intense. Written from very different perspectives are the critiques of Ridley, *Revolutionary Syndicalism*; Bernard H. Moss, *The Origins of the French Labor Movement, 1830–1914*; and Peter N. Stearns, *Revolutionary Syndicalism and French Labor* and *Workers and Protest* (with Harvey Mitchell). Because he has attacked not only heroic syndicalism specifically but conventional labor history generally, Stearns's work has stirred the most controversy. Stearns, who claims to study the working class "from the bottom up," has directed his attention to strike activity, arguing that the key to what the French worker thought can be better deduced from his actual behavior than from the pronouncements made in his name by the syndicalist leadership. The record of this behavior, Stearns concludes, reveals that revolutionary syndicalism was not expressive of the attitudes held by most French workers; in Stearns's acid phrase, revolutionary syndicalism was a "cause without rebels." The reactions to Stearns's thesis have run the gamut, but clearly the heaviest concentration has been on the negative side. For a sample of the reaction against Stearns, see the book reviews by Allen Binstock in the *Mouvement social*, no. 93 (October–December 1975), pp. 115–17; Edward T. Gargan in *Journal of Modern History* 44 (1972): 436–37; and Bernard H. Moss in *Science and Society* 36 (1972): 492–96. It seems clear that, however shaken, heroic syndicalism, at least for the present, has weathered Stearns's attack from below.

8. Jacques Julliard has published—in addition to several articles—two important works to date, *Fernand Pelloutier et les origines du syndicalisme d'action directe* and *Clemenceau, briseur de grèves*.

9. This distinction was first made in Julliard, *Clemenceau*, pp. 68–71.

10. See Julliard, *Clemenceau*, and his "Théorie syndicaliste révolutionnaire et pratique gréviste."

11. It is not, of course, to be inferred that this study is the first to present such a reassessment. It is, however, hoped that it offers new evidence and a new perspective, strengthening the revisionist argument vis-à-vis what I have described as the heroic version. Further, the reader must also be forewarned that, because this study is a political and intellectual study of the interaction between the syndicalist and royalist leadership elites (and not a social history of either syndicalism or royalism), it cannot address itself to the problem raised by Stearns, namely, to what extent the rank and file shared the revolutionary syndicalist ideas.

12. Once again, there is no claim put forward that this study is the first to document the existence of this "reformist" group. Rather, it contributes fresh information and perspective to an ongoing revision. For an apprecia-

tion of the small but growing literature on the development of this important reformist tendency, see: Gras, "La Fédération des métaux"; and two doctoral dissertations, Michael DeLucia, "The Remaking of French Syndicalism, 1911–1918," and Nicholas C. Papayanis, "Alphonse Merrheim and Revolutionary Syndicalism, 1871–1917."

13. Julliard dismisses the possibility with a kind of righteous indignation (Julliard, *Clemenceau*, pp. 194–95).

14. Charles Péguy, *Oeuvres en prose*, 2:16.

15. As with revolutionary syndicalism, the most inspiring efforts have not come from native French historians—a curious lacuna in the light of achievements of the French historical profession generally. Part of the reason, no doubt, has been the intense partisanship surrounding Maurras and the Action française. For a recent bibliographical essay surveying the state of Maurrassian research both inside and outside France, see Victor Nguyen, "Situation des études maurrassiennes," pp. 503–38.

16. René Rémond, *The Right Wing in France from 1815 to de Gaulle*, pp. 233–53.

17. Edward Tannenbaum, *The Action française*.

18. Eugen Weber, "France," pp. 97–98; Eugen Weber, *Action française*, p. viii; Nguyen, "Etudes maurrassiennes," pp. 504–5.

19. Ernst Nolte, *The Three Faces of Fascism*, pp. 26, 87.

20. Ibid., pp. 100–141.

21. See, for example, Erich Fromm, *Escape from freedom*.

22. One could argue that Nolte stacks the deck by using terms such as "transcendence." The liberal notion of history as a progression of one sort or another permeates the book. For a different view of the origins of fascism, from an anthropological perspective rather than a liberal-progressive one, see Karl Polanyi, *The Great Transformation*.

23. George Mosse, review of *The Three Faces of Fascism* by Ernst Nolte, *Journal of the History of Ideas* 27 (1966): 621–25.

24. Ibid., p. 624; Eugen Weber has long argued this "dynamic" aspect, calling fascism—somewhat too provocatively, perhaps—"the Jacobinism of our time" (Eugen Weber, *Varieties of Fascism*, p. 139).

25. Weber, *Action française*, pp. 1–88, 133–35, 205–18, 528–34.

26. For the orthodox French view, see Rémond, *Right Wing*, pp. 205–32, 273–85. See also Jean Plumyène and Raymond Lasierra, *Les Fascismes français, 1923–1963*.

27. See Zeev Sternhell, "Paul Déroulède and the Origins of Modern French Nationalism," pp. 46–70; Peter Rutkoff, "The Ligue des patriotes, pp. 585–603; Robert J. Soucy, "The Nature of Fascism in France," pp. 27–55; Zeev Sternhell, "Barrès et la gauche," pp. 77–130 and *Maurice*

Barrès et le nationalisme français; Eugen Weber, "Nationalism, Socialism, and National-Socialism in France," pp. 273–307. Recently there has been some controversy over whether Barrès was a genuine fascist before the letter or merely a fleeting "protofascist" on his way from socialism to conservative nationalism. Cf. Robert J. Soucy, *Fascism in France*, and Charles Stewart Doty, *From Cultural Rebellion to Counterrevolution*.

28. J. L. Talmon, "The Legacy of Georges Sorel," and John L. Stanley, ed., *From Georges Sorel*.

29. Talmon, "Legacy," p. 58.

30. Stanley, *From Georges Sorel*, pp. 1–5.

Chapter 2

1. Frederic H. Seager, *The Boulanger Affair*, p. 202; this was also the case in Nancy, where it has been estimated that three-quarters of the Boulangist militants were workers (Charles Stewart Doty, *From Cultural Rebellion to Counterrevolution*, p. 46).

2. Zeev Sternhell, "Barrès et la gauche," pp. 77–130. Friedrich Engels shared this opinion (Robert J. Soucy, *Fascism in France*, p. 230). As has been recently pointed out by Charles Stewart Doty, the remnant of the Boulangist movement—still some thirty deputies strong in the early 1890s—was considered by contemporaries to be part of a socialist coalition. And not without reason. Given their voting record, their advocacy of social reform, and the inchoate and factionalized state of French socialism in the early 1890s, the Boulangists found themselves comfortable using the designation "socialist." In fact, by the time Boulangism had collapsed definitively as a political force many ex-Boulangists had formally joined the socialists (Doty, *Rebellion to Counterrevolution*, pp. 70–99).

3. Seager, *Boulanger Affair*, p. 202; Doty, *Rebellion to Counterrevolution*, pp. 73–74.

4. David Robin Watson, "The Nationalist Movement in Paris, 1900–1906."

5. Ibid., p. 71.

6. Henri Vaugeois, *Notre Pays*, pp. xxii–xxiii.

7. Manouvriez was to become director of the Etudiants d'Action française; he was a frequent royalist orator and, according to the police, had a "tempérament très frondeur" (Préfecture de police [hereafter cited as PP], Carton B^a 1341, 22 May 1908, from a sheet entitled "Rapport au sujet de l'agitation des étudiants").

8. Abel Manouvriez, "L'Action française au Quartier Latin," p. 41.

9. Ibid.

10. Thierry Maulnier, "Le 'fascisme' et son avenir en France," p. 17.

11. Louis Dimier, *Vingt Ans d'Action française et autres souvenirs*, p. 8.

12. Ibid., p. 17.

13. Ibid., pp. 17–18.

14. Charles Maurras to Maurice Barrès, 8 May 1890, in *La République ou le roi* by Maurice Barrès and Charles Maurras, pp. 31–32.

15. Charles Maurras, "Sur le nom de socialiste," pp. 859–67. For extended treatment of Maurras's critique of liberalism, see Paul Mazgaj, "The Social Revolution or the King," pp. 33–38.

16. Charles Maurras, *Enquête sur la monarchie, 1900–1909*, p. xlv.

17. Thierry Maulnier, "Charles Maurras et le socialisme," p. 170.

18. F. F. Ridley, *Revolutionary Syndicalism in France*, p. 1.

19. Ibid., pp. 63–79.

20. For the anarchist influx into the syndicalist movement, see Jean Maîtron, *Histoire du mouvement anarchiste en France, 1880–1914*, pp. 249–310.

21. The controversial question of Sorel's relation to syndicalist militants is discussed in chap. 7.

22. Georges Valois, *D'un siècle à l'autre*, p. 107.

23. Georges Sorel, *L'Avenir socialiste des syndicats*, p. 28.

24. See Georges Sorel, *Reflections on Violence*, p. 248. One of the earliest commentators on Sorel's thought could conclude: "The more one tries to penetrate Sorel's thought, the more convinced one becomes that moralism is, without doubt, the most characteristic feature of his temperament and of his work" (Gaétan Pirou, *Georges Sorel (1847–1922)*, p. 58).

25. Irving Louis Horowitz, *Radicalism and the Revolt against Reason*, p. 162.

26. A sympathetic analyst of Sorel's thought has fitted this conservatism on sexual matters into a more general framework, arguing that Sorel, being a realist, rejected all forms of "idealism," intellectual or emotional: "He [Sorel] fears everything that surrenders the mind to its fantasy, the soul to its passions; everything that makes man lose a precise, immediate, and constant perception of the exigencies and the limits of the real; everything that corrupts the consciousness of good and evil" (Georges Goriely, *Le Pluralisme dramatique de Georges Sorel*, p. 34).

27. First published in book form in 1908.

28. Georges Sorel, *Les Illusions du progrès*, p. 30.

29. Horowitz, *Radicalism*, pp. 146–63.

30. Sorel quotes Proudhon approvingly: "'When man only looks for the pleasure of exercise in work, he will soon stop working, for he is playing. . . . The faculty of work, which distinguishes man from brutes, has

its source in the very depths of reason: how could it become a mere manifestation of life, a voluptuous act of our sensibility?' " (Georges Sorel, "Essai sur la philosophie de Proudhon," p. 633).

31. Neil McInnes, "Georges Sorel," in *Encyclopedia of Philosophy*, 7:496–99.

32. Sorel, *Reflections*, pp. 239–41.

33. Horowitz, *Radicalism*, pp. 101–10.

34. Georges Sorel to Hubert Lagardelle, 31 August 1898, in *Educazione fascista* 11:321.

35. Ibid.

36. Hubert Lagardelle, "Déclaration," pp. 1–3.

37. René de Marans, "La Grève générale et les deux socialismes," pp. 315–24.

38. René de Marans, "Les *Réflexions sur la violence* de M. Georges Sorel," p. 537.

39. Jean Rivain, "La Patrie des prolétaires," pp. 189–94; "Les Socialistes antidémocrates," pp. 412–18, 470–87; "L'Avenir du syndicalisme," pp. 467–84.

40. Eugen Weber, *Action française*, pp. 38–39, 79.

41. Rivain, "L'Avenir du syndicalisme," p. 468.

42. Rivain, "Les Socialistes antidémocrates," pp. 470–72, 486–87.

43. Rivain, "L'Avenir du syndicalisme," pp. 473–77.

44. Ibid., p. 479. For a fuller treatment of the early work of de Marans and Rivain, see Mazgaj, "Social Revolution," pp. 41–50.

45. Agathon is a pseudonym for Henri Massis and Alfred de Tarde.

46. Agathon [Henri Massis and Alfred de Tarde], *Les Jeunes Gens d'aujourd'hui*, p. 3.

47. Ibid., pp. 2–12.   48. Ibid., p. 115.

49. Ibid., p. 21.   50. Ibid., p. 110.

51. Georges Bernanos, *Correspondance*, 1:88.

52. In February 1907 the police reported a meeting of the "groupe Joseph de Maistre" at the Institut d'Action française where Rivain discussed the worker alliance project. Seventeen persons were in attendance (PP, carton B^a 1341, 3 February 1907).

53. For the staff of the new review, see Weber, *Action française*, p. 79.

54. Maurice Barrès, "Les Diverses Familles spirituelles de la France," *Echo de Paris*, 2 March 1917.

55. Henri Clouard, "Une Jeune Elite sacrifiée," *Renaissance: Politique, économique, littéraire et artistique*, 12 May 1917.

56. Para later went over to the *Bonnet rouge*, a leftist newspaper.

57. Emile Para, "Le Mouvement syndicaliste," p. 85, n. 1.

58. Para was not afraid to take on themes not often found in reviews of the Right. On private property, for example, Para was unambiguous: "But then if, through the conquest of power or through the general strike, the socialists manage to suppress private property, its legitimacy will disappear. Shall we not then recognize that the sole justification of the present social order is the police?" (Emile Para, "Review of *Le Socialisme: Exposé du pour et du contre*," p. 366).

59. Para, "Le Mouvement syndicaliste," p. 88.

60. Georges Sorel, "Modernisme dans la religion et dans le socialisme," pp. 177–204.

61. See, for example, Dimier, *Vingt Ans*, pp. 223–26.

Chapter 3

1. It is only recently that Valois has attracted scholarly attention. See Yves Guchet, *Georges Valois*, and "Georges Valois ou l'illusion fasciste;" Zeev Sternhell, "Anatomie d'un mouvement fasciste en France"; Jules Levey, "Georges Valois and the Faisceau." Also see Jules Levey's doctoral thesis, "The Sorelian Syndicalists."

2. *Almanach de l'Action française, 1923*, pp. 171–72.

3. Georges Valois, *D'un siècle à l'autre*, p. 10. We have only Valois's word—in the form of this autobiography—for much of his early life. When it concerns incidents in his later life, which can be checked against other sources, Valois emerges as basically trustworthy; distortions are usually due to his tendency to overdramatize.

4. Georges Valois, *L'Etat syndical et la représentation corporative*, p. xiv.

5. Valois, *D'un siècle*, p. 40.   6. Valois, *L'Etat syndical*, p. xiv.

7. Valois, *D'un siècle*, p. 43.   8. Ibid., p. 28.

9. Ibid., pp. 37–38.   10. Ibid., p. 98.

11. Ibid., p. 104.   12. Ibid., pp. 108–32.

13. Ibid., p. 133.

14. Cf. Georges Valois, *L'Oeuvre de Georges Valois*, 3:261; Valois, *L'Etat syndical*, p. xvi; Valois, *D'un siècle*, pp. 131–36.

15. Georges Valois, "Georges Sorel," *Action française*, 4 September 1922.

16. Valois, *D'un siècle*, pp. 137–47.

17. Ibid., pp. 128–29.

18. Quoted in Frédéric Lefèvre, "Une Heure avec M. Georges Valois," *Nouvelles littéraires*, 16 February 1924.

19. Valois, *D'un siècle*. p. 149.

20. Ibid., p. 151. This is a good example of an idea promoted by Valois as coming largely from his own experience, yet presented earlier by Sorel.

In 1898 Sorel wrote: "The true vocation of intellectuals is the exploitation of politics; the role of the politician is very similar to that of the courtier, and it does not require any industrial talent" (Georges Sorel, *L'Avenir socialiste des syndicats*, p. 16). Valois is not guilty, in this writer's opinion, of deliberate misrepresentation, but he had "learned from experience" what his influential mentor had prepared him to learn.

21. Valois, *D'un siècle*, pp. 165–66.

22. Ibid., p. 171.

23. Levey speculates that Valois came across the *Protocols of the Elder of Zion*, then circulating in Russia (Levey, "The Sorelian Syndicalists," p. 108, n. 1).

24. Valois, *D'un siècle*, p. 189.

25. Ibid., p. 190.

26. Georges Valois, "Au jour le jour: Charles Louis-Philippe," *Action française*, 27 December 1909.

27. See Georges Valois, "Notice," in *Parmi les hommes* by Lucien Jean, pp. v–xi.

28. Valois, *D'un siècle*, p. 113.   29. Ibid., p. 118.

30. Ibid., pp. 199–200.   31. Ibid., p. 211.

32. Ibid., p. 223.

33. Georges Valois, *L'Homme qui vient*, pp. 1–6; Valois also sees other uses for "surplus value" (ibid., pp. 7–11).

34. Eugen Weber, *Action française*, p. 74.

35. Lefèvre, "Une Heure avec Valois," *Nouvelles Littéraires*, 16 February 1924.

36. Valois, *L'Homme*, p. 141.   37. Ibid., pp. xx–xxi.

38. Ibid., p. 37.   39. Ibid., p. 213.

40. The reason men have been led away from following the dictates of their instincts, according to Valois, is that for too long they have followed teachers and writers who have destroyed their sense of reality. But the damage is not permanent because men "saw being respected in life everything that [teachers and writers had] taught [them] to despise: wealth, action, elevation by strength, faith in the instincts" (ibid., p. 148).

41. Even a cursory reading of *L'Homme qui vient* reveals how uncomfortably the principle of legitimacy fits with the principle of the most energetic. Valois's historical argument is the best indicator of this strain. Pursuing his argument of the legitimacy of the most energetic, he readily concedes the demise of the aristocracy: with their real force spent by the time of the Revolution, their claim to legitimacy, he admits, had rung hollow. But he fails to apply the same logic to the monarchy itself, which at the time of the Revolution certainly seemed to have lacked sufficient

energy for the task at hand. As for Napoleon, who, it would appear, was the energetic one—the man with the whip par excellence—Valois is ambivalent. Clearly, he had a great admiration for the man who, single-handedly, created a new order out of the quarrelsome factionalism that to Valois was the Revolution. Yet, reversing the logic of his argument to that point, Valois asks whether Napoleon could have replaced the king: "Can we call 'father' the man who enters our house when we are revolting against paternal authority, helps us kill our father, then restores order in the house and says: 'I am the head of the family and the master of property'?" (ibid., p. 24). One is tempted to speculate that originally *L'Homme qui vient* was written without its legitimist conclusions, which were added—and rather clumsily—when Valois saw that Maurras and the Action française might be his only route to publication. I have, however, no real evidence to support this speculation.

42. Against democratic politics, that is. Maurras's dictum, "politics first," was in no way contradictory. Under a democracy, Maurras argued, the entire society was caught up in the struggle for the control of the state, as the very essence of democracy was that this control be open to competition. What was required, according to Maurras, was that a new political system be instituted that would remove this divisive struggle for the state from the center of society. A political change—the change of regime—was a necessary prerequisite to all others; hence, "politics first."

43. Georges Valois, *La Monarchie et la classe ouvrière*, p. viii.

44. But he did try. See, for example, the introduction to Valois, *La Monarchie*, where he thanks Maurras for directing him to the work of La Tour du Pin. It is an embarrassingly transparent apology for being such an unreconstructed Sorelian.

45. Ibid., pp. 23–24.

46. Ibid., pp. 24–25. Valois inserts a footnote to this passage, attempting to demonstrate that La Tour du Pin is also an advocate of *esprit de classe*. Valois continually tries to impress upon the mind of the reader—rather unconvincingly—that there is really very little difference between Sorel and La Tour du Pin.

47. We know that Valois read this. See Valois, *L'Oeuvre*, 3:261.

48. The only case that Valois cites as proof is an anti-Semitic article by Robert Louzon, which appeared in the *Mouvement socialiste* in 1906. For Louzon's relationship to syndicalism, see Jacques Julliard, *Clemenceau, briseur de grèves*, p. 136.

49. Valois, *La Monarchie*, p. 47.

50. Ibid., p. 48.

Chapter 4

1. See William Buthman, *The Rise of Integral Nationalism in France*, p. 294; cf. Beau de Loménie, who claims that before 1914 Maurras's domination was not complete (Emmanuel Beau de Loménie, *Maurras et son système*, pp. 8–9).

2. Theodore Zeldin, rejecting the conventional view, has argued that social issues were already a main preoccupation in the 1890s. Whatever truth there is in this cannot hide the fact that the bloody confrontations after 1906 greatly heightened tensions and gave the social question a new sense of urgency (Theodore Zeldin, *France, 1848–1945*, 1:640–41).

3. L'Abbé de Pascal, "Chronique sociale: Le Syndicalisme: la doctrine," *Action française*, 2 July 1911.

4. L'Abbé de Pascal, "Chronique sociale: Les Déviations du mouvement social," *Action française*, 16 July 1908.

5. Firmin Bacconnier, "Le Mois corporatif: Affirmation du lien professionnel, le syndicalisme et la démocratie," *Action française*, 13 March 1909.

6. Archives nationales (hereafter cited as AN), carton $F^7$12862, no. 4, 23 December 1909, pp. 161–65.

7. Ibid.

8. George Mosse reports that membership estimates range from less than 100,000 to over 300,000. The Jaunes were first organized when several unions were expelled from the Paris bourse du travail for their refusal to toe the revolutionary syndicalist line. Paul Lenoir, secretary of one of the expelled unions, formed the Jaunes in 1901. The tone of the new organization was set by the kind of support it attracted: the Ligue de la patrie française and large industrialists. Mosse has contended that this "stifling conservatism" led to a revolt of dissident followers and ended in Lenoir's ouster as president of the Jaunes (George Mosse, "The French Right and the Working Classes," pp. 193–95, 201–2). Police reports suggest worse: Lenoir was a fraud. Not only did he invent membership figures to lure conservative money, but charges were raised, though not substantiated, that he was collaborating with the minister of interior (AN, carton $F^7$13568, "L'Organisation ouvrière: Exercices, 1912–14," pp. 63–71; AN, carton $F^7$12793, 11 October 1904).

9. AN, carton $F^7$12793, from an undated printed pamphlet entitled "Discours de P. Biétry."

10. Ibid., 18 August 1906.

11. A police report of late 1905 notes that Biétry was having difficulty holding together his federation (ibid., 6 October 1905).

12. Louis Dimier, *Vingt Ans d'Action française et autres souvenirs*, p. 125.

13. Ibid., p. 126; Dimier does not spell out what kind of agreement the royalists had reached with Biétry.

14. A police report of December 1908 estimates that of the 180 men that the Action française could muster for street action 50 were from the Accord social (cited in Eugen Weber, *Action française*, p. 54).

15. AN, carton F⁷12861, no. 6, 4 November 1907.

16. PP, carton Bª1342, agent "Lesueur," 5 January 1908.

17. AN, carton F⁷12862, no. 2, 22 April 1908, p. 26.

18. AN, carton F⁷12793, 11 October 1904.

19. It seems that Léon Daudet was most responsible for exposing Biétry. Daudet's antipathy toward the president of the Jaunes was noted in reports filed at both the Préfecture and the Sûreté (cf. AN, carton F⁷12861, no. 6, 4 November 1907; and PP, carton Bª1342, agent "Lesueur," 5 January 1908). Because Daudet was well traveled in the world of the anti-Semitic leagues before coming to the Action française, he doubtless had an opportunity to see Biétry in operation. Further, as this study will later demonstrate, Daudet had very definite ideas of his own about how to reach the working class.

20. Not only could Valois claim to be a pupil of Sorel, but he also prided himself on being a militant worker. While with the Action française, he continued to work for a publishing house and belong to a syndicat. For a time at least, he was quite active in the syndicalist movement (Georges Valois, *D'un siècle à l'autre*, pp. 250–52).

21. Dimier, *Vingt Ans*, p. 224.

22. Ibid., p. 27.

23. Charles Maurras, "La Violence," *Action française*, 12 August 1908.

24. Valois, *D'un siècle*, pp. 244–45.

25. Ibid., p. 245.

26. The only testimony available on this meeting is Valois's own—given on two different occasions. The first, written when he was still with the Action française, depicts disagreement within the context of a friendly discussion. The second, published after his break with the Action française, stresses only the disagreement (cf. Valois, *D'un siècle*, pp. 244–45, and *Basile: Ou, la politique de la calomnie*, p. x).

27. Dimier, *Vingt Ans*, p. 225.

28. Valois, *Basile*, pp. x–xi.

29. Yves Guchet, *Georges Valois*, p. 64.

30. David Robin Watson, *Georges Clemenceau*, p. 183.

31. Edouard Dolléans, *Histoire du mouvement ouvrier*, 2:145.

32. For an analysis of how the Radical party stood on the question of social reform, see Richard Wayne Sanders, "The Labor Politics of the French Radical Party, 1901–1909."

33. Clemenceau entered the Sarrien government in March 1906 as minister of interior; he formed his own government in October of the same year.

34. Quoted in Jacques Julliard, *Clemenceau, briseur de grèves*, p. 23, and Georges Bonnefous, *Histoire politique de la troisième république*, 1:15; both unattributed.

35. The reactionaries implicated were from Jacques Piou's Action libérale. Not even Bonnefous, who is quite openly hostile to the Confédération générale du travail, suggests that there was anything to the charges of complicity (Bonnefous, *Histoire politique*, 1:15).

36. Julliard, *Clemenceau*, pp. 55–62.

37. Watson, *Clemenceau*, p. 170.

38. Ibid., p. 168.

39. Ibid., pp. 204–5.

40. This fact is not emphasized in most standard French accounts, leaving the impression that the mood of confrontation was the creation of the government alone.

41. Julliard, *Clemenceau*, pp. 47–53.

42. Ibid., pp. 9–10.

43. Ibid., pp. 55–71.

44. From clippings contained in PP, carton B^{a}1602, June 1908.

45. This is apparent from a police report reproduced by Julliard (*Clemenceau*, p. 70).

46. Ibid., p. 74.

47. AN, carton F^{7}13195, from a folder entitled "Les Réactionnaires et les syndicats, 1908–1914," 10 August 1908, pp. 2–3.

48. AN, carton F^{7}12861, no. 6, 24 June 1908, p. 36.

49. AN, carton F^{7}12862, no. 1, 30 October 1906, p. 40.

50. For Daudet's own account, see his *Souvenirs des milieux littéraires, politiques, artistiques et médicaux*, 2:181–82.

51. PP, carton B^{a}1341, 7 June 1908.

52. AN, carton F^{7}13195, from a folder entitled "Les Réactionnaires et les syndicats, 1908–1914," 10 August 1908, p. 4.

53. See especially "Ligue d'Action française," *Action française*, 27 July 1908, where the degree to which the royalists had incorporated Valois's ideas is apparent.

54. AN, carton F^{7}13195, from a folder entitled "Les Réactionnaires et les syndicats, 1908–1914," 10 August 1908, p. 5.

55. Julliard, *Clemenceau*, pp. 72–94.

56. Ibid., pp. 143–96; see also Watson, *Clemenceau*, pp. 202–5.

57. Quoted in Julliard, *Clemenceau*, p. 95.

58. Ibid., p. 98.

59. The lead editorials of 30 July and 1 August form a two-part exposition of this new policy.

60. Charles Maurras, "La Question ouvrière," *Action française*, 30 July 1908.

61. Ibid.

62. Charles Maurras, "Causes politiques," *Action française*, 1 August 1908.

63. As recently as 28 July 1908, Maurras had professed his loyalty to the person and ideas of La Tour du Pin (Charles Maurras, "Corporation," *Action française*, 28 July 1908).

64. Julliard, *Clemenceau*, pp. 111–12.

65. Charles Maurras, "Le Quatre-août des conservateurs," *Action française*, 3 August 1908.

66. Charles Maurras, "Liberté d'esprit," *Action française*, 4 August 1908.

67. Charles Maurras, "Hors de France," *Action française*, 8 August 1908.

68. Ibid.

Chapter 5

1. See chap. 2.

2. Georges Valois, *La Monarchie et la classe ouvrière*, pp. 67–77.

3. Georges Valois, "Faits et documents: Syndicalisme et démocratie. Une Note de M. Hubert Lagardelle," p. 87; Berth, who by 1911 had come over to Valois's nationalism, has a quite different recollection: "Just as you are about to publish a new edition of your *Monarchie et la classe ouvrière*, you ask me to give you the answer that I should have given you at the time of the first edition, and that I would certainly have sent you if, through a stroke of bad luck—but should one really talk of bad luck?—your questionnaire had not been misplaced at the hands of a *third* party, who did not fail to live up to the habits of this type of person whose main virtue is, as you know, not to fill the mission entrusted to him" (Jean Darville [Berth] to Georges Valois, in *Cahiers du Cercle Proudhon*, 2d ser., no. 1, p. 7). Presumably, the *third* party referred to by Berth is Hubert Lagardelle.

4. Valois, *La Monarchie*, pp. 78–91.

5. Ibid., p. 122.

6. Ibid., p. 124.

7. Ibid., p. 125.

8. Of the seven, only one, Emile Janvion, was an important figure in the syndicalist movement; it is not known how many letters Valois solicited and never received.

9. Valois, *La Monarchie*, p. 135.   10. Ibid., p. 133.

11. Ibid., p. 190.   12. Ibid., p. 224.

13. Quoted in "Ligue d'Action française," *Action française*, 8 August 1908. This apprehension concerning a possible search at the headquarters of the Action française was also reported by the police (PP, carton B[a]1341, 2 August 1908 [two separate reports of the same day]).

14. J., "Notes du jour," *Indépendance belge*, 11 August 1908.

15. See, for example, "Ligue d'Action française," *Action française*, 8 August 1908, 21 August 1908.

16. Ibid., 8 August 1908.

17. AN, carton F[7]13195, from a folder entitled "Les Réactionnaires et les syndicats," 10 August 1908, p. 10.

18. PP, carton B[a]1341, agent "Drossier," 12 August 1908; AN, carton F[7]12915, 12 August 1908, and report sent from the Préfecture, 28 September 1908.

19. PP, carton B[a]1341, agent "Lesueur," 26 October 1908.

20. PP, carton B[a]1342, agent "Finot," 14 January 1909.

21. PP, carton B[a]1341, agent "Lesueur," two reports, 5 and 7 November 1908. This disparity in the quality of police reports raises the larger issue of the general reliability of police informers as a historical source, no small consideration in the light of their extensive use in this study. After reading day-to-day police reports on both the royalist and the syndicalist movements and comparing them with a variety of other sources, I believe them to be perhaps no better but certainly no worse than most other sources. Used judiciously—when possible with the corroboration of other sources —they are an indispensable tool for the understanding of movements such as the Action française and revolutionary syndicalism. As in the above case, it is often rather transparent, if not explicitly stated, whether a given agent is working on the basis of hard, precise information or whether his report is largely conjectural. The tendency for certain historians, in the name of the critical use of sources, to dismiss all police spies as agents provocateurs is, in this writer's judgment, to overlook a rich, often irreplaceable, historical source. This is all the more distressing when the same historians accept at face value, and without the least corroboration, the statements of syndicalist leaders, apparently assuming that only those outside the working class are capable of constructing self-serving rationalizations. For a fuller treatment of the police reports of late 1908 and early 1909, see Paul Mazgaj, "The Social Revolution or the King," pp. 157–75.

22. No indication is given as to who supported the first idea.

23. PP, carton B^{a}1341, agent "Lesueur," 5 November 1908.

24. Ibid., 7 November 1908. This corresponds with the formation of the Camelots du roi. It seems clear, however, that from the beginning the Camelots were conceived of as serving a broader function than indicated in this report (see Eugen Weber, *Action française*, pp. 53–55).

25. See chap. 6.

26. AN, carton F^{7}13195, 15 September 1908.

27. Ibid.

28. Edouard Dolléans, *Histoire du mouvement ouvrier*, 2:151–52.

29. Henri Dubief, *Le Syndicalisme révolutionnaire*, pp. 42–44.

30. Jacques Julliard, *Clemenceau, briseur de grèves*, p. 44.

31. Ibid., pp. 70–71, n. 2.

32. Griffuelhes was secretary-general of the Confédération générale du travail from 1902 to 1909; Pouget was its assistant secretary from 1901 to 1908 and editor of the *Voix du peuple*, its organ.

33. F. F. Ridley, *Revolutionary Syndicalism in France*, pp. 84–85.

34. Emile Pouget, "Tribune syndicale: Le Cas Janvion," *Humanité*, 16 May 1907; "Les Manifestations du ler mai," *Voix du peuple*, 5–12 May 1907; both from clippings in the Dossier Janvion at the Archives de la Seine (hereafter cited as AS). Several of the newspaper references cited below were also taken from this dossier.

35. From a single, undated sheet entitled "Notice concernant M. Janvion," AS, Dossier Janvion.

36. He returned to the municipal service only in 1913, where he worked until his death in 1927.

37. See Pouget, "Tribune syndicale," *Humanité*, 16 May 1907. Janvion, always his own best spokesman, went beyond the syndicalist press to bring attention to his cause (see Emile Janvion, "Conseils de guerre administratifs," *Matin*, 10 May 1907; "Les Impressions d'un révoqué," *Presse*, 6 May 1907; "Les Fonctionnaires de 'digestion,'" *Liberté*, 15 April 1907).

38. From various clippings (some unmarked) in a file labeled "Cabinet du Préfet de la Seine," AS, Dossier Janvion.

39. "Les Fonctionnaires révoqués en plein conflit," *Patrie*, 15 March 1908; J. St.-L., "L'Incident Janvion-Clemenceau," *Libre Parole*, 14 March 1908.

40. Emile Janvion and Emile Pouget, *Matin*, 12 August 1907.

41. Ibid.

42. Ibid.

43. Quoted in Daniel Ligou, *Histoire du socialisme en France, 1871–1961*, p. 209. Hervé's subsequent conversion to nationalism has significantly influenced the kind of press he has had among French historians of the

Left. Non-French scholars have been more sympathetic. See Maurice Rotstein, "The Public Life of Gustave Hervé," and especially Michael Roger Scher, "The Antipatriot as Patriot."

44. Scher, "Antipatriot as Patriot," p. 560.

45. *Histoire générale de la presse française*, 3:296.

46. Scher, "Antipatriot as Patriot," pp. 560–65.

47. Hervé's profound impact on the politics of the French Left has been succinctly summarized by Eugen Weber: "The Socialist Party had to move steadily toward the extreme Left to avoid losing the mass of its followers, whom the extreme antimilitarism and antipatriotism of men like Hervé seemed to inspire. There was thus a progressive Hervéization of the Socialist Party, while the Radicals, largely as a reaction to this, moved further to the right" (quoted in Scher, "Antipatriot as Patriot," p. 423).

48. Julliard, *Clemenceau*, p. 173.

49. Pierre Monatte, "La C.G.T. a-t-elle rectifié son tir?" p. 129.

50. Un Sans-Patrie [Hervé], "Le Fiasco du ler mai," *Guerre sociale*, 6–12 May 1908.

51. See "Du péril maçonnique dans le syndicalisme," *Guerre sociale*, 27 May–3 June 1908 issue through 29 July–4 August 1908 issue.

52. Ibid., 24–30 June 1908.

53. Ibid., 27 May–3 June 1908.

54. PP, carton Ba1602, agent "Finot," 4 May 1908.

55. Ibid., agent "Lyon," 4 June 1908.

56. Julliard says that many outside the movement had hopes that the reformists would finally triumph, but they overplayed their hand. The revolutionaries were able to win so handily (741 votes to 383) because "proportional representation enjoyed compromising sympathies" (Julliard, *Clemenceau*, pp. 131–32).

57. P. Tesche and A. Morizet, "Antimilitarisme," *Humanité*, 11 October 1908; PP, carton Ba1606, agent "Drossier," 12 October 1908.

58. P. Tesche and A. Morizet, "Antimilitarisme et antipatriotisme et la représentation proportionnelle," *Humanité*, 10 October 1908.

59. Louis Perceau, "Le Congrès de Marseille," *Guerre sociale*, 14 October 1908.

60. A police report of mid-November describes the extent to which the situation had degenerated. At one syndicalist conclave, Jean Latapie, one of the secretaries of the powerful metalworkers' federation, directing his comments at the ultras, claimed that a minority was trying to prevent all opinions from being heard. While making his statement, he was attacked physically by two "comrades," one of them being the ultra Blanchard; the meeting very nearly ended in a "general brawl" (PP, carton Ba1602, agent "Drossier," 15 November 1908).

61. Ibid., two reports, 14 and 19 December 1908.

62. Julliard, *Clemenceau*, pp. 135–40.

63. Ibid., p. 139.

64. Weber, *Action française*, p. 30.

65. Not only publicly but also privately. See PP, carton B^{a}1602, agent "Achard," 8 October 1908.

66. A consistent tack of the daily *Action française* was to attack the parliamentary socialists and praise the revolutionaries. See, for example, Claude Villars, "Les Antiparlementaires s'organisent," *Action française*, 1 March 1909.

67. Criton [Charles Maurras], "Revue de la presse," *Action française*, 1 April 1908.

68. "La Franc-Maçonnerie et les syndicats," *Action française*, 6 July 1908.

69. PP, carton B^{a}1342, agent "Drossier," 12 January 1909.

70. Ibid., 17 January 1909.

71. AS, Dossier Janvion, from outer cover, a summary of his career.

72. Emile Janvion, "Un Boycottage bien tassé," *Terre libre*, 15–31 March 1912.

73. Many of these indications became apparent only when Janvion began publishing his newspaper, *Terre libre*. They are therefore taken up in the next chapter, which considers this project.

74. Un Sans-Patrie, "La Mort du dreyfusisme," *Guerre sociale*, 16–22 September 1908.

75. Gustave Hervé, "Souhaits du nouvel an," *Guerre sociale*, 30 December 1908–5 January 1909. Hervé refers to the famous incident during the Dreyfus affair, when the proletariat had rallied after the president of the Republic, Loubet, had been attacked at Auteuil racetrack by anti-Dreyfusard nationalists, and his hat had been smashed.

76. Ibid.

77. Madeleine Pelletier, "Défendrons-nous la république?" *Guerre sociale*, 3–9 February 1909.

78. Criton, "Revue de la presse," *Action française*, 7 February 1909.

Chapter 6

1. See chap. 5, p. 81.

2. Eugen Weber, *Action française*, p. 46.

3. Ibid., p. 45.

4. "L'Action française dans les faubourgs: A l'Alcazar d'Italie," *Action française*, 27 March 1909.

5. Cf. ibid., with PP, carton B^{a}1342, agent "Lesueur," 2 April 1909.

6. PP, carton B^{a}1342, agent "Lesueur," 2 April 1909.

7. Ibid.

8. AN, carton F⁷12864, no. 2, 1 July 1909.

9. Victor Méric, *Coulisses et tréteaux*, 1:30–79.

10. La Bastille [pseud.], "Au jour le jour: Nos prisons," *Action française*, 25 May 1909.

11. Méric, *Coulisses et tréteaux*, 1:44.

12. Ibid., p. 52.

13. "Echos," *Révolution*, 23 March 1909.

14. Méric, *Coulisses et tréteaux*, 1:55.

15. Ibid., p. 64.

16. During the most desperate period of the First World War, a feud erupted between the fanatically prowar *Action française* and the "defeatist" *Bonnet rouge* where some of the revolutionaries had drifted after a split with Hervé. It involved a campaign of slander on both sides and ended with the mysterious death of Almereyda. See Weber, *Action française*, pp. 101–7.

17. Méric, *Coulisses et tréteaux*, 1:55.

18. Henri Bibert, "Vers la grève générale," *Autorité*, 5 April 1909; see also "Le Meeting de l'hippodrome," *Action*, 5 April 1909, and "A l'hippodrome," *Radical*, 5 April 1909.

19. "Contre les délits d'opinion," *Action française*, 10 June 1909.

20. Terre Libre [pseud.], "Pourquoi ce journal," *Terre libre*, 15 November–1 December 1909.

21. For a Darien sampler, see Georges Darien, *L'Ennemi du peuple*.

22. Ibid., pp. 123–46.

23. See entries under "Marius Blanchard" and "Benoît Broutchoux" in *Dictionnaire biographique du mouvement ouvrier français* for the importance of these two figures in the syndicalist movement.

24. Marius Riquier, "Messieurs les intellectuels," *Terre libre*, 28 February–15 March 1910.

25. Marius Riquier, "Scepticisme," *Terre libre*, 15 March–1 April 1910.

26. Emile Janvion, "Vive la république! . . . et les républirequins!" *Terre libre*, 15–30 July 1910.

27. Emile Janvion, "Les Mirlitons du pacifisme: A Paul Adam," *Terre libre*, 1–15 June 1910.

28. In fact, in Janvion's early and unorthodox antimilitarism one can already detect the realism that would make him comfortable with the men of the *Revue critique*. He argued for an end to *éducationisme*: let those who have not by now come over to antimilitarism have their war and exterminate each other. "Long live wars in which our friends do not participate" (Darien, *L'Ennemi*, pp. 100–101).

29. "Ils avouent!" *Terre libre*, 15–28 February 1910. *Youpin* could be translated as *kike*, and *calotin* is a derogatory reference to a person whose life is closely connected with the church.

30. Quoted in "Pour mémoire," *Terre libre*, 15 March–1 April 1910.

31. E. J., "Notes rétrospectives sur l'affaire Dreyfus," *Terre libre*, 15–31 May 1910.

32. Ibid., 1–15 June 1910.

33. E. J., "Pour mémoire." *Terre libre*, 15 March –1 April 1910.

34. Literally, the skullcap worn by a priest, but also derisive slang for the clergy in general.

35. E. J., "Pour mémoire," *Terre libre*, 15 March–1April 1910.

36. E. J., "Notes rétrospectives sur l'affaire Dreyfus," *Terre libre*, 15–31 May 1910.

37. "En Angleterre," *Terre libre*, 15–30 January 1910.

38. "Dreyfus et Del Sarte," *Terre libre*, 15 April–1 May 1910.

39. Pierre Gilbert, "La Réponse des syndicalistes à Briand," *Action française*, 4 June 1910.

40. Ibid.

41. Janvion said that at the high point he had 357 subscribers ("Notre Santé administrative," *Terre libre*, 1–15 February 1914). This must be seen in the context of extremely low subscription rates for syndicalist publications in general. The *Mouvement socialiste*, for example, could count only about 700 subscribers.

42. By September 1910, Janvion was complaining of a "ferocious boycott" but pledged to fight on (*Terre libre*, 15–30 September 1910, p. 4).

43. See chap. 5, pp. 90–92.

44. Two reports from PP, carton B^a1603, both from agent "Drossier," 9 April and 28 May 1909.

45. Albert Thomas, "Pour l'unité," *Humanité*, 27 May 1909.

46. PP, carton B^a1603, agent "Drossier," 15 June 1909.

47. Ibid., agent "Finot," 28 May 1909.

48. Ibid., 17 June 1909; corroborating evidence here is lacking, and police speculations on this point almost certainly exaggerated Janvion's chances.

49. Louis Dimier, *Vingt Ans d'Action française et autres souvenirs*, pp. 224–26.

50. It seems at first that this role was played by Emile Para. However, it is clear that by early 1910 Para and Janvion had a falling-out due to the former's indiscretion (E. J., "L'Appropriation du sol et la plus-value," *Terre libre*, 28 February–13 March 1910). Later, police reports indicate that Valois was the new intermediary and that the duke's political bureau was

providing the money (PP, carton Bª1342, agent "Drossier," 5 November 1910; carton Bª1343, agent "Chatenet," 17 January 1911).

51. They collaborated on projects at the *Revue critique*.

Chapter 7

1. Quoted in Edouard Dolléans, *Histoire du mouvement ouvrier*, 2:127.

2. Gaétan Pirou, "A propos du syndicalisme révolutionnaire," pp. 130–42.

3. Taken from handwritten, undated manuscripts at the Institut français d'histoire sociale, Fonds Delesalle, carton 14AS 12–14.

4. Ibid.

5. Ibid., carton 14AS 153bis.

6. When syndicalists were preparing to launch a daily newspaper, *La Révolution*, Pouget, badly in need of names that would build subscription lists, secured a promise from a reluctant Sorel to contribute occasional articles (Georges Sorel to Hubert Lagardelle, 24 July 1908, in *Educazione fascista* 11:963).

7. Sorel to Lagardelle, 11 June 1906, ibid., p. 773.

8. Sorel to Lagardelle, 18 September 1908, ibid., pp. 965–66.

9. Sorel to Lagardelle, 31 October 1908, ibid., p. 968.

10. At one point Sorel wrote: "Until now you have spent a great deal of energy only in order to make people with little talent and no morality successful; one only has to look at the list of collaborators of the *Mouvement* to perceive it" (Sorel to Lagardelle, 2 March 1908 [this letter is certainly dated erroneously; it was written sometime late in 1908], ibid., p. 969).

11. Ibid., pp. 969–70.

12. Ibid., p. 968.

13. See chap. 1. James H. Meisel has commented on Sorel's logic in this matter: "It is not easy to follow Sorel in his argument: the fine distinction which he draws between contributing a new article to the organ of the 'enemies' of yesterday (a reprehensive act) and letting them use the original for a translation, is too clearly self-defeating as to require any further comment" (James H. Meisel, *The Genesis of Georges Sorel*, p. 176).

14. Georges Sorel to Benedetto Croce, 18 September 1908, in *La Critica, rivista di letteratura, storia e filosofia*, 26:108.

15. For a very good short review of Sorel's work, connecting his social philosophy with the prevailing philosophy of science, see entry under "Georges Sorel" by Neil McInnes in *Encyclopedia of Philosophy*, 7:496–99, and McInnes's chapter on Sorel in his *Western Marxists*.

16. Henri Clouard, "Des Souvenirs sur Georges Sorel," pp. 1324–25.

17. As numerous commentators have pointed out, Sorel, unlike most other intellectuals who came to socialism, was not motivated by a moral revulsion toward the poverty and degradation that characterized much of working-class life.

18. The problems of Variot as a historical source are discussed by Meisel, *Genesis*, pp. 167–68; just as Meisel, I have found nothing in other sources that would lead me to question the reliability of Variot's account.

19. Jean Variot, *Propos de Georges Sorel*, 12 November 1908, p. 25.

20. Ibid., 14 November 1908, p. 25.

21. Ibid., pp. 25–27.

22. Georges Goriely, who likes Sorel a great deal, says of *La Révolution dreyfusienne*: "Let us say it frankly, it is Sorel's worst writing" (Georges Goriely, *Le Pluralisme dramatique de Georges Sorel*, p. 180).

23. Georges Sorel, *La Révolution dreyfusienne*, p. 57.

24. Ibid., p. 56.

25. Ibid., pp. 57–64.

26. Variot, *Propos*, 16 June 1909, p. 101.

27. Ibid., p. 103.

28. Georges Sorel to Charles Maurras, 6 July 1909, in *Notre Maître, M. Sorel* by Pierre Andreu, p. 325.

29. Literally, the snout of an animal.

30. Andreu, *Notre Maître*, pp. 67–68, n. 1.

31. Reproduced in Eric Cahm, *Péguy et le nationalisme français de l'affaire Dreyfus à la grande guerre*, p. 164.

32. Hans A. Schmitt, *Charles Péguy*, p. vii.

33. Variot, *Propos*, pp. 260–61.

34. Sorel to Croce, 22 August 1909, in *La Critica* 26:334–35.

35. On their different conceptions of religion, see Jean Onimus, "Péguy et Sorel," pp. 7–13.

36. See Georges Sorel, "Le Confessioni," published in *Divenire sociale* in the spring of 1910 and partially reproduced in his *Matériaux d'une théorie du prolétariat*, pp. 239–86.

37. Georges Sorel to Edouard Berth, 1 April 1910, in *L'Amitié Charles Péguy*, no. 77, p. 27.

38. Maurice Reclus, "Le Cas Charles Péguy," *Gil Blas*, 23 May 1910.

39. "Une Lettre de M. Georges Sorel," *Action française*, 8 June 1910.

40. Variot, *Propos*, p. 261. Sorel, never generous with compliments, said of Berth: "I not only love Berth like a son, because of the dignity of his life and of his character, I also love him like a friend—and a friend is no less

than a son—a friend who has, of all my friends, the greatest affinities with my doctrine and my ideas—those affinities of which Goethe speaks" (Variot, *Propos*, 15 May 1912, p. 162).

41. Ibid. For a more modest estimate of Berth's ability and degree of independence from Sorel, see Meisel, *Genesis*, pp. 253–54.

42. In his bibliography of Berth, Pierre Andreu counts at least twenty major articles contributed by Berth to the *Mouvement socialiste* (Pierre Andreu, "Bibliographie d'Edouard Berth," pp. 196–204).

43. Sorel to Berth, 24 April 1910, in *L'Amitié Charles Péguy*, no. 77, pp. 27–28.

44. In fact, the article was never published anywhere and is now lost (ibid., editor's note).

45. Sorel to Croce, 28 June 1910, in *La Critica* 26:341.

46. Sorel to Berth, 12 November 1909, in *L'Amitié Charles Péguy*, no. 77, pp. 25–26.

47. Sorel to Croce, 28 June 1910, in *La Critica* 26:341.

48. Reproduced in Andreu, *Notre Maître*, p. 327.

49. Ibid., p. 328.

50. Ibid., p. 330.

51. Ibid., p. 331.

52. Sorel to Berth, 9 July 1910, in *L'Amitié Charles Péguy*, no. 77, p. 30.

53. Cf. Variot, *Propos*, p. 262; Sorel to Croce, 25 January 1911, in *La Critica* 26:343; Jules Levey, "The Sorelian Syndicalists," pp. 133–36.

54. Hubert Lagardelle, *Le Socialisme ouvrier*, p. xv. Sorel responded to this statement in a letter to Croce (Sorel to Croce, 25 January 1911, in *La Critica* 26:344).

55. Lagardelle, *Socialisme ouvrier*, p. xiv.

Chapter 8

1. "La Politique: L'Idée d'avenir," *Action française*, 1 December 1909.

2. Léon Daudet, "Chantefourbe," *Action française*, 5 January 1910; B. Fournier, "L'Action française dans les faubourgs," *Action française*, 24 May 1910; "L'Action française dans les faubourgs," *Action française*, 15 December 1909; Léon Daudet, "Une Blague qui meurt," *Action française*, 24 December 1909.

3. Léon Daudet, "Chantefourbe," *Action française*, 5 January 1910.

4. See the regular *Action française* column: "Ligue d'Action française," 23 December 1909, 10 February 1910, 22 May 1910. See also AN, carton F⁷13195, "Les Réactionnaires et les syndicats," 7 and 10 February 1910, 21 November 1910; PP, carton Bᵃ1342, 24 October 1910.

5. The rail workers had not had a raise in thirty years (Edouard Dolléans, *Histoire du mouvement ouvrier*, 2:177).

6. Cf. ibid., pp. 177–81, with Georges Bonnefous, *Histoire politique de la troisième république*, 1:198–201.

7. The whole controversy is reprinted in the *Vie ouvrière* (See P. M., "Vierge et martyre," pp. 766–84, 824–53).

8. Ibid., p. 828.

9. Michael DeLucia, "The Remaking of French Syndicalism, 1911–1918."

10. Francis Delaisi, *La Démocratie et les financiers*, p. 181.

11. Delaisi, who continued to be influential on the French Left during the interwar years, had two great antipathies: a European war and the "200 families." This led him to support Briand as a friend of peace in the 1920s, Blum as a foe of the 200 families during the Popular Front era, and, finally, Déat, who would presumably fight for peace and against the plutocrats, during the Occupation. He never outlived the charge of being a collaborationist and died in relative obscurity in 1947. Henry Coston, who shared Delaisi's conspiratorial bent, was able to put Delaisi's checkered career into some perspective. Delaisi, Coston wrote, with his belief in the conspiracy of the 200 families was part of a tradition that included such disparate figures as the historian Emmanuel Beau de Loménie and Edouard Drumont. The common denominator is the belief that the apparent complexity of history can be dissolved once the long conspiratorial thread that informs it has been laid bare (Henry Coston, *Dictionnaire de la politique française*, 1:345).

12. Cratès [Francis Delaisi], "Le Camp capitaliste," p. 565.

13. There were exceptions, of course, but they were without great influence. Delaisi, by his connections with the *Guerre sociale* and the *Vie ouvrière*—especially his close relations with Merrheim—was near the center of power on both the syndicalist and nonsyndicalist Left.

14. P. M., "Vierge et martyre," p. 829.

15. "One can see there," Delaisi wrote, "that, out of 2,844 shares, 2,120 exactly, that is, *three-quarters* of them, have been subscribed by three people, whose names must be kept in mind. One is M. Salomon Reinach, Joseph Reinach's brother, who was assigned as Gambetta's secretary by the Rothschilds. Another is M. Lévy-Bruhl, a prominent philosopher, professor at the Sorbonne where he earns about 10,000 francs a month. One would wonder at his investing, *at a loss*, 125,000 in a socialist newspaper if one did not know that he is supposed to be the bestower of Rothschild's generosity among the young reviews, which bloom and die like leaves around the Odéon. As for the third one, Picard, alias Le Pic, a talented

publicist and polemicist, he had just presided over the collapse of his newspaper, *Les Droits de l'homme*, and, if he had had 125,000 francs of his own, would not he have used it to prevent the death of his own newspaper?" (ibid., p. 833).

16. Marius Riquier, "La Race persécutée," *Terre libre*, 15 November–15 December 1910.

17. Included were Robert de Jouvenel, Urbain Gohier, Georges de la Fouchardière, and Séverine.

18. Gustave Téry, "Les Juifs au théâtre . . . et ailleurs," pp. 7–8.

19. Ibid., p. 11.

20. Le Prolétaire conscient [Gustave Téry], "Le Ministère Rothschild," pp. 6–12.

21. PP, carton Bª1343, agent "Achard," 22 April 1912; AN, carton F⁷12863, no. 1, 29 June 1912.

22. The report of this agent and those of several other agents are mentioned in a very important summary on the state of royalist-syndicalist relations. It is signed by the commissaire de police (contained in PP, carton Bª1605, 31 May 1913).

23. Christian Gras, *Alfred Rosmer, 1877–1964 et le mouvement révolutionnaire international*, pp. 62–63.

24. That member was Robert de Boisfleury (PP, carton Bª1341, 19 August 1908).

25. AN, carton F⁷12862, 2 February 1909, 27 May 1909, 23 December 1909.

26. PP, carton Bª1342, agent "Chatenet," 11 June 1910, and agent "Brasseur," 12 June 1910.

27. Eugen Weber, *Action française*, pp. 56–57.

28. PP, carton Bª1342, agent "Lesueur," 7 July 1910, 20 August 1910.

29. Ibid.

30. Ibid.

31. See almost the entire issue of the *Action française* for 21 and 22 November 1910.

32. For a running account of the feud, see the *Action française* from 30 November through 31 December 1910.

33. Charles Maurras, "Briand," *Action française*, 30 June 1910.

34. Les Comités directeurs de l'Action française, "Enjuivement," *Action française*, 13 December 1910.

35. "Contre l'or juif," *Action française*, 13 December 1910.

36. Marc Sangnier, "Où aboutira le 'nationalisme intégral,'" *Démocratie*, 17 December 1910.

Chapter 9

1. Marc Sangnier, "Où aboutira le 'natioanlisme intégral,'" *Démocratie*, 17 December 1910.

2. Georges Guy-Grand, *Le Procès de la démocratie*, p. 80.

3. Léon Vannoz, "La Crise de la démocratie," p. 366.

4. For samples of the contemporary literature concerning this crisis, see Theodore Zeldin, *France, 1848–1945*, 1:713, n. 2.

5. Roger Martin du Gard, *Jean Barois*, pp. 313–14.

6. Quoted in Eugen Weber, *The Nationalist Revival in France, 1905–1914*, pp. 126–27.

7. See, for example, Pierre Gilbert, "Le Sémitisme au théâtre," pp. 290–99.

8. Gustave Téry, "Le Déserteur Bernstein," p. 6.

9. PP, carton B^{a}1343, agent "Lesueur," 3 March 1911.

10. Ibid., 8 March 1911.

11. Marcel Sembat, "Sa Fiole," *Humanité*, 8 March 1911.

12. Léon Daudet, "Après la bataille," *Action française*, 12 March 1911.

13. Un Sans-Patrie, "La Réponse des Rothschild," *Guerre sociale*, 8–14 February 1911.

14. Emile Janvion, "Devant les hébreux . . . ," *Terre libre*, 15 February–1 March 1911.

15. Ibid.

16. Victor Méric, "Au parterre: Houle de juifs," *Guerre sociale*, 22–28 February 1911.

17. Un Sans-Patrie, "Le Ministère Rothschild," *Guerre sociale*, 8–14 March 1911; *radicaille* is a play on two words: *radical* (politician of the Radical party) and *canaille* (rabble).

18. Ibid.

19. E. P. [Emile Para], "Pataud et Rothschild," *Action française*, 6 March 1911.

20. André Tridon, an observer of prewar syndicalism, writes of the militant electrical worker: "Bourgeois France and bourgeois Europe may know but little of the C.G.T. and its leaders. They cannot help knowing Pataud" (André Tridon, *The New Unionism*, p. 87). Pataud did much to establish his reputation by periodically threatening to darken Paris in the midst of government-syndicalist disputes. With Emile Pouget, he was the author of one of the most successful syndicalist prewar propaganda pieces: *Comment nous ferons la révolution*.

21. As early as April 1909, a police informer reported that royalist money had gone from a Camelot directly to Pataud (PP, carton B^{a}1603, agent "Mauve," 13 April 1909).

22. PP, carton B^{a}1343, agent "Lesueur," 25 March 1911.

23. Ibid., agent "X, 2e brigade," 28 March 1911.

24. Gustave Téry, "Et maintenant, qu'allons-nous faire?" p. 20.

25. Ibid., p. 17. This brand of "realism" was not confined to *L'Oeuvre*. In Sangnier's *Démocratie*, an article condemning anti-Semitism brought the following reply: "There is a great difference between squarely denying the Jewish question . . . and practicing a violent anti-Semitism, which consists of crying 'Death to the Jews!' at every turn" (Claudius Colas, "La Question juive: Réponse à M. Jean Guerner," *Démocratie*, 21 April 1911).

26. Téry, "Et maintenant," p. 21.

27. Gustave Téry, "L'Oeuvre de défense française," pp. 7–9.

28. The police estimated 1,500 in attendance (AN, carton F^{7}12862, no. 7, 5 April 1911).

29. From an edited reprint of Emile Janvion's *La Franc-Maçonnerie et la classe ouvrière*, p. 30. The pamphlet erroneously dates the meeting as 3 April 1910; it occurred 3 April 1911.

30. "Meeting antijuif et antimaçonnique," *Libre Parole*, 4 April 1911.

31. Victor Méric, "La Tourbe," *Guerre sociale*, 5–11 April 1911. Not that Pataud was acting as a foe of anti-Semitism. According to Téry, Pataud said at one point: "They have been feeding us priests for forty years, even in school; we now realize that it's a lean diet. Isn't our right to check for ourselves if the Jew is not more nourishing for the working class?" (Gustave Téry, "Potins et pantins," p. 34).

32. Cf. "Pataud et Janvion aux sociétés savantes," *Action française*, 4 April 1911; Un Sans-Patrie, "Ni antisémite ni antifranc-maçon," *Guerre sociale*, 5–11 April 1911; AN, carton F^{7}12862, no. 7, 5 April 1911.

33. "Dernière Heure," *Démocratie*, 4 April 1911.

34. "Meeting antijuif et antimaçonnique," *La Libre Parole*, 4 April 1911.

35. Ibid.; J. L., "Dernière Heure: Une Manifestation antisémite et réactionnaire," *Humanité*, 4 April 1911.

36. AN, carton F^{7}12862, no. 7, 5 April 1911.

37. Un Sans-Patrie, "Ni antisémite ni antifranc-maçon," *Guerre sociale*, 5–11 April 1911. This information is based upon the reports of his lieutenants, because Hervé at the time was serving one of his innumerable prison sentences.

38. Alfred Naquet, "L'Antisémitisme," p. 181.

39. Ibid., p. 183.

40. Sébastien Faure, "Pour Pataud," *Guerre sociale*, 5–11 April 1911.

41. Ibid.

42. "Exemple à suivre," *Humanité*, 10 April 1911.

43. Parti socialiste (SFIO), *Compte rendu du 8e congrès national, tenu à Saint-Quentin, les 16, 17, 18 et 19 avril, 1911*, p. 166.

44. Téry quoted Myrens on why the Jewish capitalist is more dangerous than the Christian capitalist: "For the *youtre* [another derogatory term for Jew], his heart is just a useless or even inconvenient visceral organ. Sentiment, which makes men capable of the most beautiful acts, is for him a sign of weakness; his sole aim is to cheat, plunder, steal, all this out of love for the gold that makes him rich and allows him to triumph, to be the king of the capitalist plutocracy" (Gustave Téry, "De gauche à droite," p. 28).

45. Parti socialiste, *Compte rendu du 8ᵉ congrès*, p. 187.

46. Cf. Jean Rabaut, "Charles Rappoport déconfit ou le coup manqué du congrès de Saint-Quentin (Avril, 1911)," pp. 1–14; Harvey Goldberg, *The Life of Jean Jaurès*, pp. 552–53, n. 127.

47. Rabaut, "Charles Rappoport," pp. 5–12.

48. See chap. 8, n. 15.

49. Rabaut, "Charles Rappoport," p. 12.

50. Un Sans-Patrie, "Le Réveil de l'antisémitisme," *Guerre sociale*, 15–21 March 1911.

51. Un Sans-Patrie, "Ni antisémite ni antifranc-maçon," *Guerre sociale*, 5–11 April 1911.

52. "Une Lettre de Pataud," *Guerre sociale*, 12–18 April 1911.

53. PP, carton Bᵃ1343, 20 April 1911.

54. Pseudonym for Eugène Vigo, later of the *Bonnet rouge*.

55. PP, carton Bᵃ1343, agent "X, 2ᵉ brigade," 17 January 1911.

56. See especially "Aux prolétaires juifs," *Terre libre* 15 April–1 May 1911.

57. "Dernière Heure: Les Juifs contre Pataud," *Démocratie*, 7 April 1911; "Dernière Heure: Contre l'antisémitisme," *Humanité*, 7 April 1911.

58. "Dernière Heure: A la Bellevilloise," *Humanité*, 14 April 1911.

59. PP, carton Bᵃ1343, agent "Lesueur," 3 April 1911.

60. Ibid., 20 April 1911.

61. With this in mind, the Camelots were being reorganized (ibid., 22 April 1911).

62. Maurice Pujo, "Au jour le jour: Nos prisons," *Action française*, 7 May 1911.

63. Am. D., "Mise au point," *Bataille syndicaliste*, 18 May 1911.

64. "Mouvement syndical," *Action française*, 16 May 1911.

65. L'A. F., "Notre Mise au point," *Action française*, 19 May 1911.

66. PP, Carton Bᵃ1343, agent "Lesueur," 30 April 1911.

67. See chap. 8.

68. PP, carton Bᵃ1605, agent "17," 30 May 1913.

69. Ibid., report of the commissaire de police, 31 May 1913.

70. The commissaire de police, at least, seems sure of this: "I have been told that articles written at the 'Bataille syndicaliste' had first been trans-

mitted to the Action française, which returned them with corrections in order to be published in the 'Bataille syndicaliste'" (ibid.).

71. Ibid.

72. Ibid.; the report of the commissaire de police ended, unfortunately, on an abrupt note: because the staff of the *Bataille syndicaliste* had recently moved its files outside of the newspaper's offices, more information concerning royalist-syndicalist relations, the report concluded, would probably not be forthcoming. The question of how far back relations between royalists and the director of the *Bataille syndicaliste* extended was not dealt with in this report or in any subsequent police reports. However, one cannot easily dismiss those police agents who had been insisting for several years—though without documentation—that there existed conspiratorial activities between royalists and syndicalists.

Chapter 10

1. Pierre Andreu, "Demain sur nos tombeaux."

2. Maxime Brienne, "Le Témoignage de la génération sacrifiée," p. 12.

3. Eugen Weber, *Action française*, p. 76, n. d; Maurice Barrès, "Les Diverses Familles spirituelles de la France," *Echo de Paris*, 7 March 1917.

4. Weber, *Action française*, p. 81.

5. On Rivain's early interest in syndicalism, see chap. 2.

6. Georges Valois, "Notre Première Année," p. 157.

7. Georges Guy-Grand, *Le Procès de la démocratie*, pp. 49–122.

8. See Pierre Gilbert, "Les Nuées," *Revue critique des idées et des livres* 11:477–80, 12:227–33; Georges Guy-Grand,"Les Livres," pp. 252–54.

9. Edouard Berth, "Le Procès de la démocratie," pp. 9–46.

10. Ibid., pp. 22–23.   11. See chap. 7.

12. Berth, "Le Procès," p. 28.   13. "Déclaration," p. 1.

14. "Ligue d'Action française," *Action française*, 18 January 1909.

15. See Edmund Silberner, "Proudhon's Judeophobia," pp. 61–80. For a recent Proudhon scholar's evaluation of the Cercle Proudhon, see Robert L. Hoffman, *Revolutionary Justice*, pp. 274, 347–49. See also Daniel Halévy's more favorable estimate, "Variétés: Sur l'interprétation de Proudhon," *Journal des débats, politiques et littéraires*, 2–3 January 1913.

16. Pierre Andreu, *Notre Maître, M. Sorel*, p. 85.

17. If he did not know, the first formal meeting of the Cercle Proudhon should have disabused him of any illusions. The appreciations of Proudhon delivered there were not designed to excite scholarly interest. See the first issue of the *Cahiers du Cercle Proudhon*.

18. Besides Lagrange and Valois, there were Gilbert Maire from the

Revue critique, René de Marans, who had been an early rightist student of syndicalism, and André Pascalon, a law student.

19. Notebooks 3 and 4.

20. Valois, "Notre Première Année," p. 151.

21. Once again, this low figure should be seen in the light of relatively low subscription rates for French periodicals of this genre.

22. For a sampling of attendance, see "Déclarations du Cercle," p. 175.

23. See chap. 1.

24. "Déclaration," p. 1.

25. Albert Vincent, "Le Bilan de la démocratie," pp. 98–99.

26. Ibid., pp. 100–104.

27. Ibid., p. 103.

28. Edouard Berth, *Les Nouveaux Aspects du socialisme*, pp. 34–35.

29. Ibid., pp. 35–36.

30. Edouard Berth, *Les Méfaits des intellectuels*, p. 338.

31. Georges Valois, "Les Enseignements de cinq ans, 1909–1914," reprinted in *L'Oeuvre de Georges Valois*, 3:255.

32. Ibid., pp. 255–56. 33. Berth, "Le Procès," p. 27.

34. Ibid., pp. 26–27. 35. Andreu, "Demain."

36. Georges Guy-Grand, *La Philosophie nationaliste*, p. 46.

37. Andreu, "Demain."

38. Henri Lagrange, *Vingt Ans en 1914*, p. 195.

39. Georges Valois, "Pourquoi nous rattachons nos travaux à l'esprit proudhonien," pp. 44–45. Valois abruptly dismissed the fact that Proudhon's book ended in a castigation of war; despite its conclusion *antiguerrière*, Valois argues, *La Guerre et la paix* is a "martial book." Robert Hoffman, fair to both Proudhon and the neo-Proudhonians, writes of those who drew from Proudhon's book a "mystique of violence": "This was not as great an abuse of the original as was much of the nonsense written about Proudhon, although it was a distortion of his ideas. His tribute to war and to force is more than a device of rhetorical method; it is intended seriously but it is also tied indissolubly to a final reprobation of all war" (Hoffman, *Revolutionary Justice*, p. 211).

40. Berth, *Nouveaux Aspects*, p. 4.

41. Jean Darville [Edouard Berth], "Satellites de la ploutocratie," p. 177.

42. Ibid., p. 207.

43. Ibid., pp. 207–8.

44. See Edouard Berth's essay entitled "La Victoire de Pascal," in his *Méfaits*, pp. 295–358.

45. Jean Darville, "La Monarchie et la classe ouvrière," pp. 10–15.

46. Berth, *Méfaits*, p. 344.

47. Ibid., p. 346.

48. The "early fascism" of the Cercle Proudhon did not escape the attention of commentators writing from the perspective of the 1930s. Pierre Andreu, in 1936, wrote an article entitled "Fascisme 1913," and Pierre Drieu La Rochelle could write: "Some elements of the fascist atmosphere could already be found in France before 1913. . . . Some young men from various classes of society were animated by the love of heroism and violence. . . . Already the marriage of nationalism and socialism was in the offing" (quoted in Zeev Sternhell, "Anatomie d'un mouvement fasciste en France," p. 7). Both of these examples are cited in the above article by Sternhell, who agrees: "The first French fascism continues in fact the work of the Cercle Proudhon, which had been deserted by the Action française, because of [the latter's] drift to the right." (ibid., p. 8). Valois himself admitted in the 1920s that the Cercle Proudhon had "laid the foundation" for his Faisceau, and Berth, despite the fact that he had moved back to the revolutionary Left and unsympathetic to fascism in the 1920s, agreed that the Cercle Proudhon had created a fascism "avant la lettre" (J. L. Talmon, "The Legacy of Georges Sorel," p. 58, n. 15, and Georges Valois, *L'Homme contre l'argent*, p. 61.)

49. In a strict sense, of course, it would be a national syndicalism; the Cercle Proudhon avoided the term "socialism" because of its humanitarian and social-democratic implications.

50. Valois, "Notre Première Année," p. 157.

51. Ibid., p. 159, n. 1.

52. Georges Valois, "La Bourgeoisie capitaliste," pp. 219–20.

53. Berth, *Méfaits*, pp. 53–54.

54. Valois, "Notre Première Année," pp. 161–63.

55. PP, carton B^a1343, agent "Delnard," 28 February 1912.

56. Louis Dimier, *Vingt Ans d'Action française et autres souvenirs*, pp. 226–30.

57. Valois, *L'Homme contre l'argent*, p. 62.

Chapter 11

1. The background articles on this affair are too numerous to be listed. See the *Bataille syndicaliste*, the *Guerre sociale*, and the *Action française* from the end of November 1912 through early January 1913, especially Maurice Pujo, "L'Affaire Bintz," *Action française*, 24 November 1912; Le Jeune Major, "L'Affaire Bintz," *Bataille syndicaliste*, 3 December 1912; and E. Tissier, "L'Affaire Bintz," *Guerre sociale*, 27 November through 3 December 1912.

2. "Notre Correspondance," *Terre libre*, 15–29 February 1912.

3. Le Vieux Major, "Le Frère commandant," *Terre libre*, 1–15 March 1912.

4. "La Franc-Maçonnerie et le parti," *Humanité*, 22 February 1912.

5. Jules Uhry, *Socialisme et franc-maçonnerie*, p. 16.

6. The postal workers' syndicat, for example. See G. Sarda, "L'Antimaçonnisme dans les P.T.T.," *Terre libre*, 16–31 August 1911.

7. AN, carton $F^7 13616$, 21 June 1912, 14 August 1912, 22 August 1912; AN, carton $F^7 13617$, 16 January 1913.

8. Pujo, "L'Affaire Bintz," *Action française*, 24 November 1912.

9. "L'Affaire Bintz," *Action française*, 22 November 1912.

10. Le Jeune Major, "L'Affaire Bintz." *Bataille syndicaliste*, 3 December 1912.

11. For Pujo's explanation, see Maurice Pujo, "L'Affaire Bintz," *Action française*, 5 January 1913.

12. "Le Meeting des sociétés savantes," *Bataille syndicaliste*, 12 December 1912.

13. "L'Affaire Bintz," *Bataille syndicaliste*, 4 January 1913.

14. Cf. "A nos amis, aux lecteurs," *Bataille syndicaliste*, 3 January 1913, with Emile Janvion, "Le Sac de la 'B.S.,'" *Terre libre*, 1–15 December 1913.

15. "L'Affaire Bintz," *Bataille syndicaliste*, 6 January 1913.

16. "A propos du sac de la 'B.S.,'" *Guerre sociale*, 8–11 January 1913.

17. Ibid.

18. The police had noted, as early as October 1910, that there were stirrings in the long-dormant Bonapartist camp. The leaders of the Bonapartist party were "in the process of completely reorganizing for political struggle" (PP, carton $B^a 1342$, agent "Lesueur," 14 October 1910).

19. Gustave Hervé, "La Crise du régime," *Guerre sociale*, 28 June–4 July 1911.

20. "Face aux barbares," *Guerre sociale*, 5–11 July 1911.

21. Maurice Pujo, "Jeunes Gardes ministériels?" *Action française*, 3 June 1911; Maurice Pujo, "Les 'Jeunes Gardes,'" *Action française*, 5 June 1911; Maurice Pujo, "Une Lettre de M. Gustave Hervé," *Action française*, 6 June 1911.

22. PP, carton $B^a 1343$, 16 June 1911.

23. "Expliquons-nous!" *Guerre sociale*, 8–14 May 1912.

24. Jean Texcier, "Le Quartier Latin," *Guerre sociale*, 3–9 July 1912.

25. Un Sans-Patrie, "Après la fête de Rousseau," *Guerre sociale*, 3–9 July 1912.

26. See the issues of the *Guerre sociale* for July 1912.

27. Maurice Rotstein, "The Public Life of Gustave Hervé," p. 112.

28. Ibid., pp. 119–25.

29. PP, carton Bᵃ1343, agent "R. S.," 6 January 1912.

30. Rivarol, "Echos," *Action française*, 16 January 1912.

31. "Après la grève des gens de mer," *Action française*, 24 August 1912.

32. PP, carton Bᵃ1343, agent "Lesueur," 11 September 1912.

33. Quoted in Eugen Weber, *The Nationalist Revival in France, 1905–1914*, p. 111.

34. Harmel, "Les Sauvages," *Bataille syndicaliste*, 10 March 1913.

35. "Notice," *Bataille syndicaliste*, 14 March 1913.

36. "C'est une déroute nationaliste," *Bataille syndicaliste*, 15 March 1913.

37. Ibid.

38. B. S. "Pour M. Maurice Pujo," *Bataille syndicaliste*, 18 March 1913.

39. Maurice Pujo, "Le Syndicalisme saboté," *Action française*, 30 March 1913.

40. See chap. 9, pp. 168–69.

41. The significance of this change in the character of syndicalism has been persuasively argued in a dissertation by Michael DeLucia, "The Remaking of French Syndicalism, 1911–1918." See also Nicholas C. Papayanis, "Alphonse Merrheim and Revolutionary Syndicalism, 1871–1917."

42. First appeared as a policy statement in the *Bataille syndicaliste*; reprinted in "La Revue sociale du mois," p. 282.

43. Besides Pierre Monatte, Alfred Rosmer and Georges Dumoulin started at the *Vie ouvrière*.

44. The debate was carried on in the *Bataille syndicaliste* in late January and early February. For a summary, see Papayanis, "Alphonse Merrheim," pp. 226–28.

45. Pierre Monatte, "La C.G.T. a-t-elle rectifié son tir?" pp. 129–30.

46. Ibid., p. 137.

47. Ibid., p. 138.

48. Bernard Georges and Denise Tintant, *Léon Jouhaux, cinquante ans de syndicalisme*, 1:88; my italics.

Chapter 12

1. AN, carton F⁷13617, 17 Janaury 1913.

2. Ibid., 21 and 23 January 1913.

3. Victor Griffuelhes, "Où va-t-on?" *Bataille syndicaliste*, 23 January 1913.

4. See chap. 8, pp. 139–40.

5. See chap. 9, pp. 168–69. This does not necessarily implicate everyone at the *Bataille syndicaliste*. From Gras's evidence, Merrheim was outraged by Delaisi's methods.

6. Gustave Téry, "France d'abord," p. 14.

7. Henri Clouard, "Une Jeune Elite sacrifiée," *Renaissance: Politique, économique, littéraire et artistique*, 12 May 1917.

8. See chap. 1.

9. The essay on the various European "radical Rights" in Eugen Weber and Hans Rogger, eds., *The European Right*, gives a good indication of the frequency with which disenchantment with the Left could lead to radical nationalism. In France, Valois's long evolution from anarchism to fascism was not without parallel. The two leading figures of French fascism during the 1930s and the Occupation, Jacques Doriot and Marcel Déat, came, respectively, from the Communist and Socialist parties.

Bibliography

1. Manuscript Sources

Paris, France
  Archives nationales
    F⁷12459 Mouvement antisémite (1890–1907)
    F⁷12538 Association des fonctionnaires
    F⁷12723 Agitation révolutionnaire (1893–1914)
    F⁷12793 Groupements et syndicats jaunes (1901–1909)
    F⁷12861 Royalistes (1900–1912)
    F⁷12862 Action française (1899–1911)
    F⁷12863 Action française (1912–1915)
    F⁷12864 Camelots du roi (1909–1913)
    F⁷12915 Grève de Draveil-Vigneux (1908)
    F⁷12916 Grève de Draveil-Vigneux (1908)
    F⁷13195 Action française (diverses années)
    F⁷13568 Confédération générale du travail (diverses notes)
    F⁷13616 Notes et presse sur bourse de Paris (1909–1912)
    F⁷13617 Notes et presse sur bourse de Paris (1913–1916)
  Archives de la Seine
    Dossier Janvion
  Institut français d'histoire sociale
    Fonds Delesalle, carton 14AS 12–14
    Fonds Delesalle, carton 14AS 153bis
  Préfecture de police
    Bª1341   Bª1603
    Bª1342   Bª1605
    Bª1343   Bª1606
    Bª1602

2. Letters

Barrès, Maurice, and Maurras, Charles. *La République ou le roi: Correspondance inédite, 1888–1923*. Edited by Hélène and Nicole Maurras. Paris: Plon, 1970.

Bernanos, Georges. *Correspondance*. Vol. 1, *1904–1934*. Edited by Albert Beguin and Jean Murray. Paris: Plon, 1971.

Darville, Jean [Edouard Berth], to Valois, Georges. Letter, undated, under the title: "La Monarchie et la classe ouvrière." *Cahiers du Cercle Proudhon*, 2d. ser., no. 1 (January–February 1914), pp. 7–34.

"Lettere di Georges Sorel a B. Croce." *La Critica, rivista di letteratura, storia e filosofia* 25 (1927): 38–52, 101–8, 168–76, 300–312, 360–72; 26 (1928): 31–39, 92–108, 187–97, 334–48, 432–42; 27 (1929): 47–52, 114–25, 289–97, 353–61, 438–46; 28 (1930): 42–52, 118–21, 189–95.

"Lettere di Giorgio Sorel a Uberto Lagardelle." *Educazione fascista* 11 (March 1933): 229–43; (April 1933): 320–34; (June 1933): 506–18; (August–September 1933): 760–83; (October 1933): 956–75.

"Lettres de Georges Sorel à Edouard Berth (extraits)." *L'Amitié Charles Péguy*, monthly sheets, no. 77 (May 1960), pp. 23–33.

Marans, René de, to Valois, Georges. Letter, 25 May 1912, in *Cahiers du Cercle Proudhon*, notebooks 3 and 4 (May–August 1912), pp. 117–20.

Sorel, Georges, to Maurras, Charles. Letter, 6 July 1909. In *Notre Maître, M. Sorel* by Pierre Andreu. Paris: Bernard Grasset, 1953.

3. Newspapers

L'Action	*L'Action française*
L'Autorité	*La Bataille syndicaliste*
Le Bonnet rouge	*La Démocratie*
L'Echo de Paris	*Gil Blas*
La Guerre sociale	*L'Humanité*
L'Indépendance belge	*Le Journal*
Le Journal des débats, politiques et littéraires	*Le Libertaire*
La Libre Parole	*La Liberté*
Les Nouvelles littéraires	*Le Matin*
La Presse	*La Patrie*
La Renaissance: Politique, économique, littéraire et artistique	*Le Radical*
Le Temps	*La Révolution*
La Voix du peuple	*Le Siècle*
	La Terre libre

4. *Books, Articles, and Dissertations*

Agathon [Henri Massis and Alfred de Tarde]. *Les Jeunes Gens d'aujourd'hui*. Paris: Plon, 1913.

Almanach de l'Action française, 1923. Paris: Nouvelle Librairie nationale, 1922.

Andreu, Pierre. "Bibliographie d'Edouard Berth." *Bulletin of the International Institute for Social History* 7–8 (1952–53): 196–204.

————. "Demain sur nos tombeaux." *Combat*, no. 4 (April 1936).

————. *Notre Maître, M. Sorel*. Paris: Bernard Grasset, 1953.

"A nos lecteurs." *La Revue critique des idées et des livres* 1 (1908): 5–6.

Bacconnier, Firmin. "Ce que je dois à Charles Maurras." *Cahiers Charles Maurras*, no. 1 (April 1960), pp. 25–26.

————. *Manuel du royaliste*. Paris: Bureau de la "Gazette de France," 1903.

Beau de Loménie, Emmanuel. *Maurras et son système*. Bourg, Ain: E.T.L., 1953.

Berth, Edouard. *Les Méfaits des intellectuels*. 2d ed. Paris: Marcel Rivière, 1926.

————. *Les Nouveaux Aspects du socialisme*. Paris: Marcel Rivière, 1927.

————. "Le Procès de la démocratie." *La Revue critique des idées et des livres* 13 (1911): 9–46.

Bonnefous, Georges. *Histoire politique de la troisième république*. Vol. 1, *L'Avant-guerre, 1906–1914*. 2d ed. Paris: Presses universitaires de France, 1965.

Brécy, Robert. *Le Mouvement syndical en France: Essai bibliographique, 1871–1921*. Paris: Mouton, 1963.

Brienne, Maxime. "Le Témoignage de la génération sacrifiée. 1, Henri Lagrange." *Les Essaims nouveaux*, nos. 2–3 (September–October 1917), pp. 11–12.

Buthman, William. *The Rise of Integral Nationalism in France*. New York: Columbia University Press, 1939.

Cahm, Eric. *Péguy et le nationalisme français de l'affaire Dreyfus à la grande guerre*. Cahiers de l'Amitié Charles Péguy, notebook 25. Paris: Cahiers de l'Amitié Charles Péguy, 1972.

Clouard, Henri. "Des Souvenirs sur Georges Sorel." *Le Progrès civique*, no. 161 (16 September 1922), pp. 1324–25.

Collinet, Michel. *Esprit du syndicalisme, essai; l'Ouvrier français*. Collection "Masses et militants." Paris: Les Editions ouvrières, 1952.

Coston, Henry. *Dictionnaire de la politique française*. Vol. 1. Paris: Publications H. Coston, 1967.

Cratès [Francis Delaisi]. "Le Camp capitaliste: Les Compagnies, Rothschild et Briand." *La Vie ouvrière*, no. 27 (November 1910), pp. 562–88.

Darien, Georges. *L'Ennemi du peuple*. Classiques de la subversion, vol. 4. Paris: Editions Champ libre, 1972.

Darville, Jean [Edouard Berth]. "La Monarchie et la classe ouvrière." *Cahiers du Cercle Proudhon*, 2d ser., no. 1 (January–February 1914), pp. 7–34.

————. "Satellites de la ploutocratie." *Cahiers du Cercle Proudhon*, notebooks 5 and 6 (n.d.), pp. 177–213.

Daudet, Léon. *Souvenirs des milieux littéraires, politiques, artistiques et médicaux*. Vol. 2. Paris: Nouvelle Librairie nationale, 1926.

"Déclaration." *Cahiers du Cercle Proudhon*, notebook 1 (January–February 1912), pp. 1–2.

"Déclarations du Cercle." *Cahiers du Cercle Proudhon*, notebooks 3 and 4 (May–August 1912), pp. 174–75.

Delaisi, Francis. *La Démocratie et les financiers*. Paris: Editions de "La Guerre sociale," 1910.

DeLucia, Michael. "The Remaking of French Syndicalism, 1911–1918: The Growth of the Reformist Philosophy." Ph.D. dissertation, Brown University, 1971.

Dictionnaire biographique du mouvement ouvrier français. Edited by Jean Maîtron. Paris: Les Editions ouvrières, 1964–.

Dimier, Louis. *Vingt Ans d'Action française et autres souvenirs*. Paris: Nouvelle Librairie nationale, 1926.

Dolléans, Edouard. *Histoire du mouvement ouvrier*. Vol. 2, *1871–1920*. 6th ed. Paris: Librairie Armand Colin, 1967.

Doty, Charles Stewart. *From Cultural Rebellion to Counterrevolution: The Politics of Maurice Barrès*. Athens: Ohio University Press, 1976.

Dubief, Henri. *Le Syndicalisme révolutionnaire*. Collection U. Paris: Armand Colin, 1969.

Encyclopedia of Philosophy. New York: Macmillan Company and Free Press, 1967.

Fromm, Erich. *Escape from Freedom*. New York: Farrar & Rinehart, 1941.

Georges, Bernard, and Tintant, Denise. *Léon Jouhaux, cinquante ans de syndicalisme*. Vol. 1, *Des Origines à 1921*. Paris: Presses universitaires de France, 1962.

Gilbert, Pierre. "Les Nuées." *La Revue critique des idées et des livres* 2 (1908): 138–50.

————. "Les Nuées." *La Revue critique des idées et des livres* 11 (1910): 477–80.

————. "Les Nuées." *La Revue critique des idées et des livres* 12 (1911): 227–33.

————. "Le Sémitisme au théâtre." *La Revue critique des idées et des livres* 12 (1911): 290–99.

Girardet, Raoul. "Notes sur l'esprit d'un fascisme français, 1934–1939." *Revue française de science politique* 5 (July–September 1955): 529–46.

Goetz-Girey, Robert. *La Pensée syndicale française: Militants et théoriciens.* Cahiers de la fondation nationale des sciences politiques, vol. 3. Paris: Librairie Armand Colin, 1948.

Goldberg, Harvey. *The Life of Jean Jaurès.* Madison: University of Wisconsin Press, 1962.

Goriely, Georges. *Le Pluralisme dramatique de Georges Sorel.* Paris: Editions Marcel Rivière, 1962.

Gras, Christian. *Alfred Rosmer, 1877–1964 et le mouvement révolutionnaire international.* Bibliothèque socialiste, vol. 20. Paris: François Maspero, 1971.

————. "La Fédération des métaux en 1913–1914 et l'évolution du syndicalisme révolutionnaire français." *Le Mouvement social*, no. 77 (October–December 1971), pp. 85–111.

————. "Merrheim et le capitalisme." *Le Mouvement social*, no. 63 (April–June 1968), pp. 143–63.

Guchet, Yves. *Georges Valois: L'Action française, le Faisceau, la république syndicale.* Paris: Editions Albatros, 1975.

————. "Georges Valois ou l'illusion fasciste." *Revue française de science politique* 15 (December 1965): 1111–44.

Guy-Grand, Georges. "Les Livres." *Les Annales de la jeunesse laïque*, no. 104 (January 1911), pp. 252–54.

————. *La Philosophie nationaliste.* Paris: Bernard Grasset, 1911.

————. *Le Procès de la démocratie.* Paris: Librairie Armand Colin, 1911.

Histoire générale de la presse française. Vol. 3, *De 1871 à 1940.* Paris: Presses universitaires de France, 1972.

Hoffman, Robert L. *Revolutionary Justice: The Social and Political Theory of P.-J. Proudhon.* Urbana: University of Illinois Press, 1972.

Horowitz, Irving Louis. *Radicalism and the Revolt against Reason: The Social Theories of Georges Sorel.* Carbondale: Southern Illinois University Press, Arcturus Books, 1968.

Janvion, Emile. *La Franc-Maçonnerie et la classe ouvrière.* Paris: Imprimerie spéciale de "Terre libre," 1912.

Jean, Lucien. *Parmi les hommes.* Paris: Mercure de France, 1910.

Julliard, Jacques. *Clemenceau, briseur de grèves: l'Affaire de Draveil-Villeneuve-Saint-Georges.* Collection Archives, vol. 14. Mesnil-sur-l'Estrée: Julliard, 1965.

————. *Fernand Pelloutier et les origines du syndicalisme d'action directe.* Paris: Editions du Seuil, 1971.

————. "Théorie syndicaliste révolutionnaire et pratique gréviste." *Le Mouvement social*, no. 65 (October–December 1968), pp. 55–69.

Lagardelle, Hubert. "Déclaration." *Le Mouvement socialiste* 1 (January 1899): 1–3.

———. *Le Socialisme ouvrier.* Collections des documents politiques, vol. 9. Paris: V. Giard & E. Brière, 1911.

Lagrange, Henri. *Vingt Ans en 1914.* Paris: Nouvelle Librairie nationale, 1920.

Landauer, Carl. *European Socialism: A History of Ideas and Movements from the Industrial Revolution to Hitler's Seizure of Power.* Vol. 1, *From the Industrial Revolution to the First World War and Its Aftermath.* Berkeley and Los Angeles: University of California Press, 1959.

Lefranc, Georges. *Le Mouvement syndical sous la troisième république.* Bibliothèque historique. Paris: Payot, 1967.

Levey, Jules. "Georges Valois and the Faisceau: The Making and Breaking of a Fascist." *French Historical Studies* 8 (1973): 279–304.

———. "The Sorelian Syndicalists: Edouard Berth, Georges Valois, and Hubert Lagardelle." Ph.D. dissertation, Columbia University, 1967.

Ligou, Daniel. *Histoire du socialisme en France, 1871–1961.* Paris: Presses universitaires de France, 1962.

Louzon, Robert. "La Faillite du dreyfusisme ou le triomphe du parti juif." *Le Mouvement socialiste,* no. 176 (July 1906), pp. 193–99.

Lucchini, Pierre [Pierre Dominique]. *Léon Daudet.* Paris: Editions du Vieux Colombier, 1964.

McInnes, Neil. *The Western Marxists.* New York: Library Press, 1972.

Maîtron, Jean. *Histoire du mouvement anarchiste en France, 1880–1914.* Paris: Société universitaire d'éditions et de librairie, 1955.

Manouvriez, Abel. "L'Action française au Quartier Latin: Les Premiers Pas d'une conquête, 1905–1909." *Cahiers Charles Maurras,* no. 1 (April 1960), pp. 39–44.

Marans, René de. "La Grève générale et les deux socialismes." *L'Association catholique* 59 (1905): 315–24.

———. "Les *Réflexions sur la violence* de M. Georges Sorel." *L'Association catholique* 62 (1906): 531–39.

Martin du Gard, Roger. *Jean Barois.* Translated by Stuart Gilbert. New York: Viking Press, 1949.

Maulnier, Thierry. "Charles Maurras et le socialisme." *La Revue universelle* 68 (1937): 166–71.

———. "Le 'Fascisme' et son avenir en France." *La Revue universelle* 64 (1936): 13–26.

Maurras, Charles. *Le Dilemme de Marc Sangnier.* Paris: Nouvelle Librairie nationale, 1907.

———. *Enquête sur la monarchie, 1900–1909.* Paris: Nouvelle Librairie nationale, 1909.

———. "Sur le nom de socialiste." *Revue de l'Action française* 3 (1900): 859–67.

Mazgaj, Paul. "The Social Revolution or the King: The Initiatives of the Action française toward the Revolutionary Left, 1906–1914." Ph.D. dissertation, University of Iowa, 1976.

Meisel, James H. *The Genesis of Georges Sorel: An Account of His Formative Period Followed By a Study of His Influence*. Ann Arbor, Mich.: George Wahr, 1951.

Méric, Victor. *Coulisses et tréteaux: A travers la jungle politique et littéraire*. Vol. 1. Paris: Librairie Valois, 1930.

Monatte, Pierre. "La C.G.T. a-t-elle rectifié son tir?" *La Vie ouvrière*, no. 93 (August 1913), pp. 129–39.

Moss, Bernard H. *The Origins of the French Labor Movement, 1830–1914: The Socialism of Skilled Workers*. Berkeley and Los Angeles: University of California Press, 1976.

Mosse, George. "The French Right and the Working Classes: Les Jaunes." *Journal of Contemporary History* 7 (1972): 185–208.

Naquet, Alfred. "L'Antisémitisme." *Le Courrier européen*, 25 March 1911, pp. 181–84.

Nguyen, Victor. "Situation des études maurrassiennes: Contribution à l'étude de la presse et des mentalités." *Revue d'histoire moderne et contemporaine* 17 (October–December 1971): 503–38.

Nolte, Ernst. *The Three Faces of Fascism: Action française, Italian Fascism, National Socialism*. Translated by Leila Vennewitz. New York: Holt, Rinehart & Winston, 1966.

Onimus, Jean. "Péguy et Sorel." *L'Amitié Charles Péguy*, monthly sheets, no. 77 (May 1960), pp. 3–22.

Papayanis, Nicholas C. "Alphonse Merrheim and Revolutionary Syndicalism, 1871–1917." Ph.D. dissertation, University of Wisconsin, 1969.

Para, Emile. "Le Mouvement syndicaliste." *La Revue critique des idées et des livres* 1 (1908): 85–93.

———. "Review of *Le Socialisme: Exposé du pour et du contre*." *La Revue critique des idées et des livres* 1 (1908): 365–66.

Parti socialiste (SFIO). *Compte rendu du 8ᵉ congrès national, tenu à Saint-Quentin, les 16, 17, 18 et 19 avril, 1911*. Paris: Compte rendu sténographique, n.d.

Paugam, Jacques. *L'Age d'or du maurrassisme*. Paris: Denoël, 1971.

Péguy, Charles. *Oeuvres en prose, Vol. 2, 1909–1914*. Paris: Gallimard, 1957.

Pirou, Gaétan. "A propos du syndicalisme révolutionnaire: Théoriciens et militants." *La Revue politique et parlementaire* 70 (1911): 130–42.

———. *Georges Sorel (1847–1922)*, Paris: Rivière, 1927.

Plumyène, J., and Lasierra, R. *Les Fascismes français, 1923–1963*. Paris: Editions du Seuil, 1963.

P. M. "Vierge et martyre: Les Polémiques de *L'Humanité*," parts 1 and 2. *La Vie ouvrière*, no. 29 (December 1910), pp. 766–84; no. 30 (December 1910), pp. 824–53.

Polanyi, Karl. *The Great Transformation: The Political and Economic Origins of Our Time*. New York and Toronto: Farrar & Rinehart, 1944.

Prolétaire conscient, le [Gustave Téry]. "Le Ministère Rothschild." *L'Oeuvre*, no. 45 (November 1910), pp. 6–12.

Rabaut, Jean. "Charles Rappoport déconfit ou le coup manqué du congrès de Saint-Quentin, Avril, 1911." *Bulletin de la société d'études jaurèsiennes*, no. 37 (April–June 1970), pp. 1–14.

Rémond, René. *The Right Wing in France from 1815 to de Gaulle*. Translated by James M. Laux. Philadelphia: University of Pennsylvania Press, 1966.

"La Revue sociale du mois: La Crise du syndicalisme français." *La Revue socialiste* 56 (1912): 268–82.

Ridley, F. F. *Revolutionary Syndicalism in France: The Direct Action of Its Time*. Cambridge: Cambridge University Press, 1970.

Rivain, Jean. "L'Avenir du syndicalisme." *Revue de l'Action française* 32 (1908): 467–84.

———. "La Patrie des prolétaires." *Revue de l'Action française* 21 (1906): 189–94.

———. "Les Socialistes antidémocrates." *Revue de l'Action française* 25 (1907): 412–18, 470–87.

Rotstein, Maurice. "The Public Life of Gustave Hervé." Ph.D. dissertation, New York University, 1956.

Roudiez, Léon. *Maurras jusqu'à l'Action française*. Paris: Editions André Bonne, 1957.

Rutkoff, Peter. "The Ligue des patriotes: The Nature of the Radical Right and the Dreyfus Affair." *French Historical Studies* 8 (1974): 585–603.

Sanders, Richard Wayne. "The Labor Politics of the French Radical Party, 1901–1909." Ph.D. dissertation, Brown University, 1971.

Scher, Michael Roger. "The Antipatriot as Patriot: A Study of the Young Gustave Hervé, 1871–1905." Ph.D. dissertation, University of California, Los Angeles, 1972.

Schmitt, Hans A. *Charles Péguy: The Decline of an Idealist*. Baton Rouge: Louisiana State University Press, 1967.

Seager, Frederic H. *The Boulanger Affair: Political Crossroad of France, 1886–1889*. Ithaca, N.Y.: Cornell University Press, 1969.

Silberner, Edmund. "Proudhon's Judeophobia," *Historia Judaica* 9 (1948): 61–80.

Sorel, Georges. *L'Avenir socialiste des syndicats*. Paris: Librairie G. Jacques, 1901.

————. *La Décomposition du marxisme*. Paris: M. Rivière, 1908.

————. "Essai sur la philosophie de Proudhon." *La Revue philosophique* 33–34 (June–July 1892): 622–38, 41–68.

————. *Les Illusions du progrès*. Paris: Rivière, 1908.

————. *Matériaux d'une théorie du prolétariat*. Paris: Marcel Rivière, 1921.

————. "Modernisme dans la religion et dans le socialisme." *La Revue critique des idées et des livres* 2 (1908): 177–204.

————. "Morale et socialisme." *Le Mouvement socialiste* 1 (March 1899): 207–13.

————. *Les Polémiques pour l'interprétation du marxisme: Bernstein et Kautsky*. Paris: V. Giard & E. Brière, 1900.

————. *Reflections on Violence*. Translated by T. E. Hulme and J. Roth. New York: Crowell-Collier Publishing Co., Collier Books, 1961.

————. "Response to 'La Réforme et la critique positive." *La Revue critique des idées et des livres* 10 (1910): 97–113, 193–203, 312–23, 406–16, 497–509; 11 (1910): 44–60.

————. *La Révolution dreyfusienne*. Bibliothèque du mouvement socialiste, vol. 8. Paris: Marcel Rivière, 1909.

Soucy, Robert J. *Fascism in France: The Case of Maurice Barrès*. Berkeley and Los Angeles: University of California Press, 1972.

————. "The Nature of Fascism in France." *Journal of Contemporary History* 1 (1966): 27–55.

Stanley, John L. *From Georges Sorel*. Edited by John L. Stanley and translated by John and Charlotte Stanley. New York: Oxford University Press, 1976.

Stearns, Peter N. *Revolutionary Syndicalism and French Labor: A Cause without Rebels*. New Brunswick, N.J.: Rutgers University Press, 1971.

Stearns, Peter N., and Mitchell, Harvey. *Workers and Protest: The European Labor Movement, the Working Classes, and the Origins of Social Democracy, 1890–1914*. Itasca, Ill.: F. E. Peacock, 1971.

Stern, Fritz. *Politics of Cultural Despair: A Study in the rise of the Germanic Ideology*. Garden City, N.Y.: Doubleday, Anchor Books, 1965.

Sternhell, Zeev. "Anatomie d'un mouvement fasciste en France: Le Faisceau de Georges Valois." *Revue française de science politique* 26 (1976): 5–40.

————. "Barrès et la gauche: Du boulangisme à la Cocarde (1889–1895)." *Le Mouvement social*, no. 75 (April–June 1971), pp. 77–130.

————. *Maurice Barrès et le nationalisme français*. Paris: Armand Colin, 1972.

————. "Paul Déroulède and the Origins of Modern French Nationalism." *Journal of Contemporary History* 6 (1971): 46–70.

Talmon, J. L. "The Legacy of Georges Sorel: Marxism, Violence, Fascism." *Encounter* 34 (February 1970): 47–60.

Tannenbaum, Edward. *The Action française: Die-Hard Reactionaries in Twentieth-Century France*. New York: John Wiley & Sons, 1962.

Téry, Gustave. "De gauche à droite." *L'Oeuvre*, no. 14 (April 1911), pp. 27–30.

————. "Le Déserteur Bernstein." *L'Oeuvre*, no. 7 (February 1911), pp. 1–12.

————. "Et maintenant, qu'allons-nous faire?" *L'Oeuvre*, no. 13 (March 1911), pp. 17–21.

————. "France d'abord." *L'Oeuvre*, no. 19 (May 1911), pp. 11–17.

————. "Les Juifs au théâtre . . . et ailleurs." *L'Oeuvre*, no. 39 (September 1910), pp. 1–11.

————. "L'Objection portugaise." *L'Oeuvre*, no. 41 (October 1910), pp. 20–22.

————. "L'Oeuvre de défense française." *L'Oeuvre*, no. 14 (April 1911), pp. 7–9.

————. "Potins et pantins." *L'Oeuvre*, no. 15 (April 1911), p. 34.

Tridon, André. *The New Unionism*. New York: B. W. Huebsch, 1913.

Uhry, Jules. *Socialisme et franc-maçonnerie: Discours prononcé au congrès national du parti socialiste*. N.p.: Librairie de "La Guerre sociale," n.d.

Valois, Georges. *Basile: Ou, la politique de la calomnie*. Paris: Librairie Valois, 1927.

————. "La Bourgeoisie capitaliste." *Cahiers du Cercle Proudhon*, notebooks 5 and 6 (n.d.), pp. 214–48.

————. *D'un siècle à l'autre: Chronique d'une génération*. Paris: Nouvelle Librairie nationale, 1921.

————. *L'Etat syndical et la représentation corporative*. Paris: Librairie Valois, 1927.

————. "Faits et documents: Syndicalisme et démocratie. Une Note de M. Hubert Lagardelle." *La Revue critique des idées et des livres* 12 (1911): 87–90.

————. *L'Homme contre l'argent: Souvenirs de dix ans, 1918–1928*. Paris: Librairie Valois, 1928.

————. *L'Homme qui vient: Philosophie de l'autorité*. Paris: Nouvelle Librairie nationale, n.d.

————. *La Monarchie et la classe ouvrière*. Paris: Nouvelle Librairie nationale, n.d.

_____. "Notre Première Année." *Cahiers du Cercle Proudhon*, notebooks 3 and 4 (May–August 1912), pp. 150–69.

_____. "Une Nouvelle Mystification dreyfusienne: L'Affaire Ferrar en France." *La Revue critique des idées et des livres* 7 (1909): 227–39.

_____. *L'Oeuvre de Georges Valois*. Vol. 3, *Histoire et philosophie sociales*. Collection des écrivains de la renaissance française. Paris: Nouvelle Librairie nationale, 1924.

_____. "Pourquoi nous rattachons nos travaux à l'esprit proudhonien." *Cahiers du Cercle Proudhon*, notebook 1 (January–February 1912), pp. 34–47.

Vannoz, Léon. "La Crise de la démocratie." *Les Annales de la jeunesse laïque*, no. 108 (May 1911), pp. 364–71.

Variot, Jean. *Propos de Georges Sorel*. Paris: Gallimard, 1935.

Vaugeois, Henri. *Notre Pays*. Paris: Nouvelle Librairie nationale, 1916.

Vincent, Albert. "Le Bilan de la démocratie." *Cahiers du Cercle Proudhon*, notebook 2 (March–April 1912), pp. 98–104.

Watson, David Robin. *Georges Clemenceau: A Political Biography*. Plymouth, Eng.: Eyre Methuen, 1974.

_____. "The Nationalist Movement in Paris, 1900–1906." In *The Right in France, 1890–1919*, edited by David Shapiro, pp. 49–84. London: Chatto & Windus, 1962.

Weber, Eugen. *Action française: Royalism and Reaction in Twentieth-Century France*. Stanford, Calif.: Stanford University Press, Stanford Books, 1962.

_____. "France." In *The European Right: A Historical Profile*, edited by Hans Rogger and Eugen Weber, pp. 71–127. Berkeley and Los Angeles: University of California Press, 1965.

_____. "Nationalism, Socialism, and National-Socialism in France." *French Historical Studies* 2 (1962): 273–307.

_____. *The Nationalist Revival in France, 1905–1914*. University of California Publication, vol. 60. Berkeley and Los Angeles: University of California Press, 1959.

_____. *Varieties of Fascism: Doctrines of Revolution in the Twentieth Century*. Princeton, N.J.: D. Van Nostrand, 1964.

Willard, Claude. *Les Guesdistes: Le Mouvement socialiste en France, 1893–1905*. Paris: Editions sociales, 1965.

Zeldin, Theodore. *France, 1848–1945*. Vol. 1, *Ambition, Love, and Politics*. Oxford: Oxford University Press, 1973.

Index

fascism, 17–18, 50, 222; and the conservatism of, 18, 27–31, 116–27 passim; and work, 18, 29–30; and sexual puritanism of, 18, 29–30; and nationalism, 18, 116–27 passim; and the anarchists, 27–28; and his interpretation of syndicalism, 27–31; and the nouvelle école, 28–29; and the moral dogmatism of, 28–30; and the Enlightenment, 28, 29, 30, 116–17; and the family, 29–30; and the pessimism of, 29, 116–17; and Proudhon, 29, 176; and *Illusions du progrès*, 29, 182; contributes article to the *Revue critique*, 37; and impact on Valois, 41–42, 50, 51; and Maurras, 60, 118, 120, 184; and response to Valois's enquête, 76; and his influence on syndicalism, 113–14; and *Avenir socialiste des syndicats*, 114, 116; and his disenchantment with syndicalism, 115; and the basis for his interest in the working class, 117; and the Dreyfus affair, 117, 118–19, 122; and his complicity with the Action française, 118–27 passim; on the Action française, 118, 120, 122; and *Révolution dreyfusienne*, 118–19, 122; and Péguy, 120–22; and Berth, 123–24; and the *Cité française*, 123–27; and anti-Semitism, 127; and the Cercle Proudhon, 177–78

Stanley, John L., 17–18
Sûreté générale, 79–82
Syndicalism, revolutionary: general

description of, 4, 25–26; and complicity with the Action française, 5, 11, 79–82, 92–94, 142–43, 165–69, 214–19; and historiography of, 6–12; and crisis of, 6–11, 82–92, 110–12, 135–40, 198–99, 208–12, 213–14, 216–19; and the Amiens congress (1906), 6, 83; and the ultras, 7–9, 10, 83–92, 103, 110–12, 135, 208–9; and the politiques, 7–9, 68–69, 83–92, 110–12, 135–36, 209; and the reform-revolutionary division, 7, 83, 90–92, 103, 110–11, 135–37; and reinterpretation of, 8–11; and impact of anarchists upon, 9–10; and direct action, 9, 31, 36, 51, 136; and the "new reformists," 10, 135–37, 209–12; and anti-Semitism, 11, 82, 137–42, 156–68 passim, 215–17, 218; and anarchist interpretation of, 27–28; and Sorel's interpretation of, 27–31; and the early interest of the Action française, 31–38, 45–46, 51–54, 62–75 passim; and relations with Clemenceau, 62, 65–68, 71–74; and the Dreyfusard coalition of the Left, 62–67, 132–35, 138–42, 162–65, 205–6; and growing reformism of, 84–85, 136, 208–12; and the Marseille congress (1908), 90–91, 110; and antimilitarism, 90–91; the impact of Sorel upon, 113–14; and the distinction between "militants" and "theoreticians," 113–